*Frontispiece: Galvanized
iron shadehouse at Ard
Choille, Mount Macedon*

Historic Gardens of Victoria

A RECONNAISSANCE

FROM A REPORT OF THE NATIONAL TRUST OF AUSTRALIA (VICTORIA) BY *Peter Watts*   EDITED BY MARGARET BARRETT

OXFORD UNIVERSITY PRESS   MELBOURNE

OXFORD UNIVERSITY PRESS

Oxford London Glasgow New York Toronto
Delhi Bombay Calcutta Madras Karachi
Kuala Lumpur Singapore Hong Kong Tokyo
Nairobi Dar es Salaam Cape Town
Melbourne Auckland
and associates in
Beirut Berlin Ibadan Mexico City Nicosia

National Library of Australia
Cataloguing-in-Publication data:

Watts, Peter, 1949–.
Historic gardens of Victoria.
Bibliography.
Includes index.
ISBN 0 19 554397 1.
1. Historic gardens — Victoria.
I. Barrett, Margaret. II. Title.
635'.09945

Designed by Alison Forbes
Typeset by Davey Graphics Pty Ltd
Printed by Nordica, Hong Kong
Published by Oxford University Press, 7 Bowen Crescent, Melbourne
OXFORD is a trademark of Oxford University Press

To Professor-Emeritus John Turner

Contents

ACKNOWLEDGEMENTS

When the idea of surveying Victoria's remaining historic gardens was first put forward, it received early encouragement from the then Premier, the Hon. R. J. Hamer, E.D., M.P., subsequently Sir Rupert Hamer. The State Government, through the Garden State Committee, provided most of the funding. Contributions were also made by the Council of the National Trust of Australia (Victoria) and the Myer Foundation. The task of overseeing and advising on the survey fell to a joint committee of the National Trust and the Garden State Committee chaired by Professor John Turner. Members of the committee were Professor T. C. Chambers, Warwick Forge, John Jack, Alan Thatcher and George Wright.

The Council and staff of the National Trust assisted throughout in a variety of ways. Dr Carlotta Kellaway filled in many gaps through her meticulous research, while Barbara Martella, who typed both the report and this manuscript, assisted in a hundred other ways.

Without co-operation – and often the most generous hospitality – from the owners or custodians of Victoria's oldest gardens, this book would not have been possible. Many of those whose gardens are described here contributed further by unearthing and making available plans, paintings, photographs and other records. Finding the gardens involved helpers all over Victoria. Loma Pescott (Ballarat district), Diana Allen, Bardie Mercer and Meredith Bell (Western District), Helen Vellacott (Castlemaine), and Barney Hutton and Harold Rutherford (Mount Macedon) were particularly generous with knowledge of their local areas.

Appreciation is expressed to all who gave assistance of any kind, among them personnel from various municipal councils and other public authorities, and members of the Australian Heritage Commission and of various historical and horticultural societies. Individuals deserving special mention include James Broadbent, Howard Tanner, Warwick and Suzie Forge, George Tibbits, Geoffrey Stilwell, Dr Alan Roberts, Ron Hodges, John Patrick, Dame Elisabeth Murdoch, Richard Aitken, Art Truter, Tom Garnett, Dr Jim Willis, Frank Keenan, Peter Perry, Dr Miles Lewis, P. L. Brown, R. T. M. Pescott, Ruth Sanderson, Ian Rogers and Louise Sweetland. Special credit must go to designer Alison Forbes for her skill in making a fine book of it all. Permission was kindly granted by Angus & Robertson Publishers to reproduce a passage from The Letters of Rachel Henning, edited by David Adams.

Detailed acknowledgement of the origin of illustrations is made separately, but particular thanks are due to the Library Council of Victoria, the Principal Librarian, State Library of Victoria, and to the La Trobe Librarian and her Picture Collection staff. Map Collection staff were similarly helpful. We are grateful to several members of the Photographic Committee of the National Trust of Australia (Victoria) for their work, and most of all to the committee's chairman, Brian Hatfield, for his enormous personal effort.

The author and editor also wish to thank their respective families for tolerance of an unreasonable preoccupation with historic gardens over many months.

In 1966 the National Trust of Australia (Victoria) was
responsible for the publication of a book called *Historic Buildings
of Victoria*. It was a pioneering work, which attempted to
record photographically a number of Victoria's important
historic buildings; providing a few pertinent details about each,
it was informative as well as a means of stimulating interest
in the built environment.

Historic Gardens of Victoria attempts an encore. It, too, is a
record and a guide, based in this case on the first survey of
historic gardens undertaken in Victoria. Part I, which sets
Victoria's notable old gardens in context, is written primarily
from a study of the surviving examples, which are described in
Part II. All that remain of a once rich collection, they are
almost certainly not representative of their respective periods.
But – as Part III makes plain – their conservation is a worthy
objective for the government and people of Victoria. Since we
can rarely be sure of the intention of a garden's original
designer, early plans, photographs, paintings and descriptions

have been used to provide some clues. These records are often
as fascinating as the gardens themselves.

The introductory chapters of the Trust's 1966 book may
today appear rather sketchy, because their authors did not have
the benefit of research findings accumulated over the subsequent ten to fifteen years. As interest in our historic gardens
grows, and as further research into the lives of designers, the
history of individual gardens and the influences on them is
completed, this story too will become richer and better
balanced.

Though comparatively few historic gardens survive in
Victoria, the number being properly cared for is pathetically
small. They are not all beautiful. But gardens of every kind and
in varying condition are included because they are all part of
the picture. Regrettably, a small but significant number of
Victoria's best nineteenth-century gardens have not been described or even mentioned here. Their owners, in order to
protect their privacy, or for other reasons, have not allowed
their inclusion. Other notable gardens were destroyed by the
bushfires of early 1983 – more of them lost in minutes than
might have disappeared in a decade of neglect.

Gardens have been described as man's idealized view of life,
revealing the dream world of any particular period. For what
they tell us of our forebears and often also for their mellowed
charm, those historic gardens that remain deserve study and
care. Glancing through the pages of *Historic Buildings of Victoria* in
1982, one is struck by the unfamiliarity of many of the entries.
Rated highly in 1966, scores of those buildings have long since
been demolished. It would be a sad reflection on all who love
gardens and respect the lessons of history if this book, like its
sister volume, should also become an obituary.

Peter Watts

Private gardens described in this book are normally closed to the
public, and readers are urged to respect the privacy of owners.
Inquiries about this or any other historic gardens matter
may be directed to the National Trust of Australia (Victoria)

Introduction
The historic gardens study

CREATING GARDENS seems always to have been a pre-occupation of civilized man. Born of necessity at times, with gardens supplying food and little else, this activity has generally met a much wider range of human needs – aesthetic, philosophical, emotional and physical. Public gardens have embellished cities and refreshed city-dwellers, and domestic gardens have provided pleasant settings, grand or modest, for houses all over the world.

Australia's earliest man-made gardens, in and around Sydney, were devoted to survival, yet there was already a fine natural garden of angophoras, banksias, eugenias and eucalypts on land adjoining the first Government House – the site-to-be of Australia's first official botanic garden. By the 1820s the Colonial Botanist and Superintendent of the Botanic Gardens, Charles Fraser, was working hard at introducing new plants to the gardens, whose size was nearly doubled between 1821 and 1825 by Sir Thomas Brisbane, Governor Lachlan Macquarie's successor. Thus developed a garden of supreme historical interest. Few of Australia's old gardens date back so far, or are so significant, but they are all very much part of our history.

Melbourne from the south side of the Yarra, 1839 (detail). J. Carmichael's engraving from an ink drawing by J. Adamson is Victoria's earliest known illustration showing gardens, with Commissary Erskine's at the centre

Opposite: Flowers, vegetables and at least one fruit tree are growing around this very early hut, which is surrounded by a stout fence

At Australia's first Garden History Conference in 1980 David Yencken, then Chairman of the Australian Heritage Commission, acknowledged that 'In the pantheon of Australian heritage historic gardens have until very recently held a very lowly place'. The conference was also told that Britain itself had had a Garden History Society for a mere fifteen years or so. It was only in the 1970s, in fact, that there arose a remarkable world-wide interest in the past, present and future of historic gardens.

The International Council on Monuments and Sites, a non-government organization closely linked with UNESCO and having members and national branches in over fifty countries, began in this same period to prepare an international inventory of important historic gardens. Its sponsorship of a number of conferences attracted a great deal of attention, especially in Britain and Europe.

There had been concern in Victoria for one historic garden more than ten years before this. Soon after the National Trust of Australia (Victoria) acquired the South Yarra mansion Como in 1959, a garden committee was established to care for the grounds. The committee set out to retain, as far as possible, the planting and Victorian character of long-established parts of the garden and to develop neglected areas sensibly. Research into gardens of the Western District – undertaken by Kate Hattam in 1975–76 with a grant from the Australian Heritage Commission – indicated the wealth of material available and the paucity of adequate documentation. In 1976, in an endeavour to explore this field further, the National Trust offered a series of lectures on 'The History and Development of Gardens in Victoria'. These drew considerable support, and demonstrated the interest of the public in all aspects of the subject.

The National Trust's long and bitter campaign against destruction of the garden at the Elsternwick mansion Rippon Lea focused attention on historic gardens as never before. The Australian Broadcasting Commission had compulsorily acquired the most important part of that garden – the lake, grotto, waterfall and several fine garden buildings – to extend its television studios, and it must have been astounded at the reaction.

Opposite: Less than half a century after settlement of the colony, gardening on a lavish scale was not uncommon in Victoria. At Rippon Lea in Elsternwick, the outer beds of the orangery were planted with citrus trees of several kinds, and the inner with heaths suitable for the warm situation and sandy soil. One of the windmills that pumped water around the garden is visible in this 1880 photograph

It was normal, at the time, for the demolition of buildings of historic value to be strongly opposed by conservation groups. But a mere garden! This was, of course, one of the most important surviving nineteenth-century gardens in Australia, and the National Trust won the battle. Its acquisition of Rippon Lea in 1974 helped the Trust itself to recognize the treasures that often lay out of sight behind fences, as well as around the buildings it had been fighting to save for twenty years.

In August 1977 the National Trust took one more step. Seeing the great need for research in the area of historic gardens, and aware of public concern and likely support, it made a submission to the Premier of the day, the Hon. R. J. Hamer, E.D., M.P. (now Sir Rupert Hamer). The personal enthusiasm of the Premier was gratifying to the Trust, as was a grant of $30 000 subsequently made by the Victorian Government, through the Garden State Committee, to enable the commencement of a two-year survey of historic gardens in Victoria.

Developments abroad in the study, control and care of historic gardens were obviously relevant to the Victorian survey, and since some countries had been engaged in this field for a number of years their activities were examined thoroughly. The terms of reference for the project placed particular stress on the analysis of overseas 'trends and techniques' for solving the problems of rehabilitation, management and finance of gardens.

IT IS PERHAPS WORTH NOTING in some detail what was found in Britain, since in many ways British legislation is a good model, and non-government conservation bodies there are similar to our own.

The National Trust in Britain is the custodian of the most important collection of historic gardens anywhere in the world. Its procedures and standards for restoration are therefore of great interest. The policy and development of each of its gardens are guided by a group of people knowledgeable and skilled in gardening, garden history, property management, fine arts

and administration. The restoration philosophy for each garden is different, and is based on many factors including its documentation, relative importance and condition. The approach can vary from a pure one that rigorously restores a garden to its condition at an earlier date, or one that accepts the alterations and additions from different periods.

The National Trust for Scotland has begun a School of Gardening to train young people for the specialist work required in its own gardens. Despite the expertise in Britain, the Trust considered that the special skills and attitudes necessary for working in an historic garden were not always taught in the conventional horticultural and gardening courses. The National Trust for Scotland also runs two of its gardens as Gardening Advice Centres, which hold lecture series and courses on practical gardening.

A programme that reaches many more people is the National Gardens Scheme, run as a fund-raising exercise by the Queen's Institute of District Nursing. This scheme arranges for private owners to open their gardens to the public. In 1978 about 1400 owners were co-operating, with annual attendances of over half a million. The scheme has greatly increased knowledge and enjoyment of the nation's old gardens.

The Historic Houses Association is an organization made up of the owners of historic houses and gardens. It sets out to provide a forum for discussion and to enable these people to speak to government with a united voice. Its main aim with regard to historic gardens has been to obtain tax concessions for owners.

The Garden History Society, formed in 1965, began as a learned society but has rapidly become an influential pressure group. It campaigns actively to increase public awareness of the amenity value of historic gardens and of the need to protect them as an important component of the nation's cultural heritage. The society gives evidence at inquiries, its opinion is sought by government, the National Trust, planning authorities and individuals, and it acts as a watchdog for the nation's gardens.

There are several fairly recent pieces of British legislation relating (in most cases indirectly) to historic gardens. These include the Historic Buildings and Ancient Monuments Act 1953 and the Town and Country Planning Act 1971. However, the Town and Country Amenities Act 1974 is perhaps the most important piece of legislation affecting historic gardens in Britain since it has been the first to make specific reference to gardens. Section 12 of the Act provides for grant aid to gardens of outstanding historic importance even when they are not attached to a building of historic or architectural merit. This is a notable recognition of their intrinsic significance. The Garden History Society was responsible for securing the inclusion of the clauses relating to historic gardens.

By means of the Civic Amenities Act 1978, provision is made for the preservation of *areas* as distinct from buildings. It was never intended that the Act would be used for the protection of individual gardens. However, in the absence of any more specific legislation, it is being invoked by an increasing number of planning authorities to designate some of the larger historic gardens and parks, and may prove to be the best safeguard for the landscaped garden.

A recent amendment to the Finance Acts enables gardens, like buildings of outstanding importance, to be exempt from capital transfer tax and death duties, a concession partly due to the efforts of the Historic Houses Association.

It is generally felt by responsible organizations in Britain that gardens should be listed officially and be eligible for the same grants and benefits as historic buildings. In the meantime many owners see a partial palliative to their problems in the opening of their gardens to the public, though the provision of parking facilities, lavatories, advertising and guides can outweigh the potential economic advantages.

Most British authorities, including the National Trust and the Garden History Society, believe that gardens lose something of their individuality when taken from the personal care of their owners. Tony Venison summed this up in the 9 September 1976 issue of *Country Life* by saying that 'A garden's individual character and evolving entity are still best cherished in private ownership rather than in the ossified layouts and mummified plantings now becoming despairingly commonplace in public and corporately held gardens'. But, given the current difficulties, a number of alternatives are being explored. These include commercial use – for hospitals, private schools, public agencies, private company headquarters, university premises and hotels; government appropriation (the British Government has accepted property in lieu of death duties and in some instances the property has been handed to the National Trust for management); and National Trust acquisition. The National Trust is not actively seeking to take on further properties, but will do so where the property is of outstanding significance and where a sufficient endowment is also made to allow for its development and maintenance. In 1976 it was estimated that a garden requiring four full-time gardeners would need an endowment of at least £200 000 to make it viable. Such demands naturally militate against owners' leaving gardens to the Trust, and some gardens have been lost through its inability to accept property without adequate accompanying funds. In some cases where the garden has been of particular significance, the Trust has acquired this while the owner has retained the house for his own use.

In a number of instances property has been left to local government authorities, or they have stepped in to save a garden where its imminent loss has become apparent. In all such known cases the gardens have then been used for public pleasure and recreation.

The number of people visiting historic gardens in Britain has risen steadily over the past few years; there has been a growing interest in the history of gardening and a concern for the future of the country's best historic gardens. Books on garden history have poured forth. Coupled with all this has been a rising level of professional interest in the philosophical and practical aspects of garden restoration.

IN THE LIGHT OF so much activity in the U.K., a study of the historic gardens movement there was valuable in many ways, but the Victorian project had to be planned in detail, and within guidelines that suited the local scene. The terms of reference for the Victorian study were set out in February 1978. It aimed to identify, document and assess important historic gardens in Victoria; to determine the problems facing them; to recommend on future assistance and/or legislation required to preserve and protect them; to analyse overseas experience in solving these problems; to obtain a general understanding of the development of Victoria's garden heritage; to gather information to assist the Trust and other bodies in undertaking accurate and informed restoration of historic gardens; to establish a photographic record of such gardens in the state; and to encourage a general awareness of Victoria's garden heritage.

At the beginning of the survey it was evident that Victoria had some very significant historic gardens, such as the Royal Botanic Gardens, the Fitzroy Gardens, Mawallok at Beaufort and Dalvui at Noorat. It was also clear that some historic gardens were being lost. Caravan parks had infiltrated the Botanic Gardens at Camperdown, Koroit, Port Fairy and Kyneton. Some privately owned gardens such as Ercildoune at Burrumbeet were known to have degenerated sadly. But generally there was far too little information about the state's historic gardens, and it was necessary to establish the location, ownership and condition of those gardens so that they could be 'documented and assessed'. Visiting the gardens would allow some of the other aims of the study to be fulfilled at the same time: the photographic record could be established (weather permitting), and specific problems recorded.

It was necessary, of course, to try to define the term 'historic garden'. The difficulties involved in such a definition had been among the chief reasons why the Garden History Society in Britain was so slow to prepare an authoritative list of gardens. In 1971 the International Council on Monuments and Sites declared an historic garden to be 'an architectural and horticultural composition of interest to the public from the historical and artistic point of view'. Feeling that this did not adequately cover the *jardin Anglais*, the Garden History Society produced its own definition three years later. It reads: 'An historic garden (or park) is a defined area deliberately created as an orna-

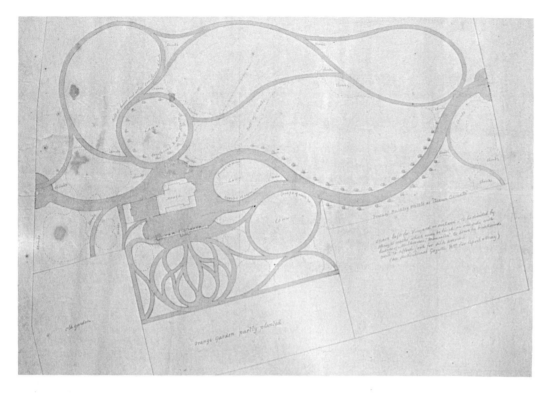

One of the earliest domestic garden plans surviving, this was submitted by George O'Brien for the great homestead Bontharambo, Wangaratta, in the 1860s. A design by John Hotson (too faint to reproduce here) seems to have been the one actually followed, but the two layouts are both notable for their baroque exuberance

mental environment and of historical interest as such. The term includes designed landscapes . . .'

Both of these attempts are distinctly preferable to Lawrence Fricker's 1975 description in the *Town Planning Review* – 'An assemblage, principally of vegetation, kept in a preferred state of ecological arrest by the craft of gardening' – but they all seemed appropriate to European conditions rather than to Australian. It was decided therefore to avoid a strict definition, adopting instead simple criteria that could be readily understood by members of the public who were being asked to suggest gardens. Thus, in its general character an 'historic garden' in Victoria had to predate 1920; it was essential that something remained of its original layout; and it had to retain part of its original planting or of the character of that planting. The first criterion was later altered to include exceptional gardens, such as those of Edna Walling, up to the late 1930s.

A basis for selection having been established, the next step was to search out gardens that fell into at least some of the categories laid down. It seemed a forbidding task.

It was decided that the project was of considerable interest to the public and could only benefit from receiving as much exposure as possible. The press was used extensively, and some of the gardening and environment writers in the main metropolitan daily papers took a continuing interest in the study over several years.

Each of the 212 municipal councils in the state was asked to assist with the survey and nominate gardens in its area. The historical and horticultural societies were similarly contacted. Although some of these organizations were enthusiastic and co-operative, many of the approaches drew little response. Individuals, however, were most helpful. Many were already known to the National Trust and were active on its various committees, and such people, especially those in the more remote country areas, proved to be an invaluable source of information as well as of hospitality. The Trust's own staff, its various honorary architects, historians and planners, who among them have a good knowledge of the state, also added much to the stock in trade of historic gardens.

Talks and lectures on the study were delivered to groups as diverse as the Lyceum Club and classes of the Council of Adult Education, and on most of these occasions new information came to light.

The National Trust in Victoria holds several thousand files on individual historic buildings in the state and each of these was examined. In many cases the file contained photographs of the building, photographs that gave a glimpse of the garden and made it possible to establish quickly whether a visit was warranted. This research was time-consuming but one of the most productive sources of information. The National Trust had also collected material over the previous few years for a proposed publication on historic gardens Australia-wide. The list of gardens nominated for this project covered most of the large private gardens in the state and was a valuable starting-point.

Nineteenth-century photographs in the La Trobe Collection of the State Library of Victoria were also a good reference source, though they were more useful for checking known gardens than locating new ones.

Nearly all the terrace house gardens and most of the villa gardens included in the survey were found by accident – they were simply noticed from the street and could easily have been overlooked. This surely suggests that many more such gardens are waiting to be discovered. The majority of the state's really important gardens were known, of course, but a few very significant and previously unrecorded ones did come to light.

In order to make the assessment of gardens as objective as

An early stage in the transformation of a 'dreary waste sparsely sprinkled with aged gum trees' into an English paradise: the main east-west walk in the Fitzroy Gardens in 1861

possible, a simple scoring system was devised. Gardens received marks out of 4 under each of the following headings:

Original form	Intact (4 marks)
	Substantially intact (3)
	Recognizable (2)
	Recognizable with minor alterations (1)
Original planting	Characteristic (4 marks)
	Substantially characteristic (3)
	Recognizable period or designer (2)
	Recognizable but in poor condition (1)
Atmosphere	This was a matter of the garden's general design, relationship with buildings, setting etc.; a degree of emotional response was allowed for here
Condition	Excellent (4 marks)
	Good (3)
	Fair (2)
	Retrievable (1)

This gave a total out of 16. A further mark was given for each of the following points of interest:

The garden was planned by a notable designer
It was representative of a characteristic style
It contained an outstanding plant collection
It was associated with an important historic building

These sub-totals were added to give a score out of 20. Since the total score could be weighted excessively because of the four bonus points, the first sub-total, and the total score out of 20, were calculated on a percentage basis out of 16 and 20 respectively and the higher percentage figure of the two was the final score allocated to that garden. The gardens were then put into groups according to their score. Gardens considered 'very important' had to score 78 to 100 per cent; those with 66 to 77 per cent were rated 'important'; any between 53 and 65 per cent were 'of considerable interest'; and those with 35 to 52 per cent were regarded as being 'of interest'. Some gardens came close to the borderline between two categories, of course, and further subjective evaluation was needed to determine their rank.

Before most of the gardens nominated for the study were visited, their status was checked wherever possible. Inevitably, however, many gardens were found to be of no historic interest at all. Nevertheless, in the initial stages these visits were important, as they helped establish a standard by which later gardens could be measured.

In many instances early photographs were available to compare the state of an old garden with its present condition. Sometimes this information was not forthcoming and speculation was necessary. This, of course, may be dangerous, although in most cases it is probably fairly accurate. Aerial photographs of many of the larger gardens facilitated the drawing of simple plans. Information from the owner, the style of the garden, the physical evidence of any changes, and the apparent age of the plant material all helped to substantiate guesswork about the authenticity of a garden. While for the purposes of the survey such speculation is probably acceptable, much more detailed study is clearly to be desired. This would be particularly the case if a preservation controversy arose or if a garden was to be restored.

In cases where modern gardens have been superimposed on much earlier gardens, as at Bolobek, Macedon – the modern garden having been begun in 1969 and the older one in 1908 – it was difficult to judge the degree to which the character and quality of the garden derived from the latter. Substantial changes have also been made to several other gardens (including Woolongoon at Mortlake and Murrindindi Station at Yea) that have nevertheless been regarded as meeting the historic gardens criteria.

The distinction between garden and park was not always clearcut, and as a general guide a garden was thought of as an area where horticulture is practised with some intensity. Private parklands, where they are associated with houses, were included. Public parklands such as Royal Park were not.

Finding and assessing historic gardens in Victoria constituted the primary aim of this survey. In the course of the work various avenues were investigated in a random manner, rather than a systematic one, simply to find out what information was available from various sources or to check on a particular aspect. A cursory glance at some of this information, especially in nineteenth-century newspapers and gardening journals, indicated that there is undoubtedly a good deal of material available about individual designers, gardens, horticultural societies and so on. Plant catalogues, private diaries and papers, and general reference books also provide useful information.

The collections of the National Gallery of Victoria and the various regional galleries were checked for illustrations of early gardens. Most of the best of these were shown in the exhibition 'Converting the Wilderness: The Art of Gardening in Colonial Australia', which was taken to Queensland, New South Wales, Victoria, Tasmania and South Australia in 1979–80. Paintings, plans and photographs held in private collections were noted.

Plans published by the Melbourne and Metropolitan Board of Works from the early 1890s to about 1920 in connection with the city's sewerage system are among the most valuable of records showing garden layouts. Especially in inner suburban areas the design of gardens, even those associated with the humblest houses, is often shown here in some detail. These plans are particularly useful for verifying the authenticity of a present-day layout thought to date back to these times.

The survey has resulted in some spin-off for other work and research. The files of the National Trust were updated considerably after visits to many properties listed on its register. A number of unknown buildings were also discovered, perhaps the most notable being Mynda in Kew, with its intact Victorian interior. Another find was an excellent private library of garden history in Castlemaine.

Most of the gardens visited were photographed, and the resulting transparencies make up an important part of the information gathered during this project. The National Trust's collection now includes approximately 5400 slides, comprising 1100 of overseas gardens, 2300 of gardens in Victoria taken during the study, and approximately 2000 taken by Kate Hat-

This 1889 drawing of the garden at Greystones, Rowsley, came from a sketchbook of Hester L. Massie

tam in the course of her Australian Heritage Commission survey of gardens in the Western District (they include some photographs of gardens in South Australia).

During the course of the study a bibliography of relevant information was maintained. This has already proved very useful, forming the basis of a bibliography of material relating to Australian gardens prepared by the Australian Heritage Commission.

There have necessarily been a number of limitations on the historic gardens study, though they are not considered to have substantially altered its conclusions. They do account for some of the omissions from the listings, however, and for some of the gaps in information considered desirable.

It has taken the National Trust over twenty years to build up its inventory of five thousand historic buildings. Although there are not as many important gardens as notable buildings surviving in the state, there are nevertheless hundreds of old gardens throughout Victoria. During the course of this study 360 were inspected and many more were viewed from the front street. It is likely that most of the main large gardens, both public and private, were included. It is more than likely

that many smaller suburban, villa and terrace house gardens
were omitted. A shortage of time and personnel was a limiting
factor on the extent of the survey.

Visits to properties were not always possible, for a number
of reasons. The state was covered municipality by municipality,
and if a garden was nominated after its area was completed it
was not at all easy to back-track. In several instances gardens
could not be found or the owners could not be contacted. In
five cases access was not permitted by the owners. Other
gardens, including several outstanding ones, were excluded
from this book at their owners' request. The Geelong region
and the Mornington Peninsula were investigated rather cursor-
ily during the survey, and might well hold a number of historic
gardens in addition to those described here.

All these limitations are relatively minor compared with the
main one. This survey was undertaken by one person and,
although a reasonably objective system of evaluation was developed, the results will inevitably reflect the biases of that one
person. For one thing, there is an emphasis here on design

rather than on plants. Some of the gardens were known to
members of the steering committee that supervised the study,
but the vast majority have been surveyed without the benefit
of outside consultation. Discussion with people who knew each
of the gardens and could make a comparative evaluation would
most likely have led to different results.

Since the commencement of the study in February 1978
there has been a steadily growing interest in historic gardens
throughout the community. Projects completed in the last few
years, or under way, include research into bandstands, pavilions and rotundas; the restoration of the Government House
garden; the collecting and propagating of old species of plants;
books on noted landscape designers Edna Walling and Ellis
Stones; and the gathering together of nineteenth-century nurserymen's catalogues from several states. Perhaps the clearest
evidence of this interest was the formation of the Australian
Garden History Society in March 1980 at the conclusion of
Australia's first Garden History Conference. Both the conference and the society arose directly out of Victoria's Historic
Gardens Study. In fact it has had wide repercussions throughout Australia. Following the lead of the Victorian Government,
the Commonwealth Government, through the Australian
Heritage Commission, has sponsored similar studies in each
state of Australia and funded two meetings of those undertaking the studies in each state. Further evidence of the increasing
interest in historic gardens was the popularity of the travelling
exhibition 'Converting the Wilderness: The Art of Gardening
in Colonial Australia'.

Some of the findings and recommendations of the Historic
Gardens Study with regard to the future are discussed in Part
III. The assembled material about the state's gardens, while
highly revealing, should be regarded as preliminary only. It
must be emphasized that there are undoubtedly many more
historic gardens in Victoria. The research is not meant to be
seen as static, but should be continually modified as circumstances change and new information emerges. With the ever-
growing interest in historic gardens there seems little reason
why this should not happen.

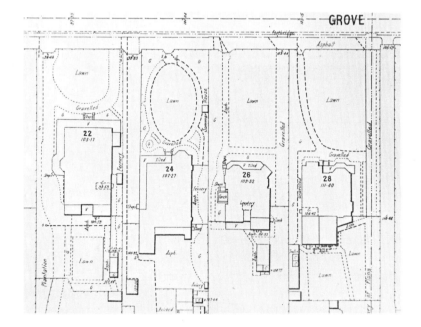

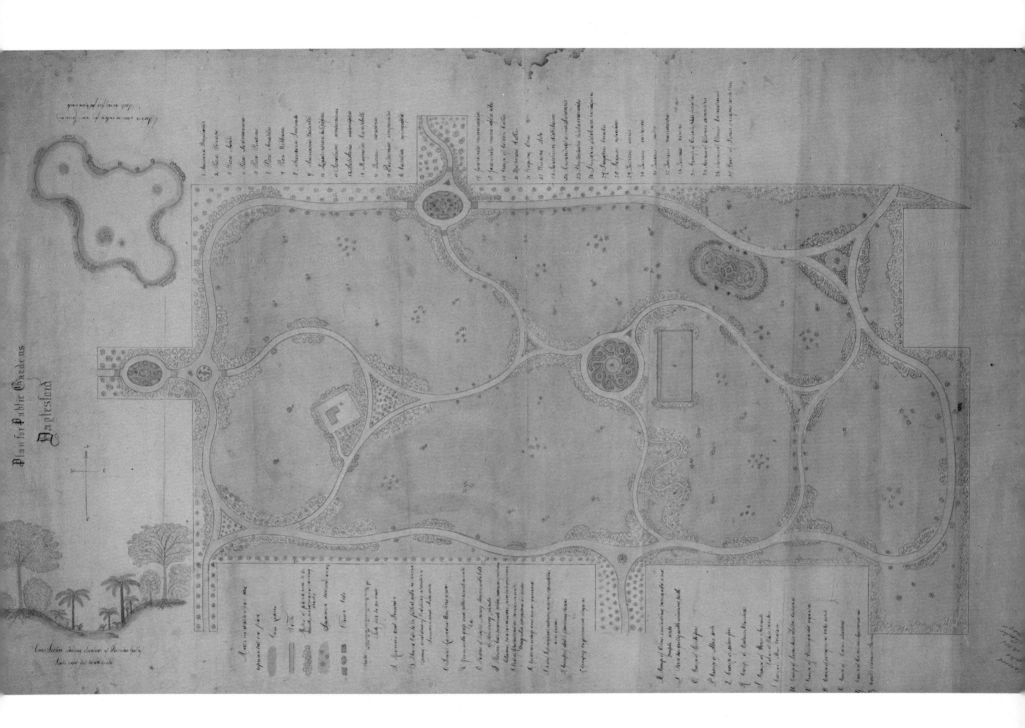

Plan for Public Gardens
Daylesford

19

Part I Historic gardens in focus

THE HISTORY of Victoria's gardens is elusive. This state, in a mere 150 years, has not known the great waves of change apparent in the history of British gardening, beginning in medieval times and ending in the twentieth century with the gardens of Gertrude Jekyll and later designers. Nor does it have the great surviving prototypes, gardens around which the history of design has pivoted: Victoria cannot boast a Stowe, Stourhead, Attingham Park or Munstead Wood. Nevertheless the years have witnessed various turns in the tide, the development of some interesting gardens that still illustrate the changes, and the emergence of a number of influential personalities.

Gardeners are not generally given to looking back. Indeed they must always be anticipating the future, imagining the results of planting those seeds or that avenue of tiny seedling trees. But to understand something of the present state of our gardens we must cast our eyes over the shifting fashions of a century and a half – for gardens have been subject to the

The South Yarra mansion Como, as illustrated in 1888. In its heyday the garden at Como was one of the finest in Melbourne

Opposite: View of Jolimont by an unknown artist, about 1844. The colony may have been only ten years old, but the fashionable gardenesque movement of the nineteenth century was already evident around Superintendent La Trobe's cottage

whims of fashion as much as any of the arts – and try to analyse the factors behind them.

Very early in its history Victoria developed a flourishing garden industry that, far from Britain and in a somewhat different environment, was quite closely related to trends there. Australia became a colony late in the eighteenth century, which had seen remarkable changes in aesthetic thinking and the most profound transformation in the great gardens of Britain. The seventeenth-century formal garden, characterized by its axial planning, avenues and ponds, and the cosiness of its embroidered floral parterres, was swept away in the eighteenth to create great landscaped parklands devoid of any decoration and with lawns sweeping up to the very foundations of the houses. Instead of looking onto an ordered scene of flower plots, gravelled walks and pleached alleys, the fashionable English aristocrat converted by the new movement gazed into a masterfully contrived bucolic landscape with deer grazing around lakes and without a single flower to interrupt the flowing lines of trees, grass and water. Never before had gardens so cleverly and ruthlessly mirrored nature. The passion for the landscape style came to an end with the death of

its greatest proponent, Lancelot 'Capability' Brown, in 1783, just four years before the First Fleet set sail for Australia.

But this is far too simple a standpoint from which to examine Australian gardens. The sheer scale of Britain's surviving great gardens has often led to misconceptions about the wider influence of the eighteenth-century landscape style. If it had been so universally understood and ingrained in the British mind, one would have expected to find strong advocates of the mode among Australia's early colonists. There should have been landscaped estates scattered throughout at least our first two colonies, New South Wales and Van Diemen's Land. But with a few exceptions they are not to be found in those places, nor were they ever.

It is doubtful whether more than a handful of those who came to Australia in its first thirty-odd years had much idea of what a landscaped garden was, even if they had seen one. And to create such a garden required land and wealth – both in large doses – as well as a commitment to a new aesthetic ideal. Inevitably it was confined to the aristocratic few and they were sparse in Australia during her formative years. In any case the fashion had long since changed by the time such luxuries were

Behind Kew Palace within the Royal Botanic Gardens, Kew, lies the Queen's Garden (right). This replica of a formal seventeenth-century English garden includes only plants that might have been seen around the palace soon after it was built in 1631

The grounds of Rousham in Oxfordshire (far right) were redesigned in 1738–41 by William Kent, a pioneer of the English landscape movement

possible. So what were the influences that shaped Australia's first gardens?

In putting to rest the 'grossly exaggerated' effect 'Capability' Brown had on the general gardening scene in Britain, the English garden historian John Harris said in 1979 that 'it is clear from a study of the gardens of the minor gentry that the formal tradition survived well into the 1770s, if not later, and that there were formal and informal flower gardens signposting the route from Wise [1653–1738] to Repton [1752–1818]'. These gardens of the minor gentry, the clergy and the rising middle classes are likely to have been the gardens known and relevant to colonists rather than were the grand estates of the aristocrats.

At the Australian Garden History Conference of February 1982 the architectural historian James Broadbent said that for the 'colonial landholder untrammelled by contemporary theories of aesthetics the ideal garden was still that simple geometric layout of beds and paths which had continued around simple farmsteads and rectories in England when grander establishments were being isolated in acres of mown grass'. Paintings of the first Government House in Sydney and that at Parramatta, and the surviving garden at Rouse Hill House, west of Sydney, bear this out. All three have simple rectangular layouts, complementing the equally simple and symmetrical facades of the houses they surrounded. And by and large Australia's earliest domestic gardens were of this kind.

There were the odd exceptions, and they are interesting as carryovers from the eighteenth century rather than as the antipodean freaks they have often been branded, gardens cut off from the mainstream of contemporary thinking on design. The convict architect Francis Greenway advertised in a Sydney paper in January 1835 that he laid out grounds 'in the landscape gardening style'. The garden he planned around the new, castellated Government House in Sydney was, he said, to have been planted 'in the manner of the celebrated Brown . . . it having great capability about it'. Louis Haghe's lithograph (from about 1835) of Panshanger in Tasmania shows a Greek Revival mansion, built four years previously, sitting on a gentle knoll surrounded by a vast stretch of grass devoid of any decoration. Another lithograph of the same year, from a painting by W. Lyttleton, confirms the extent to which the house commanded views of the surrounding landscape. Two of the other exceptions are Henrietta Villa in Sydney and Quorn Hall in Tasmania.

But perhaps the most direct evidence of influence from the eighteenth-century landscape movement is to be found in Thomas Shepherd's *Lectures on Landscape Gardening in Australia*, published in 1836. The lectures promoted the concept of broad parklands around country estates. Shepherd said that though the colony could not claim Britain's scope for landscape gardening, it did have some advantages: 'Extensive parks may . . . be made in the first style of magnificence here, at a comparatively trifling expense, when contrasted with the large sums of money which have been expended on similar objects in Britain.' He went on to say that 'we have plenty of trees already

Completed in about 1790, the natural-looking landscape at Stowe in Buckinghamshire was created by four great designers, the last of whom was 'Capability' Brown. Classical structures like Stowe's 'rotondo' added to the Arcadian quality of such gardens

growing indigenous, which only require to be thinned out to give effect to park scenery'. His lectures are somewhat incoherent, but in this matter of the landscaped parkland his intention is clear. It was, by this time, well out of date in England, of course, although the style appears to have been adopted at Fernhill, Mulgoa, 50 kilometres west of Sydney. Fernhill was built in about 1840 and in Godfrey Mundy's *Our Antipodes* (1852) was described thus:

A handsome stone house overlooks by far the most lovely and extensive landscape – as a home view – I ever met with in Australia; and its beauty is much enhanced by the taste and success of the proprietor in weeding out the thinly leafed and unsightly kinds of the gum-tree, and preserving only that species of the Eucalyptus called the apple-tree, which, with its stout gnarled branches and crisp tufted foliage, is, when standing alone or in clumps in parkish looking ground, by no means a bad representative of the English oak. Were it not for the vineyards and wine-houses at Fern Hill, a stranger might imagine himself at the country-house of some substantial English squire.

There were probably even fewer exceptions to the rule in Victoria than in New South Wales or Tasmania. Perhaps Murndal, west of Hamilton, retains something of the bold spirit of the eighteenth century. It was the product of Samuel Pratt Winter, who first settled there in 1837. Winter, who was descended from Anglo-Irish gentry, surrounded his ever-growing house with great avenues of oaks and elms. He did not build the allegorical temples or the other classical garden structures of the previous century. But, in a similar vein, he commemorated great events by planting clumps and avenues and single specimens of trees, and by transforming his estate into a sort of landscaped park. Later in the century that great pastoralist Niel Black laid out, at his property Mount Noorat, a 60 hectare parkland in front of the Italianate mansion, from which it was viewed across a lawn (inset, however, with colourful flower beds), and over a ha-ha wall.

The desire of eighteenth-century English landscapers to recreate a rural version of the natural scenery had become modified early in the nineteenth century by new theories of the sublime and the 'picturesque', the latter emphasizing the rugged qualities of the natural landscape. The classical temples of earlier days were now built in a rustic form – with thatched roofs and with tree trunks for posts. At the same time grottoes and waterfalls were conscripted to the cause of imitating wild nature. Humphry Repton, who succeeded Lancelot Brown as the most influential garden designer in Britain, began re-introducing terraces, flower beds and fountains to the gardens of the aristocracy. This trend, too, passed over the heads of the majority of those who came, voluntarily or otherwise, to Australia.

In England, however, social changes brought about by the industrial revolution were causing a redistribution of power and money. No longer was wealth associated only with the landed gentry and its vast holdings. A new monied class

Opposite: Though planted mainly with exotic trees, and reminiscent of elements of the eighteenth-century English landscape movement, Murndal, near Hamilton, is unmistakably Australian

A modern view of the grotto and waterfall at Rippon Lea, Elsternwick: constructed late in the nineteenth century, they were a reflection of the 'picturesque' style popular in England much earlier in the century

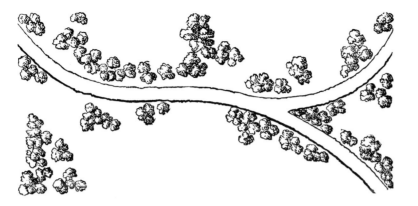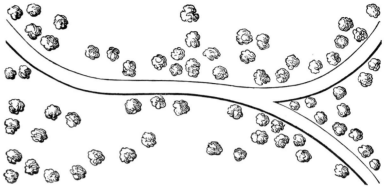

emerged that derived a substantial income from city-based commercial enterprises, and the parkland style of fashionable eighteenth-century rural estates did not suit their urban mansions. Instead, they required a more decorative approach, which included all the features of the gardens of the aristocracy in a fraction of the space. In time they demanded many other features as well. For this was the period of the great horticultural explosion that accompanied the development of conservatories and which was fuelled by the great botanical and horticultural explorations of the nineteenth century. The change in garden fashion was widespread and rapid.

Literary expression for this new style came from John Claudius Loudon. He is thought to have coined the term gardenesque to describe it; he certainly promoted its acceptance through his voluminous writings in the 1820s and 1830s. In *The Suburban Gardener and Villa Companion* (1838) he defined the gardenesque as

the production of that kind of scenery which is best calculated to display the individual beauty of trees, shrubs, and plants in a state of culture; the smoothness and greenness of lawns; and the smooth surfaces, curved directions, dryness, and firmness of gravel walks: in short, the gardenesque style is calculated for displaying the art of the gardener . . .

The very opposite had been true in the previous century: the greatest compliment that could have been paid to a designer such as Brown would have been *not* to recognize his hand in a

landscape. By the time Victoria was settled, the landscaped garden was a thing of the past in Britain and the gardenesque was in full swing. There was a time-lag due to the colonists' immediate need for survival, but the gardenesque came to have a very strong influence on gardens in Australia, and on those in Victoria particularly, when time and money became available for decorative gardening.

THE FIRST PLANTING of exotic species in Victoria occurred on Churchill Island in March 1801 when Lieutenant James Grant made the initial European landing there from the exploratory sloop *Lady Nelson*. Grant planted wheat and other grain, coffee, fruit and vegetable seeds and potatoes, but it was left to his successor on the *Lady Nelson*, Acting Lieutenant John Murray, to return and harvest what remained of the crops at the end of 1801. Soon after establishing his little garden on Churchill Island Grant planted seeds on nearby Elizabeth Island (or Margaret Island, as he called it), though he considered its soil less fertile.

Another brief mention of early European plantings in Victoria comes from James Flemming, who was with the surveyor Charles Grimes when he discovered the River Yarra on 2 February 1803. Flemming wrote in his journal for 8 February: 'Sowed some seeds by the natives' hut . . .'

A few months later, in October of 1803, David Collins, Lieutenant-Governor of the proposed Port Phillip settlement, disembarked near what is now Sorrento with the convicts and free settlers conveyed from Britain in the *Calcutta* and *Ocean*. The unsuitability of the location quickly became apparent and the settlement was abandoned less than four months later – but not before Collins had had a few acres opened up for a garden and corn crop. Of these, he told Governor King in New South Wales, 'I do not entertain much hope, but I find in it some employment for my people'. Meanwhile J. H. Tuckey, First Lieutenant on the *Calcutta*, had been exploring land close to the shores of the bay with a small party. In an account published in 1805 he provides one more record of horticultural interest:

Though this excursion added but little to the knowledge of the country, it is hoped it will not be entirely devoid of utility. In those spots which appeared best adapted to the purpose, seeds from Rio Janeiro and the Cape were sown, viz. oranges, limes, melons, pumpkins, Indian corn, and several kinds of garden seeds.

Victoria's next known gardens were planted by sealers on Phillip Island in the early 1820s. Then Captain Samuel Wright established a settlement at Western Port late in 1826, and thirteen days after his arrival reported to Governor Darling that 'an excellent garden' had been planted and that the seeds had germinated well. But this, like all the other very early exotic gardens in Victoria, was short-lived.

John Pascoe Fawkner crossed from Van Diemen's Land and commenced a garden on 18 November 1835 at the edge of the swamp near Emerald Hill, Melbourne, planting potatoes, beans, peas, radish and cabbage seeds. Fawkner also brought a varied assortment of 2500 fruit trees from his nursery at Windmill Hill near Launceston. The demand for such plants grew, and on 28 June 1848 Fawkner announced in the *Geelong Advertiser* the following for sale from the nursery he had in the meantime established in Victoria: '35 apple varieties; 20 pears; 20 plums; 10 cherries; 200+ varieties of grapevines, as well as peaches, nectarines, apricots, figs, currants, mulberries, filberts, gooseberries and also shrubs and bulbs.' Already in 1846 G. H. Haydon (*Five Years' Experience in Australia Felix*) had recorded that

Massie and Anderson were growing fruits at Western Port that included grapes, melons, apples, pears, peaches, currants, Cape gooseberries and cherries.

The first recorded picture of gardens in Victoria is thought to be in an engraving by J. Carmichael called *Melbourne from the South side of the Yarra Yarra*, dated 1839. It shows a large garden laid out adjacent to Commissary Erskine's House in Collins Street and a smaller one around John Batman's house on the Yarra River. It would be unwise to accept without question the detail supplied by the engraver, but it does at least conform with an early nineteenth-century stereotype. Carmichael depicts both gardens as axial, divided by paths into rectangular areas. Both have a circular bed in front of the house and the entire gardens seem to be laid out in furrows.

The first gardens developed in Victoria were little concerned with aesthetics. They were, as Beatrice Bligh has described

Thomas Turner's drawing of Taradale as it was in about 1868 suggests that, although there is as yet no flower garden, the owners have gone to some trouble to lay out their vegetable garden attractively

Opposite: A cottage garden, 1872. The locality was Hill End, New South Wales, but such gardens might have been seen in many developing parts of Australia. Near the house is a highly decorative area given over to shrubs and flowers; further away the garden is planted with vegetables in simple geometric style

them in *Cherish the Earth* (1973), 'gardens of survival'. As settlers spread throughout the state their primary concern was indeed survival, and the plants and seeds they took with them were mostly ones that would produce food.

Anne Drysdale was a middle-aged woman who took up the Boronggoop run near the Barwon River in about 1841. Her diary tells us that by August of that year she had established peach, plum and cherry trees in her garden. In September of the same year she records that peas, carrots, melons and onions were all planted, as well as vines, turnips, cabbage, cauliflower and potatoes. Thirty young almond trees were being transplanted. The only flowers she refers to at that stage came from the bush. Writing in her diary on 16 September 1841, she says that 'the ladies again rode after dinner. While they were away I was employed with the children bringing home roots of flowers from the bush to plant in the garden'. (Perhaps Anne Drysdale was particularly partial to the native plants: on her arrival in Victoria she had had a long, hot walk from the port, but she remarked that 'the flowers, shrubs & trees as we went along delighted us all'.)

The Midgley family settled at Yangery Grange near Koroit in 1852. Sarah Midgley too kept a diary, and gardening matters featured quite prominently in it. The orchard yielded enough plums for a pie or two by 1856, and in the same year Sarah's brother brought home from another garden in the locality 'several slips of holly'. Later she was delighted with 'Moss Rose cuttings which we have long wished for'. Flowers seem to get as many mentions as food plants in this diary.

Few of the utilitarian gardens survive, except in illustrations. They date from no particular period, but seem to have appeared when any part of the country was newly opened up. These gardens were generally rectangular in shape and mostly in front of the house. A central path controlled the arrangement with various other paths parallel or at right angles. The gardens had no lawn, the whole area being taken up in intensive cultivation and surrounded by a stockproof fence.

An interesting remnant of one of these gardens may be seen at Green Hills, Tarraville. Surrounded by a split paling fence,

the garden is divided into rectangular compartments. Immediately in front of the house is a simple geometric arrangement of flower beds surrounded by an edging of saw-tooth brickwork. This part was the flower garden, as were other sections close to the house. But most of the area was devoted to fruit and vegetables, with earthen paths dividing the garden into rectangular patches of convenient size. It is very doubtful whether the residents of this humble dwelling knew anything about the intellectual theories of Loudon who, in *The Suburban Gardener and Villa Companion*, had said:

The suitableness of this [geometric] style for a country in a wild state must, we think, be obvious to every unprejudiced mind, from the contrast which its clearly defined lines and forms offer to the irregularity of the surrounding scenery, and from the obvious expression of art and refinement which they produce . . . [It is therefore calculated] to suit newly peopled, and thinly inhabited, countries, such as the back settlements of America or Australia.

Indeed, Australian colonists would almost certainly have found such notions absurd: their reasons for creating geometric gardens were eminently practical. Sketches of gardens similar to that at Green Hills remain for the first homesteads at Bontharambo (Wangaratta) and The Gums (Penshurst).

Sometimes these first gardens were very small. Jack Redgrave's garden, in *Ups and Downs: A Story of Australian Life* by

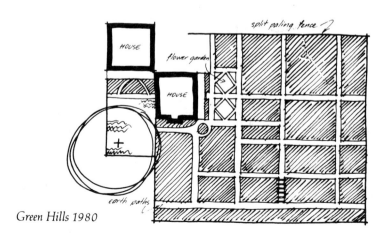

Green Hills 1980

sketched the cottage about ten years later when its profusion of plants gave it the intimacy of an English cottage and garden.

The artist Georgiana McCrae, a friend of the La Trobes, wrote in her journal for June 1841: 'Sent to Jolimont for the cuttings of creepers, geraniums, and roses promised by Mr La Trobe.' Her gardens in Melbourne and a little later at Arthurs Seat may also have been exceptions – like Jolimont – to the utilitarian rule. A list of plants from Georgiana's garden in 1843 includes several kinds of vegetables but a somewhat greater number of flowers, including nasturtiums, iris, tulips, hollyhock, wallflower, carnations, alyssum and poppies. There are no fuchsias in the inventory: four months earlier she had written that the fuchsia she had been given by a friend had been destroyed overnight – 'Mr McCrae blames Archie for allowing our cow to rove'.

Grander versions of the gardenesque than that at Jolimont appeared in Victoria when, from the 1850s, those who had begun to prosper enlarged their cottages or abandoned them in favour of bigger houses requiring more extensive gardens. A number of gardens, though all changed to some extent, survive from this period. They include Burswood at Portland, Murndal at Hamilton, The Heights at Geelong, Wombat Park at Daylesford, Como in South Yarra (painted by William Tibbits in 1875), Meningoort at Camperdown and Glenara at Bulla (two properties painted by Eugène von Guérard in 1861 and 1867 respectively).

There is little consistency in the gardens of this period except that they are generally large pleasure gardens as opposed to solely utilitarian ones. They contain some restrained decoration as in the balustraded terrace at Glenara and the fountain at Como. Their paths are usually curved. The trees shown in early pictures are small but of species that would eventually achieve gigantic proportions. Burswood, Como and Glenara are all essentially gardenesque in character. Murndal, with its 'Richmond Park', 'Cowthorp Oak' and 'Coronation Avenue', seems to attempt to recreate an English manor setting in the Australian countryside. The garden at Meningoort on the other hand was conceived with a grandeur certainly not

Rolf Boldrewood, is thought to date from the 1850s, though the tale was written in 1878. Boldrewood says of the garden:

Over there was where he had sowed his first vegetable seeds, cutting down and carrying the saplings with which it was fenced. It was, certainly, so small that the blacks believed he had buried some one there, whom he had done to death secretly, and would never be convinced to the contrary, disbelieving both his vows and his vegetables.

Prior to 1850 there were few gardens in Victoria that made any concessions to decoration or to leisure. A notable exception was that surrounding the cottage occupied by the Superintendent of the colony, Charles Joseph La Trobe. A painting of Jolimont, as the house was called, survives from about 1844 (the artist is unknown). If there was a utilitarian part of the garden, and there probably was, it is not shown in the picture. Instead, we find a picturesque cottage as the focus of a true gardenesque design. Even the flower beds cut into the lawns are in the shapes of crescents and diamonds. Loudon would have thoroughly approved. A gardener scythes the lawn on which have been left a few of the indigenous trees. La Trobe's cousin, the garden designer Edward La Trobe Bateman,

Even the comparatively small first part of the homestead at Meningoort, Camperdown (about 1860), had a grand axial drive leading up to its front steps. The boldness of this concept was enhanced when the house was extended

The front garden of Como, South Yarra, in the early 1860s. The decorative urns have long since disappeared

common in England at the time, and Bontharambo's with a baroque sense of splendour totally unprecedented.

Kitchen gardens remained of great importance, especially on the remoter country properties where there were no alternative supplies of fruit and vegetables. An early account of W. E. Stanbridge's garden at Wombat Park, Daylesford, in the *Daylesford Advocate* described the kitchen garden thus:

Here the vine thrives in all its splendor. The hop has been most successfully cultivated. Every kind of English tree is seen to the greatest advantage. The almond, hazel, walnut, filbert, and other trees of the same species, have, by their growth and productiveness, amply repaid the efforts of the careful cultivator. We were particularly struck with the amazing growth of the apple and pear trees, which had been planted only eighteen months. In this garden there are between sixty and seventy different sorts of English apple trees, which from their height, bulk, and luxuriance, prove that the red volcanic soil in which they are planted, and which abounds in this district, is destined, at no distant time, to astonish those most familiar with the exuberance of the Victorian soil generally.

Many of these homestead kitchen gardens lasted well into the

was unemployed at times and the entire backyard of her family's home at Alphington was given over to food-producing, with a chicken pen as well as vegetables and fruit trees. A man living at Fairfield, who enjoyed only intermittent work during the depression, said that his whole garden was cultivated with vegetables and that they were shared with others. (A good deal of sharing and bartering of homegrown foodstuffs went on.) A carpenter of Ballarat said his family grew all its own 'vegetables . . . fruit trees . . . currants'. Of 500 people asked whether they grew their own food at that time 365 replied; 71 per cent of these said yes. (Nearly 20 per cent also kept poultry for meat and/or eggs.) David Potts says that 'the largest acknowledged *increase* in production was amongst those most heavily affected by the depression'.

This is the story of selected gardens rather than of gardening because documentation of such day-to-day activities during

A vegetable patch surrounded by clipped cypress hedging at Mount William, Willaura (left)

Vegetable-growing was important to suburban households with incomes diminished by the Great Depression: the owner of this work of art was rightly proud of it

twentieth century, but they have mostly disappeared now. Those remaining at such places as Mount William (Willaura), Talindert (Camperdown), Woolongoon (Mortlake), Barunah Plains (Hesse) and Government House in Melbourne are reminders of what was once an essential and major part of gardening activity.

City gardens such as that of Rippon Lea had extensive orchards and kitchen gardens, and there were undoubtedly vegetable patches and fruit trees in smaller gardens throughout Victoria in the nineteenth century, though it is impossible to gauge their extent now. It is not much easier to guess how much vegetable-growing is done in the 1980s. Perhaps there will always be a substantial minority of people who want to grow as much of their own food as possible, however restricted their garden space.

One short but important period in the early twentieth century has been investigated on this score. Research by David Potts of La Trobe University shows that during the Great Depression food grown in their own gardens made an important contribution to the diet of ordinary people. One of the women interviewed for the study was born in 1911; her father

most of Victoria's history is sparse. The 'great gardens' and the publicly funded gardens often had a firm structure and semi-permanent features such as dominant drives, flights of steps, summer houses and fountains. They also had space for long-living and lofty trees. Few small gardens owned by people of average skill and means managed to be anything other than ephemeral.

FROM THE 1850s onwards, gardens quickly became an important part of life in Victoria. Vast wealth generated by the gold rush of the 1850s, a reticulated water supply in Melbourne after 1857, the temperate climate, and a widespread interest in horticulture set the stage for a boom in garden-building around many a city mansion and country homestead.

James Sinclair provided in *The Beauties of Victoria in 1856* a description of '200 of the principal gardens round Melbourne'. Kearney's map of the previous year confirms the extent of many of these gardens, which appear to have been up to 12 hectares in size. Como, for instance, is known from a descrip-

Kearney's map (right) shows the extent of some of the gardens along the Yarra Valley in 1855. Como lies immediately south-east of Bona Vista (marked), and its entrance drive appears to run off Williams Road at this stage

The gate lodge at Como was located on Toorak Road when photographed around 1910. Built by 1864, it was demolished about 1911

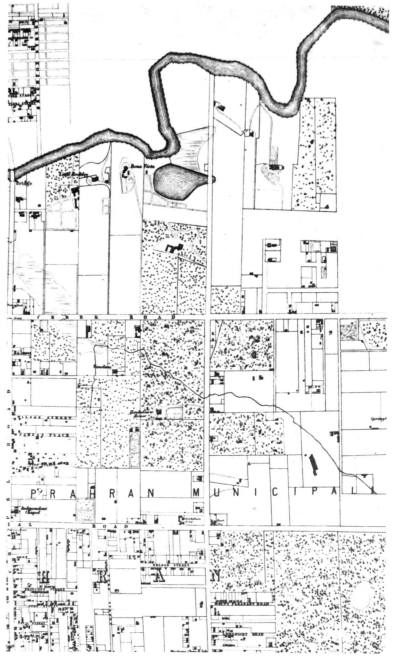

tion in 1866 to have had an intensively cultivated area of 6 hectares around a house whose nucleus had been built in 1847. It was entered through 'its massive entrance gates with Gothic pillars' adjacent to an 'octagon lodge surmounted by battlements'.

Gardeners and nurserymen arriving from Britain helped to encourage an enthusiasm for gardening. Many of them had been trained in the great gardens and nurseries of Britain and Europe, and two such men were the Scots John Arthur and John Dallachy. Arthur was an experienced landscape gardener who had been head gardener to the Duke of Argyll before emigrating with his family to the Port Phillip settlement. Appointed superintendent of the new Melbourne Botanic Gardens in 1846, Arthur seems to have given the gardens a good beginning; but he died suddenly in 1849 and a new curator was required. His successor, John Dallachy, had worked at the Royal Botanic Gardens, Kew, and been head gardener on the estate of the Earl of Aberdeen. His consuming passion, however, was botanical collecting, and preoccupation with this aspect of his work took him away from the Melbourne gardens rather too much. Thus by 1857 the directorship had been given to Dr Ferdinand Mueller, and Dallachy's role was reduced to that of field collector for a few more years.

Phillip Doran was another emigrant gardener who readily found a niche in Victoria. He had been apprenticed to the famous Joseph Paxton, at a time when the landscaper and hothouse builder who became Sir Joseph Paxton was still head gardener to the Duke of Devonshire at Chatsworth. Settling in Castlemaine in the 1850s, he later created the Botanic Gardens in that town. Doran's position might have gone to another well-trained gardener if circumstances had been a little different. On 6 November 1854 one Friedrich Hirschi wrote to Sir Charles Hotham, Lieutenant-Governor of Victoria. He described his years of study in Switzerland at an eminent institute for agriculture and gardening and asked for portion of Castlemaine's reserve land for a 'public botanical Garden, which I am willing to enclose at my own expense'. Hirschi wanted to start a nursery there for native and introduced plants, 'thereby

arriving at the exact time for planting and transplanting Trees, Shrubs, Plants, and for sowing seeds &c, which in a country so little known can only be productive of the greatest benefit to the Inhabitants and to Botanists'. Records held by the Department of Crown Lands and Survey show that the Surveyor-General's advice to Hotham was against granting the request: perhaps, though, the people of Castlemaine might employ Hirschi if and when they officially sought permission to commence botanical gardens. Those gardens were not gazetted until 1860, however. Nearly four years before that, Hirschi already had an impressive private garden of 2 or 3 hectares laid out near Castlemaine and was on the way to becoming one of the town's pioneer nurserymen.

Some emigrant horticulturists working in private gardens had a small army of assistants. They were all – as were owners – helped in their task by the numerous horticultural books and journals available by that time.

The weekly newspaper the *Victorian Farmers' Journal and Gardeners' Chronicle* had plenty of advice for its gardening readers. In

This unusual rose 'trellis' is an example of the lengths to which some gardeners went to achieve a striking effect

35

July of 1860 it suggested that they 'trench and drain the whole of their land'. Where the soil consisted of 'cold stiff clays... refrain from planting till the second year. This will give an opportunity of getting the land to a better tilth using lime, ashes...sand, bones and dung of every kind...' The garden-writer remarked that 'On the taste of individual planters, the beauty or otherwise of our suburban scenery twenty years hence will depend...', and asked readers to record the results of their garden experience for the benefit of others. Newspapers of less specifically horticultural intent also catered for gardeners; the *Australasian* was another weekly that, from 1864, supplied a good deal of information to gardeners, reporting also on gardening successes at agricultural shows.

The regular garden columns tended towards the practical, supplying detailed hints on vegetable-growing, pruning, seed-raising, mulching and weeding, and flower-combinations for carpet bedding. It might be suggested that carriage drives be given a graceful sweep rather than sharp curves, and that space should be left along boundaries for fence-concealing shrubs, but sophisticated ideas on design tended to be confined to the works of such writers as the Englishman Loudon. Readers in the colonies might not, in any case, have been able to absorb the subtleties of garden design quickly, but they could fill their gardens with what the local literature told them was the latest in off-the-shelf urns, vases, fountains and balustrades. Such garden ornaments could actually be inspected, very often, at Victoria's Exhibitions. Displaying locally produced and imported goods of all kinds, these were held in Victoria from 1854 onwards. Compared with later Exhibitions, the first is said to have been a mere bazaar, but they all attracted a great deal of attention. Terra cotta edging tiles and vases were among garden products displayed at the Victorian Intercolonial Exhibition of 1875. At the International Exhibition of 1880 the exhibit from the Melbourne Botanic Gardens received special praise in *Massina's Popular Guide to the Melbourne International Exhibition 1880–1*. There was a collection of fibres prepared from plants growing in the gardens, some of them dyed to demonstrate their suitability for use in floor coverings. Fully labelled

fruits and seeds from 1300 genera were displayed, together with 'one portfolio containing a full collection of Victorian ferns'. The published record of the Centennial International Exhibition of 1888–89 lists a host of garden products: garden seats and tables and ornamental wirework exhibited by a South Melbourne company; imported lawnmowers; an 'ornamental conservatory' from an East Melbourne firm; horticultural tools made in Sheffield; and eight-armed lawn sprinklers from a Melbourne company.

Horticultural societies were a further source of information and stimulation for the colony's gardeners. A horticultural society initiated by John Pascoe Fawkner in 1849 had arranged regular exhibitions of fruit and vegetables and claimed to have already fostered much interest in gardening when a meeting was held to discuss a falling away in attendance. A report of the meeting in the *Argus* of 26 August 1853 blamed the gold rush, which had drawn attention to 'what was to be found under the earth, [rather] than to the floral beauties which might be produced upon its surface'. The society was disbanded in 1854 but the Horticultural Society of Victoria was founded in 1856 and the Victorian Gardeners' Mutual Improvement Society (later known as the Victorian Horticultural Improvement Society and still later as the Victorian Horticultural Society) in 1859. Regional branches of the societies, like the parent bodies, conducted regular meetings and held shows at least once a year, the city groups frequently using the Botanic Gardens as venue.

The eclectic English gardening style of the nineteenth century was perfectly suited to a new, rich, and essentially urban colony. It allowed boundless individualism for an aggressively opportunist and gregarious society. William Kelly in *Life in Victoria* (1859) remarked on the implications of wealth for the gardens of one part of Melbourne:

The land in the South Yarra district, fortunately for its abiding pre-eminence, was originally in the hands of wealthy and respectable classes, free enough from the vice of avarice to resist the prevailing temptation of cutting up their properties into small allotments... the purchasers, who were mostly of the settling class, were thus

Government House, Sydney (1808–9): G. W. Evans depicted it as largely utilitarian

Similarly practical were the small gardens painted by Charles Norton in 1844 at Seven Hills (below), and in 1847 at Tooralle near Clunes (below right)

Panshanger, Tasmania, in 1835. This lithograph from a painting by W. Lyttleton indicates that Panshanger owed more to eighteenth-century English landscaping than to trends in the nineteenth century

Pioneer gardens in Victoria that expressed their owners' decorative instincts: Smeaton Hill, the station of Captain Hepburn in 1846 (far left), and a view from Charles Norton's front door at Carlsbadt on the Barwon in 1848 (left), both painted by Norton

Shoubra, Geelong, about 1875. William Tibbits was obviously aware of the prevailing wind that undid some of the formality of this hilltop garden, with its statue, fountain, and lines of conifers

enabled to build fine dwellings and surround themselves with gardens and pleasure-grounds . . . The villa residences then in existence were of a superior order, with gardens scrupulously neat and trim, after the style of Putney or Twickenham . . .

Some of the greatest horticultural extravagances were reserved for the hill station gardens, especially those at Mount Macedon. These houses and gardens were commenced in the 1870s when allotments became available for residences. The summer move to the mountain gained momentum when the government in 1888 acquired a 'cottage' for the Governor, Sir Henry Loch, and his entourage and Melbourne society shifted en masse to the cooler clime of Mount Macedon for the hot months.

The gardens at the resort competed with each other in their lavish collections of plants and their summer displays. The rich soil, cool climate and abundant water supply encouraged the introduction of an astonishing range of plants. Charles Ryan is said to have employed William Guilfoyle to lay out his extensive garden at Derriweit Heights, and to have spent a total of £30 000 on it. Others spent equally lavishly on their gardens and many owners still do.

By the 1870s a number of garden designers had emerged, some of whom were able to rationalize the Victorian passion for variety and complexity in gardens. Joseph Sayce in 1873 produced a plan for the development of the Government House garden and the Domain that showed a restraint and simplicity uncommon for the period. Virtually nothing is known of Sayce's life, but he was not a professional designer.

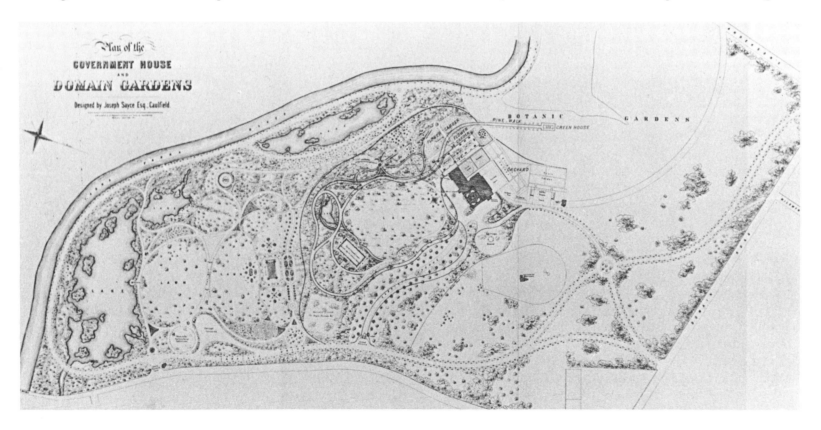

Joseph Sayce's 1873 plan for Melbourne's Government House garden shows that the present grounds owe much more to the 'amateur' Sayce than to the Botanic Gardens Director William Guilfoyle, whose modifications are marked on this copy of the plan. The two men seem, however, to have held similar ideas on design

William Guilfoyle, called in to redesign the Colac gardens in 1910, was disparaging about Bunce's original plan in several respects but felt that the drives 'could scarcely be improved upon'. It seems, however, that the drives of 1910 were not those laid down by Bunce. Isaac Hebb's series of articles written in 1888 for the *Colac Herald* and republished in 1970 under the title *The History of Colac and District* shows that alterations to the carriageway were made in about 1876, the curator of the day, C. Reeves, having consulted 'two professional gardeners' before proceeding. Reeves claimed that the original drive was not wide enough, its angles were too sharp for turning carriages, and it did not allow vehicles to enter at one end of the gardens and depart from the other. The next curator, John McDonald – appointed in 1877 – improved the carriageway further, extending it 'around the crest of the hill overlooking the lake . . . [then] along the southern edge of the gardens to the main entrance gates'.

The Hon. V. N. Hood was a peripatetic government official who frequently photographed his employers and their friends. As aide to the Governor of Victoria he would often have visited Mount Macedon and its 'Government Cottage'. Derriweit Heights, photographed by Hood in 1911, was a nearby property

Originally designed by Daniel Bunce in the 1860s, the drives in Colac's Botanic Gardens (right) were considerably altered in the 1870s

When he joined the Victorian Gardeners' Mutual Improvement Society in 1860 he was clearly designated 'amateur', a distinction of some importance in an association for 'Practical gardeners and Amateurs of acknowledged ability'. (The membership list notes his business address as 'Bank of Victoria'.) The *Australasian* also described him as an amateur in 1873, and on his death in 1876 the *Leader* called him 'one of our most intelligent and enthusiastic amateur gardeners', whose garden at Elsternwick had been 'quite a model, both in design and in the choice of the trees and shrubs with which it is planted'.

Several professional designers were working in Victoria during this period and earlier. Daniel Bunce first arrived in Victoria in 1839 after some years as a nurseryman in Tasmania. He became curator of the Geelong Botanic Gardens in 1857, planning and planting about 80 hectares at Eastern Park (the formal gardens now only occupy something like 5 hectares). Bunce also laid out the Botanic Gardens at Colac.

Little is known of Bunce's skill as a designer. Only his parkland at Geelong, some of the drives through it, and various trees planted at the heart of the gardens remain as evidence.

Bunce wrote a number of books, ranging from the *Manual of Practical Gardening* (Hobart, 1838) – quite informative, but sparse in design ideas – to what E. E. Pescott has shown to be the grossly plagiaristic *Hortus Victoriensis* (Melbourne, 1851).

Edward La Trobe Bateman, a cousin of Lieutenant-Governor C. J. La Trobe, was a draughtsman, illuminator and sketcher as well as a garden designer. In 1857 he planned two of Melbourne's public parks – the Fitzroy and the Carlton Gardens – and later a number of private gardens around Melbourne and in the Western District (including Wooriwyrite at Kolora). His

stylistic approach to the city public gardens was rather stiff, but Dr John Foster of the University of Melbourne's history department points out that Bateman was also capable of 'relaxed and natural' designs where these were appropriate.

For James Sinclair, who had been the highly regarded Scottish landscaper to a Russian prince, helping also to design the Royal Gardens at St Petersburg for Czar Nicholas, the position of curator at the Fitzroy Gardens in the Colony of Victoria must have seemed a little tame. However, he set out in 1858 to convert La Trobe Bateman's geometric design to a landscape

Daniel Bunce, author of several books and curator of the Geelong Botanic Gardens from 1857 to 1872

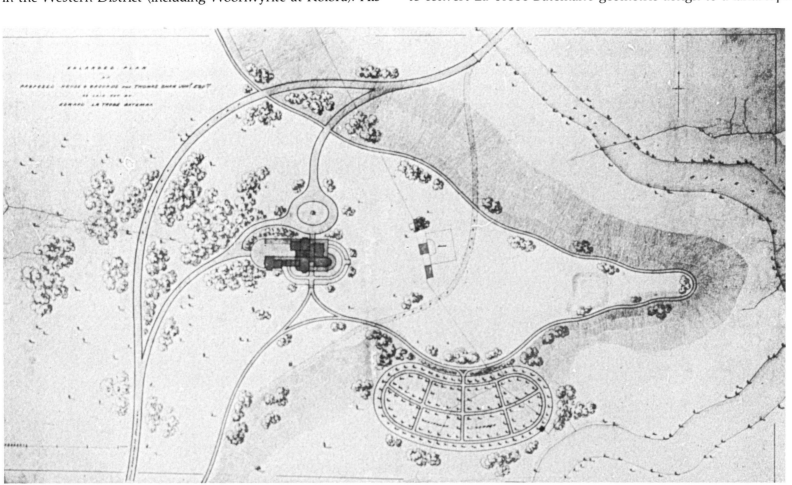

Plan by Edward La Trobe Bateman of the garden at Wooriwyrite, Kolora

of curving lines and natural contours, exploiting rather than ignoring the creek that crossed the square. Sinclair spent the rest of his life at the gardens and died there in what is still called 'Sinclair's cottage'. Like Bunce, Sinclair produced a number of books, including several on gardens and gardening. He also wrote verse and had something of a reputation at the Royal Botanic Gardens, Kew, as a plant illustrator.

A number of nurserymen were advertising plants – and sometimes also their skills at landscaping – in Victoria by the mid-nineteenth century. Newspapers published many such notices, and Rosemary Polya has listed and illustrated surviving catalogues in her *Nineteenth Century Plant Nursery Catalogues of South-East Australia: A Bibliography*. Daniel Bunce's St Kilda nursery was one of the earliest, established in 1839. John Rule set up his nursery business in 1850 and published his first catalogue in 1857. In addition to offering a wide range of flower, vegetable and agricultural (such as lucerne) seeds, Rule advertised fruit trees, vines, and what he called florists' plants. He would 'lay out and furnish orchards, vineyards, flower-gardens, pleasure-grounds at reasonable rates' and pack and

Photographed somewhere around the 1920s, the cottage in the Fitzroy Gardens built for their first curator William Sinclair still stands

From De Guchy and Leigh's isometric plan of 1866 (right), a portion of East Melbourne that includes the Fitzroy Gardens. The Melbourne Cricket Ground is one of many distinct landmarks beyond the gardens

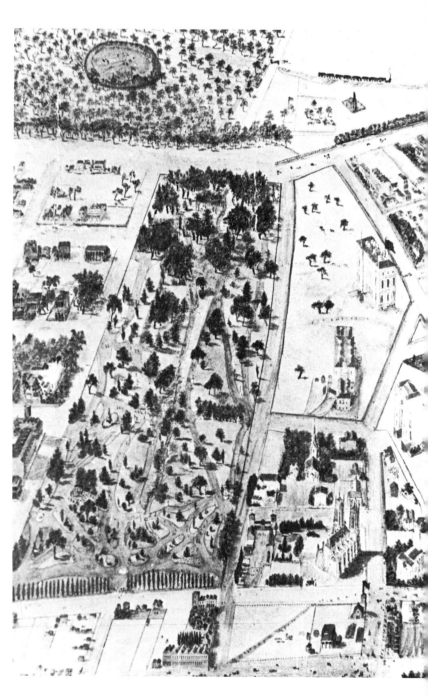

dispatch 'cases of Australian plants, seeds, and ferns . . . to any part of the globe'. The wholesale and retail seedsmen Law, Somner began business in 1850 and the seeds firm still operates as Law Sumner Pty Ltd. Other well-known companies were those of William Adamson, George Brunning, Thomas Lang, Thomas McMillan, and John Smith & Sons.

The firm of Taylor & Sangster laid out many gardens in Melbourne and in rural areas of Victoria, as well as conducting nurseries at Toorak and Mount Macedon. Both William Taylor and William Sangster had earlier been gardeners in distinguished establishments – Sangster at Como and Taylor at Government House – so that there is no doubt that the partners were highly experienced in the art of horticulture. One of their best-known landscaping projects was the redesigning of part of the Carlton Gardens around the Exhibition Building erected in 1880.

However, the dominant figure in garden design was undoubtedly William Robert Guilfoyle, who replaced Baron Ferdinand von Mueller as director of the Melbourne Botanic Gardens in 1873. Guilfoyle delighted many Victorians with his bold reconstruction of the gardens and, although despised by some sections of the press, which bitterly criticized him for undertaking private work, he was responsible for many domestic and public gardens throughout Victoria. His design idiom, like that of Sayce, was a well-controlled rationalization of Victorian garden ideals. He favoured the 'English landscape' style, as he called it in a letter to Niel Black in August 1898. This meant sweeping lawns and bold curves, but also allowed for picturesque elements such as the summer houses and arbours he designed for the Botanic Gardens. His notes for the 'Wilderness or Wild Garden' at the Palmer property near Terang (probably The Bend) show his feeling for the picturesque combined with the natural:

The pathway is shown winding through shrubbery with occasional glimpses of the interior portion of the dell . . . Each side of the path may be edged with Violets, Primroses, Cowslips, Pansies, Lily of the valley, Wild Cape geraniums, Solomons seal, Golden rod, Acanthus, Torch Lilies or any other Lilies, tube rose, Wild Hyacinths, Scillas,

Belladonna, Ixias, Iris, in fact all sorts of bulbs and Herbaceous plants in irregular masses or patches, & running into or between the smaller wild shrubs . . . Cherry-plums . . . flowering peaches, plums & Cherries will be desirable. Roses can be allowed to grow wild without pruning, especially the stronger growers. The Himalayan rose 'Brunoniana', red Climbing China rose . . . the Banksian roses, might be allowed to clamber anywhere over the fence and up into the trees. Honeysuckles, Plumbago Capensis, Clematis . . . wistarias, Tecomas and Bignonias, together with many other quick growers should be trained eventually from tree to tree or to form arches. A wild garden really means picturesque confusion of plants and no formality of any kind.

About eighty years before Guilfoyle took control of the Melbourne Botanic Gardens, Humphry Repton had started to bring decorative elements back to the English garden. By 1873,

William Guilfoyle, Director of the Melbourne Botanic Gardens from 1873 to 1909: the man whose design established the gardens in their present form

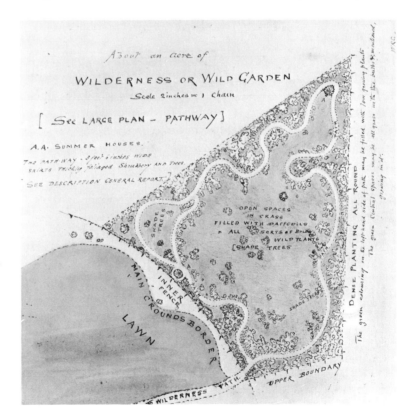

William Guilfoyle's plan for a 'wild garden', probably at The Bend, Terang

however, many gardens put undue emphasis on embellishment to the detriment of the general form. Guilfoyle was able to meet the popular demand for decoration without losing control of the overall design.

To what extent Guilfoyle influenced the design of private gardens other than those he actually laid out is not certain. One he may have had a hand in is that of Rippon Lea, which was possibly the greatest garden extravaganza in the state in the 1870s and which by the 1880s had undergone a complete transformation, much of the fussy detailing having been replaced by the sweeping lawns of today. The *Garden Gazette* of July 1902 remarked that 'Sir Frederick Sargood has not been above consulting those who have made a life's study of beautifying a home by means of well-planned and suitably planted gardens'. Guilfoyle may well have been one of those consulted. (So too may Joseph Sayce, who lived nearby.)

Almost a 'folly', and certainly an eye-catching element in the landscape: the bluestone lookout tower at Glenara, Bulla

An attractive gate lodge in the Gothic style (right) at Mount Noorat, Noorat

Opposite: The extravaganza of Rippon Lea in 1903

MANY OF THE GREAT pastoral fortunes had been made by the 1870s. Landholders abandoned the modest dwellings that had replaced the first huts and set about building the enormous stone and brick homesteads which are especially prevalent in the Western District. Some of the owners engaged professional designers – Edward La Trobe Bateman at Wooriwyrite and at Chatsworth House (Chatsworth), and Guilfoyle at Dalvui (Noorat), Mawallok (Beaufort), The Bend (Terang), Mooleric and Turkeith (Birregurra), and probably at Banongill (Skipton).

As if almost to symbolize the success of their owners, their pretensions to the status of landed gentry, some of these gardens adopted elements from the eighteenth century, but always combined them with the fashionable nineteenth-century style. Gate lodges were common, and excellent examples can still be seen at Ercildoune (Burrumbeet), Mount Hesse (Winchelsea), Mount Noorat (Noorat), Narrapumelap (Wickliffe) and Titanga (Lismore). They generally adopted a picturesque Gothic form, no matter what the style of the main homestead, but the fine lodges at Werribee Park (Werribee) and Rupertswood (Sunbury) are Italianate in style.

Ha-ha walls and variations of them were also used to give uninterrupted vistas into the landscape from the house and garden. A drop in levels, sometimes combined with a ditch at the foot of the wall that reinforced the cut, was sufficient to keep out stock without the visible barrier of a fence. Contrary to popular belief many Victorian homestead gardens were not inward-looking, attempting to shut out an alien and harsh landscape. In fact homesteads were often sited on slopes and hills to take advantage of views into the countryside. George O'Brien wrote on his plans for the pleasure garden at Bontharambo as early as the mid-1850s that 'summerhouses or grottoes [were] to be placed wherever a picturesque view upon the surrounding landscape or some patriarchal tree or other object can be obtained. . . ' Ha-ha walls served this purpose beautifully and examples can still be seen near the early bluestone farmhouse at Werribee Park, and at the homesteads Dalvui, Mawallok, Eynesbury, Glenormiston and Mount Noorat. Some of these might better be described as retaining walls – but they fill exactly the same aesthetic and practical role as the true ha-ha wall.

The great parklands that developed at Murndal and Mount Noorat, reminiscent of eighteenth-century English landscapes,

VIEW FROM THE WINDMILL

Box-hedging was quite a feature of the garden around one of the earlier homesteads at Mawallok, Beaufort

The glasshouse at Werribee Park, Werribee (right), housed ferns in 1916. Subsequently neglected, it was restored to use in the 1970s

have been discussed. Other significant parklands survive at Meningoort, Narrapumelap, Titanga and Talindert.

Box-hedged parterres, which were once common in country and city gardens alike, are now mostly found in homestead gardens. They have fared better there, away from the threat of the bulldozer. Box-hedging was certainly used in the 1870s and possibly earlier, though a comment in 1860 from the *Victorian Farmers' Journal and Gardeners' Chronicle* suggests that it was not then widespread: 'we certainly miss the nice box edgings of our English gardens'. The English Box, *Buxus sempervirens*, was widely planted in these hedges, although one or two of its cultivars are also listed in early catalogues. Often a garden devoted a special area, such as a rose garden, to a geometric parterre edged with box. A marvellous circular one survives at The Laurels near Learmonth. Others are at Rosemount near Koroit, Mount Boninyong, Scotsburn, and at Titanga, Lismore; remnants may be seen at Oakbank near Heywood and Gulf Station at Yea. There are twentieth-century examples at Delatite (Mansfield), Miegunyah (Toorak), Seven Creeks (Euroa) and Willaroo near Casterton.

Geometric flower gardens were also popular, especially in some of the larger gardens. These could be borders of flowers paralleling a driveway or path, or a much more elaborate affair such as the large circular flower garden recently restored at Werribee Park. Often beds were simply cut out of lawns and

filled with flowers. These were used to display the gardener's virtuosity at carpet bedding – a practice whereby seedling annual flowers were planted out in elaborate patterns. The plants were often selected to give excessively sculptured effects, sometimes known as mosaiculture, which needed glasshouses and shadehouses and plenty of labour behind them for success. The practice is still carried on to great effect in such places as the Fitzroy Gardens, Ballarat Botanical Gardens and the Conservatory Gardens in Bendigo. The Fletcher Jones factory garden in Warrnambool includes a mid-twentieth-century version of carpet bedding that has more of the flavour of a Victorian garden than have some of the authentic examples, whose trees have often grown to the point of dwarfing the flower beds.

Glasshouses were not only used for the production of seedlings for use in the garden. They were quite often grand affairs and frequently, as conservatories, were attached to the house, and indeed to one of the principal rooms. Mandeville Hall (Toorak), Rippon Lea (Elsternwick) and Fortuna (Bendigo)

all have beautiful conservatories with direct access from their drawing rooms. Here the choicest of ferns, flowers and palms were grown, often with the aid of elaborate heating systems. More commonly the conservatory was approached from a verandah, and excellent examples still survive at Trawalla (Beaufort), Renny Hill (Camperdown), Marida Yallock (Terang), Ingleby (Winchelsea) and Barunah Plains (Hesse). Heating systems were also used for free-standing glasshouses. There is an interesting contrast between the simple (and now almost derelict) arrangement at Warrock (Casterton) to heat what might well be one of the earliest glasshouses in the state, and the extensive underground equipment that warmed several now-demolished glasshouses at Alton (Mount Macedon), together with a number of water tanks used for growing tropical aquatic plants. Mark Girouard in his introduction to Susan Lasdun's book *Victorians at Home* (1981) has suggested that although these glazed rooms served the practical purpose of growing plants out of season, and denoting the prosperity of an owner by the richness and rarity of the display, they were also romantic, 'magically rich and sweet-scented bowers of colour and greenery...'

Members of the household could take their pleasure in the summer houses dotted around many a garden. Few of these have survived, their shingle or thatched roofs and lattice frameworks succumbing too readily to the rigours of the weather.

The conservatory of Sir Thomas Fitzgerald's house in Lonsdale Street, Melbourne in 1901 (above left)

A summer house built in 1912 at Riversdale, Geelong West (its fanlight came from a demolished building in Geelong)

47

Richard Aitken, in an exhibition at the Geelong Art Gallery in
1980–81, demonstrated through many drawings and photographs of these and other garden structures just how numerous they were in the nineteenth century and how diverse they
were in design. They ranged from the most delicate little lattice
structures to the large rustic buildings which still survive at
Rippon Lea. In large public and botanic gardens they could be a
considerable size: one such was the now-demolished bougainvillea rest house in the Royal Botanic Gardens. Most of the
surviving examples are in the rustic style with posts of tree
fern trunks or saplings and walls of interlaced branches –
occasionally of short split sticks made into complicated geometric patterns. This type of rusticity became very popular and
manifested itself also in cast-iron seats and balustrades. Examples of the latter can be seen on the bridges at Rippon Lea. At
least a few summer houses were built in more permanent
materials, and two beautiful iron structures survive at Over-
newton (Keilor) and Ard Choille (Mount Macedon).

Not so durable were the many ferneries built in private and public gardens. Like summer houses they were often built of timber lattice and few are still standing. The large ones at Belmont (Beaufort), Avoca (South Yarra) and the Ballarat Botanical Gardens now survive only in drawings and photographs. The enormous fernery at Rippon Lea, although it has lost most of its lattice, has been fortunate in having a relatively long-lasting iron framework.

By and large homestead gardens were as individualistic as their city counterparts the mansion gardens, though they tended to be less fussy. They were true pleasure gardens, laid out for both convenience and enjoyment.

BY THE 1880s the art of gardening, both public and private, had become so widespread and well practised that the English historian J. A. Froude was able to write in *Oceana* (1886) that

A sense of beauty . . . everywhere indicated itself in the gardens, in striking contrast with the U.S., where the ordinary suburban house rises bare in the midst of indifferently kept grass, and even the

THE FERNERY

palaces of the millionaires stand in ground poorly laid out. In Melbourne, and in these colonies universally, there seemed a desire among the owners to surround themselves with graceful objects, and especially with the familiar features of their old home – oaks, maples, elms, firs, planes, and apple-trees.

Not everyone lived in the mansions described by Froude. In fact the vast majority of the people of Victoria knew much humbler circumstances. But they still found time to develop simple, often geometric gardens in front of their cottages. A model made by Mr James Cowling and exhibited in Castle-maine in 1866 shows a cottage and its garden laid out in a geometric arrangement of beds bordered with white rocks. The *Castlemaine Representative* published the suggestion 'that the Exhibition Committee purchases the model and forwards it to the Paris exhibition so that the people of Europe may be enabled to form some idea of the dwellings of the middle-classes of Australia'. William Tibbits painted Cornubian House at Daylesford, which had a very similar garden to Cowling's model. The *Victorian Farmers' Journal and Gardeners' Chronicle* in 1860 had something to say, too, on this kind of garden: 'gardens laid out

A manuscript written by Frances Annie Moore and held by the State Library of Victoria suggests that the very elaborate and well-cared-for little garden around this cottage at Wandin North was the work of the middle-aged couple on the left, who moved to the newly completed house early in the 1880s

[About 1853] the town boundary was extended away into the Bush, and imaginative parks, and parades, and gardens without number, and of the most ambitious dimensions, were deliberately mapped and duly staked off. But [in 1858] the day-dream has turned out a reality, for these remote parks and pleasure-grounds are now being bounded by extensions of the original streets, lined with stately dwellings and magnificent terraces . . . surrounded with smiling parterres . . .

Nevertheless gardens such as the Fitzroy, Carlton and Treasury Gardens were developing, and by the end of the 1860s public gardens had been commenced in at least a dozen provincial centres.

The fantastic and rapid wealth gold gave to some towns and to some people now and then unleashed the full gardenesque style in public gardens. This was no more apparent than in the plan prepared for the Beechworth Botanical Gardens by Baron

James Cowling's model of a Castlemaine cottage (left). The beds are edged with white quartz

The lavish plan prepared in 1856 by a Hungarian daguerreotype artist, Baron Rochlitz, was intended for Beechworth's botanical reserve

geometrically . . . are easily planned on paper by the use of compasses and ruler, and in endless variety of shape and pattern . . . when well done, nothing for a garden of limited area can be better'.

These ordinary gardens have largely disappeared, and now mostly survive in the form of photographs – very often in family albums alone. Only a handful of simple terrace house and villa gardens dating from the 1880s remain to give us some idea of the intensity with which gardening was practised even in the smallest spaces.

As early as the 1840s a tradition of public gardens had begun in Victoria with the Melbourne Botanic Gardens, which were founded in 1846 under the curatorship of John Arthur. Superintendent Charles Joseph La Trobe was a key figure in the final choice of a location for the gardens. Enthusiastic about botany and pursuits related to it, La Trobe continued to take a keen interest in the Botanic Gardens and other gardens of the colony.

According to William Kelly in *Life in Victoria* (1859), however, the parks system envisaged in the early 1850s was blighted by the unforeseen development of subsequent years:

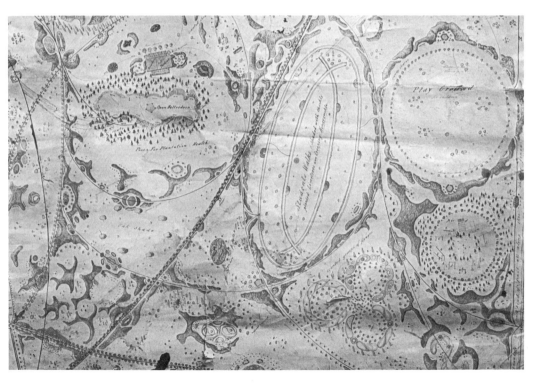

Rochlitz in 1856, though it seems to have gone no further than the paper it was drawn on. It is inscribed 'better late than never', perhaps indicating that it was an entrant in a competition. This great swirling and interlocking plan includes belvederes, playgrounds, a musicians' corner and archery ground, and caters for a host of other activities.

However, most of the public gardens were more subdued. The design of the later ones often took its cue from the Melbourne Botanic Gardens and in fact William Guilfoyle, who planned those gardens, was associated with a number of other botanic gardens in Victoria.

AS THE NINETEENTH CENTURY neared its end there was a reaction in Britain against the contrivance of the high Victorian garden. In 1870 William Robinson had published *The Wild Garden* and he followed it in 1883 with the mammoth *English Flower Garden*. In both works he promoted a style contrary to the prevailing gardening tastes. Like Loudon, Robinson paid attention to individual plants, but from this standpoint developed a mode of expression different from the gardenesque. The propo-

sition that being difficult to grow made a plant particularly desirable was dismissed by Robinson as nonsense. He found beauty in the fields and woods and hedgerows and in the natural association of plants, and he proclaimed the need for a more natural kind of gardening. His ideas were far from universally accepted, partly because of his slightly cranky nature. One of his chief opponents was the architect Sir Reginald Blomfield, who also disliked the excesses of Victorian gardens. Rejecting the resumption of a more natural style as a cure-all, Blomfield advocated a return to the simpler formality of the seventeenth century. He expressed these views in *The Formal Garden in England* (1892).

Victoria was soon similarly struggling with the two opposing points of view but its verbal blows were of a more gentlemanly kind than those being exchanged in the British press between Robinson and Blomfield. Marilyn McBriar has provided a useful analysis of the local debate (*Journal of the Australian Garden History Society*, no. 2, winter 1981). The differing standpoints were expressed in two papers read before the Royal Victorian Institute of Architects in 1903 and 1904 respectively. The first,

Charlie Hammond completed his bungalow, Winscombe at Belgrave, in 1914, and proceeded to clear land for a garden. By 1921 the house had been enlarged and the garden established (opposite). Architects and horticulturists might talk their heads off about garden design, but people like Charlie Hammond had their own ideas

entitled 'Garden Design in Relation to Architecture', was given by the architect Walter Butler. Butler had worked in England with J. D. Sedding, a supporter of Blomfield; and, not surprisingly, he approved of formal and architectural gardens. The second paper, 'Garden Design in Accord with Local Needs', was given by the principal of the Burnley School of Horticulture, C. Bogue Luffmann. He did not totally reject the formal style, but he clearly favoured for Australia a more natural style that involved paths and lawns in 'winding glades'. According to McBriar, 'Whereas Butler saw Australians as wanting (in their homes) to escape from primeval nature, Luffmann saw them as wanting to escape from their urbanized, industrialized society'.

The conflict was resolved in Britain by Gertrude Jekyll who, beginning in the 1890s and in consort with the architect Edwin Lutyens, planned formal gardens with an informal planting style to soften the architectural framework. And Edna Walling, strongly influenced by Gertrude Jekyll, and commencing in the 1920s, brought a similar harmony into some of Victoria's gardens.

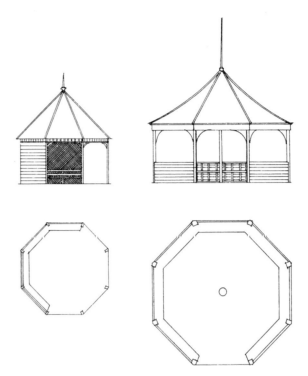

An octagonal rotunda at Kardinia Park, South Geelong, in 1880, and (far left) a summer house at Raith, Herne Hill, built by 1890

Part II Victoria's garden heritage
Botanic gardens

VICTORIA alone, of all the Australian states, developed in the nineteenth century a tradition of municipal botanic gardens in nearly every country town and city of any consequence. It was a remarkable phenomenon, and one that is still not properly understood. By the 1860s botanic gardens, some on a lavish scale, had been commenced in Castlemaine, Colac, Portland, Warrnambool, Ballarat, Daylesford, Williamstown, Kyneton, Malmsbury, Ararat, Koroit, Geelong, Bairnsdale, Alberton and Port Fairy, as well as in Melbourne. There were probably others. By the end of the 1880s Hamilton, Camperdown, Maryborough, Buninyong and Beechworth were among towns added to the list. It seems that every major country town marked the occasion of its coming of age by establishing a botanic garden.

Generally these gardens came into being when a group of local citizens formed a committee and petitioned the government for a grant of land. The approach was made through a department known at various times as the Lands Office, the Board of Land and Works, the Board of Lands and Survey, and – finally – the Department of Crown Lands and Survey. Where justification was adequate and suitable land was avail-

Melbourne's Botanic Gardens early this century and in 1982 (opposite)

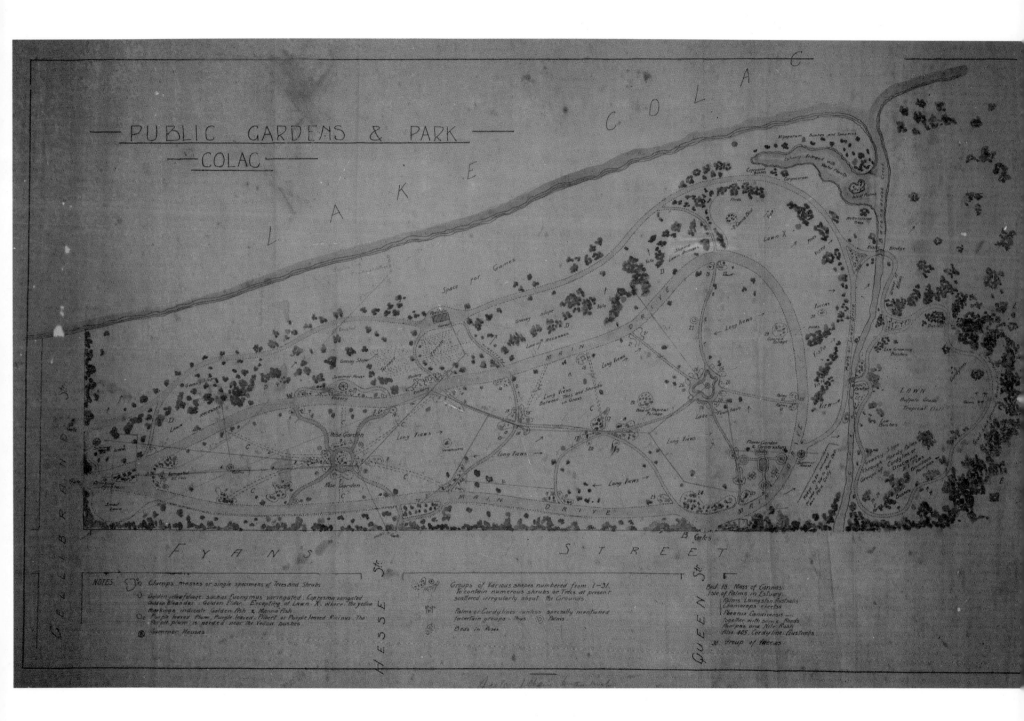

56

able (it seems often to have been already reserved for the purpose), the government was inclined to consent. On 10 March 1879 the Secretary of the Camperdown Park Committee wrote to the Minister for Lands:

This area is one of the few really beautiful and picturesque places to be found in this part of the colony, still belonging to the State. And to allow it by any mischance or other cause to be alienated from the people would be an irreparable misfortune to us and our posterity.

The grant was made and the garden laid out by William Guilfoyle. Regrettably posterity has allowed a caravan park to usurp these mature and once magnificent grounds.

Since botanic gardens were usually established following local pressure rather than representing a policy decided on by government, it is possible that there was a snowballing effect after the first few grants were made: perhaps sizeable towns came to expect land for this purpose, and governments began to apportion finance for it willy-nilly. But more likely it was simply that all the conditions were right – growing wealth in the community, an interest in botanical and horticultural pursuits, and a general stability – and sense of civic pride – as towns and cities settled down after their early and sometimes spectacular growth. The Acclimatisation Society, formed in 1861, encouraged the planting of a wide range of species from all over the world, and may have intensified the common preoccupation of ordinary men and women with the mysteries of botany. Dr Ferdinand Mueller, Director of the Botanic Gardens in Melbourne from 1857 to 1873 (by which time he was known as Baron Ferdinand von Mueller), was a voluminous correspondent and ardent traveller and probably influenced many prominent citizens to commence gardens in their own localities. He is known to have supplied trees and shrubs to the gardens of many country towns. There would have been many conifers among those trees, for Mueller – with his European background – had a special interest in them.

Whatever the reasons for so many botanic gardens being established in Victoria, little effort was spared. William Guilfoyle, who from 1873 began remodelling the Melbourne Botan-

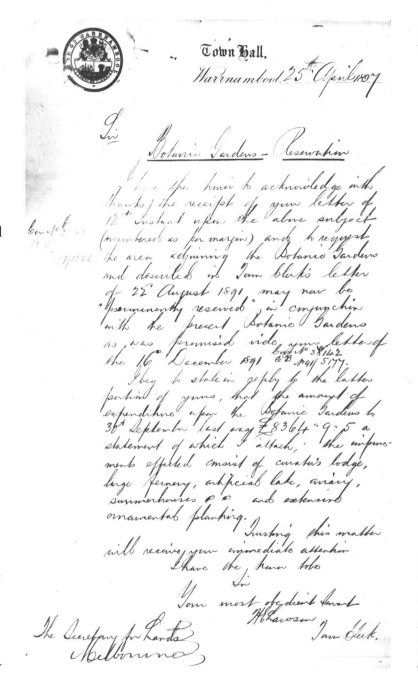

Opposite: William Guilfoyle's 1910 plan for the Colac Botanic Gardens

In the second half of the nineteenth century the Victorian Secretary for Lands was bombarded with letters from municipalities and groups of well-meaning citizens intent on setting up or extending botanic gardens

In 1880 Robert Whitworth drew up a plan for the Koroit Botanic Gardens under the direction of William Guilfoyle, who had visited Koroit to advise the council; it seems that there were government objections to Guilfoyle's doing the work himself

The famous fernery at Ballarat's Botanical Gardens in 1904 (opposite). These gardens were then, and still are, among the most elaborate in Victoria

ic Gardens, was associated with the development of five other botanic gardens – Warrnambool (1877), Horsham (about 1880), Koroit (1880), Camperdown (about 1888) and Colac (1910). Other well-known designers were engaged – William Sangster at Daylesford, Daniel Bunce at Geelong and Colac, William Allitt at Portland and William Ferguson at Hamilton.

The public is generally indiscriminate in its use of the terms 'botanic' or 'botanical' for these gardens, and even official records sometimes ignore local usage. Though the majority of botanic gardens today seem to use the shorter form, several Victorian country gardens still call themselves 'botanical'.

Some of the provincial botanic gardens were laid out in naturally spectacular surroundings. Camperdown's site is high on the edge of an extinct volcanic crater and the Daylesford gardens are also set on a hill, from which their lofty trees are a landmark over many kilometres. Most of the gardens are in the natural idiom of the English landscape revival movement, though with picturesque elements – arbours, rockeries and ponds. Others favoured more formal embellishments such as urns, fountains and statues. Ballarat, possibly the most elaborate of all, even boasts a glass-walled statuary pavilion erected in 1887. Summer houses, ferneries and bandstands were commonly found in botanic gardens and offered resting-places and entertainment to the crowds who visited them. In many ways,

in fact, most of Victoria's botanic gardens have been barely distinguishable from its municipal pleasure gardens. But in the early days plants were often carefully labelled, and curators were given the responsibility of trying out new species (some of them of potential importance commercially) for people such as Dr Mueller.

Sadly, many of these places are now ruined or in a state of neglect and abuse. Used as a convenient repository of civic memorabilia over the years, they have often lost their meaning. At Kyneton, Koroit and Port Fairy – as at Camperdown – municipal caravan parks smother what were once places of pleasure, pride and education.

A subcommittee of the Gardens and Environment Committee set up for Victoria's 150th Anniversary Celebrations was in 1981 provided with funds to begin the rejuvenation of the state's botanic gardens. Much remains to be done.

All the gardens in this section are open to the public

Royal Botanic Gardens, Melbourne

The Royal Botanic Gardens, on 36 hectares, are the focal point of 49 hectares of superbly landscaped parklands constituting the Domain in Melbourne. That they are world renowned is due both to the foresight of C. J. La Trobe, when he was Superintendent of the Port Phillip District, and to the genius of two directors, Baron Ferdinand von Mueller and William Guilfoyle.

As early as 1841, seven years after the founding of Melbourne, various citizens decided on the need for natural parklands, emulating those left behind in Great Britain, to surround the village. A botanic garden was to be part of these, a beautifully landscaped area of lawns and floral displays that would be suitable for recreation, public celebrations and charity functions.

The present site was chosen by that cultivated administrator Superintendent La Trobe, who Geoffrey Blainey says in *The Tyranny of Distance* (1966) 'exulted in trees, grasses and plains'. La Trobe's choice, which he called 'a veritable Garden of Eden', was a low ridge covered with thick shrubby plants and large eucalypts (including river red gums) and which sloped gently to the Yarra River.

By coincidence, the first two curators were both Scottish-trained gardeners and landscapers. The first, John Arthur, who was curator from 1846 to 1849, cultivated 2 hectares in the north-eastern corner, where La Trobe held official garden parties. Many of the first plantings came from Arthur's own nursery at Heidelberg. Four elms (*Ulmus procera*) which still stand on the Tennyson Lawn are said to have been planted by Arthur.

As curator between 1849 and 1857 John Dallachy, because of his avid collecting in Victoria and Queensland, introduced many native plants to the gardens. At the end of his term one thousand of the six thousand plants there were indigenous.

Dr Ferdinand Mueller, his successor, was a German-trained chemist and self-taught botanist who had been Victorian Government Botanist from 1852 to 1857, when the two positions were combined. Mueller's concept of botanic gardens differed from that of La Trobe (who had left the colony in 1854) and the public: the teaching and furtherance of botanical science were of prime importance to Mueller, so that the placement of plants was based on scientific requirements, and aesthetic considerations were low on the list of priorities. Mueller set up an exchange with many other countries and introduced a multitude of exotic plants, which included numerous conifers for his pinetum on the western slope. As well as pioneering the acclimatization of exotics, he collected, identified and established in the gardens thousands of Victorian and other Australian plants, and set up a Herbarium. By this time most of the area was under cultivation and criss-crossed by a maze of paths, lined with large trees. In 1873, in his travelogue *Australia and New*

Zealand, Anthony Trollope described the gardens as

A perfect paradise of science for those who are given to botany rather than to beauty . . . I am told that the gardens and the gardener, the botany and the baron, rank very highly indeed in the estimation of those who have devoted themselves to the study of trees, and that Melbourne should consider herself to be rich in having such a man. But the gardens though spacious are not charming, and the lessons which they teach are out of the reach of ninety-nine in every hundred. The baron has sacrificed beauty to science, and the charm of flowers to the production of scarce shrubs, till the higher authorities have interfered.

The government 'interfered' to the extent of holding, in 1873, a public inquiry into the administration of the gardens. This

resulted in Mueller (who in 1869 had received an hereditary baronetcy from the King of Württemberg) being shabbily dismissed from his post as Director of the gardens while retaining the position of Government Botanist.

Von Mueller's mantle fell to William Guilfoyle, a young horticulturist who at the time of his appointment was living at Tweed Heads in northern New South Wales. Guilfoyle, while agreeing with von Mueller on the scientific purpose of botanic gardens, was in tune with the requirements of his employers and the general public: 'I have every confidence that the results will be a garden in which facility of research and scientific classification will combine with sterling beauties of landscape scenery.'

As R. T. M. Pescott has shown in his book *The Royal Botanic Gardens, Melbourne* (1982), Guilfoyle totally transformed the gardens over the next thirty years. They became, and still remain, a celebrated example of nineteenth-century English landscaping. His vision of the gardens was formed by two experiences in particular. The first was his apprenticeship to his father, Robert Guilfoyle, who had been trained by the eminent English landscape designer Joseph Paxton. The second was a trip he made to the South Sea Islands, where he was greatly

impressed by the tropical vegetation. This penchant for such vegetation was reinforced at subtropical Tweed Heads.

The basis of his redevelopment was the wealth of exotic trees and plants that von Mueller had introduced. Boldly ignoring claims that it could not be done, he transferred mature trees of up to 15 metres. His theory was that

One of the greatest essentials in landscape gardening is the variety of foliage and disposal of trees. Nothing can excel the glimpses afforded by the openings between naturally formed clumps of trees and shrubs, whose height and contrast of foliage have been studied. At every step, the visitor finds some new view – something fresh, lively and striking especially when tastefully arranged. Where long sombre rows of trees are planted, and a sameness of foliage exists, the very reverse is the case. Nature's most favourable aspects then seem sacrificed to art, and that art often produces a chilling effect.

This deference to nature influenced his whole canvas. The myriad of paths were reduced to a few major, gently curved walkways. A balance between broad sweeping lawns and garden was established, the juxtaposition allowing either short or long vistas – from as little as 1.5 metres to the full length of an axis of the gardens. An arrangement of plants was introduced whereby large shrubs or small trees were surrounded by smaller shrubs and herbaceous specimens in such a way as to allow the visitor to read the names of each plant without walking into the group. The lagoon was redesigned and landscaped (this was completed in 1898 with the straightening of the Yarra River) so that it became the focal point of the gardens: 'glimpses will be afforded to the clear lake, studded with islands the careful plantation of which will add to the diversity and charm of the landscape.' On conspicuous promontories of the lake Guilfoyle planted specimens of the long-living Date Palm, *Phoenix canariensis*. He satisfied the public's wishes by establishing beds for floral displays:

flower gardening . . . should be concentrated in certain spots. A corner of flowers here, or a bedding out here, can be watched; but flowers everywhere amongst trees and shrubs become monotonous, and are out of place in those proportions set apart for showing various species of different orders of plants.

Most of the important landscape features of the Royal Botanic Gardens in 1982 are evident here: lawns, the lake, dense clumps of shrubbery, a predominance of ever-green trees, and con-spicuous date palms

Opposite left: A rusti-cated summer house in Melbourne's Botanic Gardens, photographed around 1880 by Charles Nettleton

64

Geelong Botanic Gardens

Geelong's Eastern Park is a beachside stretch of grass and trees within which the Botanic Gardens form an oasis of intensive cultivation. Originally the whole parkland of 80 hectares was known as the Botanic Gardens, part of the present enclosed area of about 5 hectares being 'the nursery' until at least the 1880s.

From 1850 a committee of management guided the affairs of the gardens, and in 1857 Daniel Bunce became their first curator. Bunce had been a nurseryman at Hobart's Denmark Hill Nursery before moving to Victoria, where he made various exploratory journeys as a naturalist (one with Ludwig Leichhardt), and managed a mining company in Bendigo, finally establishing a nursery at St Kilda. Before taking up the Geelong post he had written several books on horticulture and botany (and a little book listing Aboriginal names and their meanings). He had also applied unsuccessfully for the directorship of the Botanic Gardens of Melbourne. In 1865 he failed in his application for the equivalent post at Adelaide's Botanic Garden.

By 1859 Bunce was occupying a cottage in the gardens, and the planning and planting of the entire park began. Excess

But he was particularly interested in capitalizing on the variation in texture, colour and shape of foliage. This is especially evident in those sections surrounding the lake where the wall of varied vegetation looks almost like a jungle edge.

He developed the fern gully with native and exotic trees, rare and epiphytal ferns; a palmetum, the oak lawn, a rockery. In 1909 he built a small lake at the south-eastern end of the gardens and planted it with nymphaea lilies.

Several rustic summer houses were built but unfortunately only a few survive in their original form; some have been insensitively modified, others destroyed. A memorial to La Trobe, inspired by Greek architecture but with Australian epiphytal ferns as capitals for the columns, was built on the north-western corner – Guilfoyle's Temple of the Winds.

Subsequent directors have attempted to maintain Guilfoyle's design, though occasionally inappropriate modernization has been allowed. In 1958 the standard of Melbourne's magnificent Botanic Gardens was acknowledged when Queen Elizabeth II granted them the use of the prefix 'Royal'.

Eastern Park, Geelong, in about 1861: curving drives and very young planting

plants propagated in the nursery were offered to other public bodies, in spite of opposition from commercial nurserymen. Dr Ferdinand Mueller, Director of the Melbourne Botanic Gardens, exchanged plants with Bunce and visited the gardens from time to time.

The *Geelong Advertiser* of 3 July 1872 published the news of Bunce's death, together with a lengthy (and probably faulty) account of his life. This obituary concludes: 'He became curator of our Botanical Gardens 16 or 17 years ago, when it was an untilled waste just fenced in. What he has since done with the land can be seen by all, residents or visitors.' The tone of the article seems to imply that what such people saw would have pleased them.

After Bunce's death John Raddenberry was curator until 1896. A very large timber fernery designed by Raddenberry and constructed in 1885 has, like most of the early garden buildings here, long been demolished, though the paths in the vicinity today are believed to be those laid down within the fernery. A maze planned by Raddenberry and partly established by his successor James Day has also disappeared. Recently rethatched is a small latticework summer house built during Raddenberry's curatorship, possibly to his design. Two conservatories in the gardens were erected in the 1960s and 1970s respectively, and are pleasantly sited among well-kept lawns, flower beds, shrubberies and groups of trees.

There have been many changes over the last 130 years in the area now designated Botanic Gardens at Geelong, and no traces of the first curator's layout can be authenticated. A number of the very old trees, including an exceptionally large specimen of the Maidenhair Tree (*Gingko biloba*), are thought to have been planted by Daniel Bunce. Many trees in the outer parkland that made up the bulk of the original gardens almost certainly date back to Bunce's day, as do the remaining roadways.

Geelong's Botanic Gardens in 1890 (opposite), with their large fernery of timber battens at the rear

In 1982 the position of the demolished fernery is marked by the surviving palms and rather grotesque mound of rocks surmounted by a fountain

67

Portland Botanic Gardens
(Henty Park)

William Allitt, 1828–93

The rustic bridge (below) at the Portland Botanic Gardens has disappeared, but Allitt's cottage (right) remains

Though about 20 hectares of land for the Botanic Gardens at Portland had been set aside as early as 1851, their first curator, William Allitt, claimed in a letter to the *Portland Guardian* of 5 May 1893 to have found 'a bush of gum stumps, and a paddock of ferns' on the site when he began work there in 1857, under the supervision of a committee of three Portland Council members. It was land chosen by C. J. La Trobe while he was Superintendent of the Port Phillip District. Allitt also declared in the *Portland Guardian* that in 1859 'twenty-five natural orders of plants were represented', and that by the following year all the plants had been named. Some paths at the gardens were set out in 1857 by Alexander Elliott of Melbourne, but the general design for the earliest part of the gardens is attributed

to Allitt, who 'left in 1866 over 2000 species of plants, out of which fully 700 were permanent trees and shrubs'. He was succeeded as curator by Henry Hedges who, said Allitt, deserved 'great credit for his design of the lower part of the garden', although he was not a 'thorough plantsman' capable of setting up a botanic garden.

In 1876, the year in which Henty Park was permanently reserved and gazetted, A. C. Allan (Inspector of Plans and Surveys) reported the state of the gardens to the Secretary of Lands:

The whole of the reserve (a little over 50 acres) is enclosed with a paling fence . . . and a row of trees planted on the Western boundary. The Eastern portion of abt. 13 acres . . . has been laid out and planted as a flower garden with artificial ponds constructed on the South side connected with the creek and gardner's cottage erected of blue-stone. The Western portion (about 37 acres) is now being laid out with walks, preparatory to being planted with shrubs and flowers . . .

By the end of April 1876 a total of £4236 18s 2d had been spent over the years on the gardens.

A large proportion of Henty Park's remaining 13 hectares is now devoted to sporting facilities; even at the eastern end, where trees and lawns and extensive walks are still to be found, there is an area given over to a bowling green and its clubrooms.

The gardens have obviously changed considerably since they were first laid out; for one thing, the 'artificial ponds' are all gone. Nevertheless they are noteworthy for their association with the nurseryman and gardener William Allitt, whose small bluestone cottage still stands near the entrance, and for their early establishment in Victoria's first permanent settlement. A small tree of botanical interest at the Portland Botanic Gardens is *Wigandia caracasana*, and two unusual shrubs are *Iochroma grandiflora* and a species of the scrambling cactus *Perovskia*.

Ballarat Botanical Gardens

When Anthony Trollope visited Ballarat late in 1871, one of his many favourable impressions was of 'a public garden full of shrubs and flowers and a lake of its own'. The happy association of Lake Wendouree and its parkland with the Ballarat Botanical Gardens made this part of Ballarat attractive in the nineteenth century to large numbers of people from Ballarat and beyond – for picnics, fishing and boating. The British historian J. A. Froude used extravagant terms in *Oceana* (1886) to describe the gardens:

I have already expressed my admiration of the Australian gardens, but this at Ballarat excelled them all. It was as if the town council had decided to show what gold and science could do with such a soil and climate. The roses which bloom ill on the hotter lowlands were here, owing to the height above the sea, abundant and beautiful as

The Ballarat Botanical Gardens in about 1900

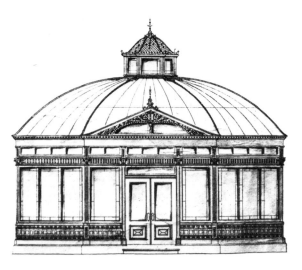

T. E. Molloy's plan, dated 1887, for the statuary pavilion (right), still a notable feature of the modern gardens (below). The splendid fernery, sketched in 1885 (far right), has been demolished

in Veitch's nurseries at midsummer. Besides roses, every flower was there which was either fair to look upon or precious for its fragrance. There were glass houses to protect the delicate plants in the winter; but oranges and camellias, which we [in Britain] know only in conservatories, grow without fear in the open air, and survive the worst cold which Ballarat experiences. A broad gravel-walk led up the middle of the grounds, with lateral paths all daintily kept. Dark shadowy labyrinths conducted us into cool grottoes overhung by tree-ferns, where young lovers could whisper undisturbed, and those who were not lovers could read novels. Such variety, such splendour of colour, such sweetness, such grace in the distribution of the treasures collected there, I had never found combined before, and never shall find again.

The Ballarat Botanical Gardens were gazetted in 1858 and planting began in that year, but the origin and date of their design are not known. There are many surviving plans of a garden on this site – all, unfortunately, undated and unsigned. In the 1860s the area of planting was gradually extended, lawn was sown, and the gardens began propagating blue gums for use around the Ballarat district. About 12 hectares were under cultivation in 1870, and 'Viator' remarked in the *Australasian* of 31 May 1873 on 'some very fine features', such as an 'acacia walk' and an avenue of wellingtonias (now *Seqoiadendron giganteum*). By the 1880s there was an enormous and elaborate lattice fernery (since demolished, though the plans survive) a fish hatchery, a glasshouse and a conservatory. Gifts of statues in the 1880s from wealthy residents like Thomas Stoddart inspired a continuing tradition of statuary that includes an avenue lined with the busts of Australian prime ministers. A pavilion was erected in 1887 to house some of the statues. A bust of F. M. Claxton, who was mayor of Ballarat on several occasions, marks among other things this man's zealous promotion of the well-being of the gardens. The curator George Longley, who looked after the gardens from their commencement in 1858 until his retirement in the 1890s, was evidently a capable and energetic man: it was in his time that the gardens became renowned as the most splendid in Victoria. Two other men, Thomas Toop and Tom Beaumont, were each in charge of the gardens for very long periods in the twentieth century.

Dr Ferdinand Mueller of the Melbourne Botanic Gardens supplied many plants for the gardens, and no doubt the most mature trees are part of his legacy. There are certainly many outstanding specimens of trees popular in the nineteenth century still standing: among them are surviving 'wellingtonias', as well as Bunya Bunya Pine (*Araucaria bidwillii*) and Norfolk Island Pine (*A. heterophylla*). Other trees in the gardens include the Deodar Cedar (*Cedrus deodara*), Maidenhair Tree (*Gingko biloba*), Douglas Fir (*Pseudotsuga menziesii*), Tulip Tree (*Liriodendron tulipifera*) and *Liquidambar styraciflua*. Shrubs include the American Mountain Laurel (*Kalmia latifolia*), Beauty Bush (*Kolkwitzia amabilis*), Pink-flowering Currant (*Ribes sanguineum*), and various hydrangeas, azaleas and rhododendrons.

The Ballarat Botanical Gardens are well known today for their fine collection of hothouse begonias and the elaborate scale of their bedding-out. Some of the twentieth-century buildings, such as the public toilets and the new conservatory, have not contributed to the Victorian flavour of the gardens. Since the history of the gardens is poorly documented, it is only possible to speculate that there have been many alterations since their inception.

Williamstown's Botanic Gardens, pictured between about 1890 and 1910. They show a richness and variety in layout and planting that are typical of Victoria's public gardens at that time

Williamstown Botanic Gardens

There has been some suggestion that Daniel Bunce, curator from 1857 and designer of the Geelong Botanic Gardens, also planned the Botanic Gardens at Williamstown. No evidence has been found for this. Borough of Williamstown minute books do, however, record donations of trees and shrubs from Dr Ferdinand Mueller of the Melbourne Botanic Gardens in 1867 and 1868. On one occasion, in fact, Dr Mueller found it necessary to ask for 'the return of flower pots from public garden'.

Four hectares of land for the gardens were first gazetted in 1856, and they were fenced and open to the public by January of 1860. Two hectares were added in 1865 and a slightly smaller area in 1878. The present size of the gardens is about 2 hectares. The council had actually asked for an extra 4 hectares in 1865, the Town Clerk in his letter to the Commissioner of Lands and Survey stating that

the Public Gardens here are now so well frequented by the inhabitants of Williamstown and by numerous visitors from Melbourne and the suburbs on holidays and fete days that the present space is

council's intentions of 1865. Part of the reserve was let for grazing in the 1860s and 1870s, the proceeds going to improvements at the gardens.

In 1889 the council decided to offer a reward of £5 for information leading to the conviction of any persons stealing trees from the gardens, and regulations to protect buildings and plants were gazetted in 1895.

The gardens were extensively reorganized in 1907. The elaborate cast-iron gates at the entrance were bought in that year from the estate of Edmond Fitzgibbon. Weighing 6 tonnes, they had originally been imported for Fitzgibbon's South Yarra residence (Fairlie, in Anderson Street) from a foundry in Glasgow. The gardens were again renovated in the 1930s.

Some very old palms and cypresses may still be seen at the Williamstown Botanic Gardens, and displays of annual flowers are maintained. It is believed that all plants at the gardens once bore name-tags. A dominant feature is the long straight walk focused on a statue of the parliamentarian A. T. Clark. It was erected by public subscription in 1891, but has unfortunately been vandalized by less responsible members of the public since then.

insufficient to afford the accommodation required. The Council therefore with a view of protecting the beds and flowers (which in consequence of the numbers attending have been much damaged,) and to afford facilities for holding the exhibitions of the Horticultural Society, also for the erection of a pavilion or orchestra for the Volunteer bands who are willing to play in the gardens if accommodation be afforded, and to give room for the gymnastic exercises and sports which are largely participated in by the visitors at the fetes and on holidays especially, – respectfully the Council request that you will be pleased to reserve ten acres additional adjoining the west side of the gardens in the line of the north and south fences.

At about this time a gardener and assistant gardener were working in the grounds at salaries of £125 and £26 (part-time) respectively. A gardener's cottage was built in 1870 but was demolished when a new residence was put up in 1907 (this too has been replaced). Another garden building erected in the 1870s and now gone was a rotunda, no doubt built to fulfil the

Castlemaine Botanical Gardens

Gazetted in 1860 after a change in the site proposed, these gardens are today quite a feature of the historic town of Castlemaine. The layout is thought to have been the work of Phillip Doran, their first curator, who had come to Victoria in 1855 in search of gold after an apprenticeship at the Duke of Devonshire's great Chatsworth estate under Joseph Paxton, designer of the gardens and conservatories there. Doran remained at the Castlemaine Botanical Gardens for forty-seven years. During this time hundreds of plants, both native and exotic, were provided for the gardens by Dr Ferdinand Mueller of the Melbourne Botanic Gardens through his friendship with the noted silversmith and goldsmith Ernest Leviny, who owned

the mansion called Buda at Castlemaine. It seems likely that Mueller also influenced the gardens' design: three rows of trees running parallel with Downes Road may well have been set out by him. Species in the rows include Chinese Weeping Cypress (*Cupressus funebris*), Holm Oak (*Quercus ilex*), Canary Islands Pine (*Pinus canariensis*) and Stone Pine (*P. pinea*).

'The Vagabond' (Julian Thomas) wrote about the Castlemaine Botanical Gardens in the *Illustrated Australian News* of 2 October 1893: 'They are admirably laid out, and are planted with a splendid variety of trees and shrubs . . . A large ornamental sheet of water is the rendezvous for a number of graceful black swans, as tame as children and the inevitable biscuit can make them . . .' Records of the Department of Crown Lands and Survey show that by the very same year

The lake, pictured in modern times (below) and early in the twentieth century (right) is an important feature of the Castlemaine Botanical Gardens

the value of improvements at the Castlemaine gardens had reached £3000.

An impressive set of cast-iron gates on fine bluestone piers marks the entrance to the gardens. There is a distinct contrast between a manicured garden of lawn, rose beds and annuals near the entrance and an extensive informal area. As is suggested by Thomas's account, the natural-looking lake in the centre of the gardens is their dominating element. The many fine exotic trees include oaks, conifers, limes and an excellent catalpa. Castlemaine's largest oak was planted in the gardens by Alfred, Duke of Edinburgh, during a visit to Australia in 1867. (A plaque now identifies this tree, but its site was established only after considerable detective work by Helen Vellacott of Castlemaine.) There are also Australian trees: kurrajongs, silky oaks and eucalypts, and examples of Queensland's Bunya Bunya Pine (*Araucaria bidwillii*).

Now reduced from about 32 to 13 hectares, the Castlemaine Botanical Gardens have seen many changes; the date at which they were given their present form is uncertain.

Daylesford Botanic Gardens (Wombat Hill)

Commenced in 1861 and remodelled by William Sangster of Taylor & Sangster in 1884–85, these gardens are notable for their dominant site on top of a steep hill near the centre of the town of Daylesford, which is in an area whose rich volcanic soil and cool, moist climate are especially favourable to horticulture. 'Tramp', writing in the *Daylesford Advocate* of 3 February 1885, remarked on the

splendid view of miles of the surrounding country . . . The gardens are under the control of the local Borough Council, and it certainly shows something for the few years labour spent in its formation. The walks are all neatly laid out, and the beds are decorated with rare flowers and shrubs of every description. There is also an artificial lake on its summit in the centre of the gardens, which serves the double purpose of beautifying the hill and storing a day's supply of water in the event of one of the main pipes bursting. Most of the old denizens of the forest have been destroyed, but a few have been preserved . . .

Mention was also made of Sangster's work on the gardens, which were expected, as a result of that work, to be able within a few months to 'hold their own against any in Victoria'.

Sangster's surviving plan shows a much more complex layout than is apparent today. Initially of 15 hectares, the gardens were certainly very elaborate in their early days, with extensive bedding-out displays (requiring the attention of two full-time gardeners at one stage) and a fern gully whose outline is still visible.

A bandstand has been moved to nearby Central Springs, below Lake Daylesford, where it survives in a state of decrepitude.

Many civic celebrations, such as local demonstrations of joy on the occasion of a Royal wedding in 1863, were held at Wombat Hill. The *Daylesford Express* of 21 May 1863 reported the latter holiday in detail:

Giant sequoias frame a view from the Daylesford Botanic Gardens

The simple act of planting two oak trees in celebration of the Royal nuptials was something more than a mere ceremony... this [was a] symbolical testimony of loyalty... The roasted bullock on the top of Wombat Hill attracted all eyes... The fire it was over was a welcome sight to those who were damped by the continually drizzling rain...

A torchlight procession led by the Fire Brigade in uniform, at about six o'clock in the evening, marched to Wombat Hill. A gigantic pile was lit... Composed as it was of an immense heap of combustibles, comprising upwards of 1000 tons of firewood carefully packed, with tar and other flammable materials, it cast its illuminating effects for miles around...

The great trees of the town's gardens delineate the skyline above Daylesford (right)

An old rest-house, now derelict, at Wombat Hill

What remains today at the Daylesford Botanic Gardens is a comparatively simple parkland of just over 9 hectares, with many fine trees and avenues still standing. About forty of the old trees, identified in the 1970s by Dr J. H. Willis, have been provided with labels. Among these trees are some quite rare

conifers, such as the Spanish Fir or Crucifix Tree (*Abies pinsapo*) and a magnificent specimen of the Himalayan Pine (*Pinus wallichiana*). There are still a number of Giant Sequoias (*Sequoiadendron giganteum*), though the tallest of them were cut down by the Defence Department during the Second World War. A very unusual shrub is the Anchor Plant (*Colletia cruciata*). Native shrubs and trees mingle with these introduced species. For the quality of their trees and the prominence of their site, the Daylesford Botanic Gardens are of considerable interest among Victoria's historic gardens. They form a dramatic backdrop for the town of Daylesford and its surrounding area, including the fine homestead garden at nearby Wombat Park.

The rotunda in the early twentieth-century view of the Warrnambool Botanical Gardens (opposite left) still stands, but the layout of the gardens has since been simplified (opposite right)

Warrnambool Botanical Gardens

Like those at Colac, the Botanical Gardens of Warrnambool owe their present form largely to William Guilfoyle. His plan for Warrnambool may have been his first design for a public garden outside Melbourne, for it was produced very early in his directorship of the Melbourne Botanic Gardens.

Botanic gardens had been begun in Warrnambool in the 1850s, but the locality chosen proved too exposed and was abandoned. About 8 hectares of gently sloping land, fenced in 1866, became the site of the present gardens. Charles Hortle, curator from 1869 to 1872, was succeeded by Charles Scobo rio, who had acted as curator of the earlier gardens and was to remain in charge of the new gardens until 1906.

The Warrnambool Council invited Guilfoyle in 1877 to prepare his plan. It was a typical Guilfoyle design, with sweeping lawns, wide, curving paths (replacing straight ones), a rockery, a lake, clumps of trees (including palms), and dense shrubberies. A former Town Clerk of Warrnambool, H. Worland, in a 1947 radio talk on the Warrnambool Botanical Gardens, referred to Guilfoyle's 'suggestions jotted on the plan', but the City of Warrnambool had no copy of that plan in 1979.

Since there was no water supply to the gardens until 1883, and full reticulation only after 1890, planting that required intensive watering in dry weather would have been severely restricted in those early days. A collection of native and exotic birds and animals attracted visitors to the gardens late in the nineteenth century, and early in the twentieth William Donald, the curator appointed in 1906, gradually dispensed with the menagerie and developed floral displays at the gardens. Beds of annuals are still a feature here, as are Guilfoyle's lawns, palms and shrubberies. A number of fine urns and the old rotunda remain. The Warrnambool Botanical Gardens are thought to be little changed from their pattern in the late nineteenth century.

Colac Botanic Gardens

In 1865 a piece of land about 15 hectares in extent was reserved on the shore of Lake Colac for the Colac Botanic Gardens. A plan prepared by Daniel Bunce, curator of the Geelong Botanic Gardens, gave them their basic form, with an internal carriageway that enabled a circuit of the area. But little progress was made. In 1876 the trustees of the gardens (appointed by the citizens of Colac who first petitioned for reservation of the land) resigned over a debt of £80 and the shire council took control. Under a new and very capable curator, John McDonald, matters improved. In 1910, however, the council asked William Guilfoyle, newly retired from the Melbourne Botanic Gardens, to examine the gardens and to suggest ways of developing them further.

Guilfoyle's report was critical of Bunce's plan: 'The locality having great natural advantages and, therefore, lending itself to artistic landscape treatment, it is to be regretted that a better scheme for its beautification and improvement was not adopted years ago, when the site was first chosen for a park.' Though he felt that the carriageway was almost entirely satisfactory, there were too many paths and beds cutting up the spaces between, and the shrubs and trees were arranged in a fashion that was 'most inartistic and perplexing to say the least of it'.

One of Guilfoyle's major – and lasting – changes was to reorganize the path system. He proposed to eliminate 'many mean looking borders' along the paths, replacing them with groups of shrubs. All healthy and well-shaped trees would be retained except where they were overcrowded, while many shrubs would be transplanted for grouping. A 'Shanks patent horse-mower' would take care of the lawns. In addition to detailed suggestions for the improvement of the gardens, Guilfoyle submitted a list of 'extra plants to be used for the decoration of the Colac Park'. They included many acacias and eucalypts as well as various shrubs and climbers (native and exotic) and the palms he was so fond of. The watercolour plan drawn under Guilfoyle's supervision cannot be said to have been completely sustained. The creek is now a mere drain, and the 'tropical dell' he envisaged for that area never eventuated.

Few trees at the Colac Botanic Gardens have name-tags now, and water shortages in summer cause maintenance problems. Nevertheless the gardens retain much of the shape given them by William Guilfoyle, and they are among a very small number of Victorian gardens of any kind to do so.

Hamilton Botanical Gardens

These gardens were gazetted in 1870, and in the same year a design was prepared by William Ferguson, the Victorian Inspector of Forests, who had recently been put in charge of landscape and practical work at the Melbourne Botanic Gardens – much to the chagrin of their Director, Baron Ferdinand von Mueller. They are similar in style to large gardens designed in Victoria soon after by Mueller's successor, William Guilfoyle: gardens based on sweeping lawns and well-grouped trees and shrub beds. If the *Cyclopedia of Victoria* (1904) may be relied on, the gardens were being kept in excellent order early in the twentieth century by their curator Mr R. Hughan, who spent

a total of forty-four years in this position. The gardens are a particularly fine asset to Hamilton today, and their present form is thought to be generally similar to their original design.

There is a system of winding paths throughout the well-drained, sloping grounds, which still cover 4 hectares as they did when gazetted. Several decorative wire arbours and a large fountain constructed in 1917–18 provide appropriate embellishments. The gardens contain many very fine trees, including specimens of Bunya Bunya Pine (*Araucaria bidwillii*), Giant Sequoia (*Sequoiadendron giganteum*), *Acacia elata*, Horse-chestnut (*Aesculus hippocastanum*) and Indian Bean (*Catalpa bignonioides*). Some bedding-out of annual flowers is still undertaken. A zoo of unknown date is located in one corner, and a modern sound shell was erected in the gardens in 1967.

Opposite: Marked on William Guilfoyle's 1910 plan (see page 56), this bed of palms is one of many features of the design that are still evident in the Colac Botanic Gardens

A peaceful corner of the Hamilton Botanical Gardens, photographed earlier this century

'Suburban' gardens

TO CALL this group of gardens suburban is perhaps misleading. Although they are nearly all found in suburbs of Melbourne or within the boundaries of country towns, the main reason for putting them in a special group is their size. They range from about 0.2 to 0.8 hectares and are generally attached to bigger than average houses. Some of the larger villa gardens might just as readily fall into the 'suburban' category. There are few similarities among these gardens apart from a generous amount of space. This is partly because of the range of styles and periods involved – from the relatively simple gardens of the 1850s to the indiscriminate featurism of the late nineteenth century and some attempts at modification in the twentieth century.

In the earlier examples such as The Heights, Geelong (only part of which is thought to date from this period) and Burswood, Portland, the character of the gardens derives largely from their geometry and the shaded walks bordered with low clipped hedging. Essentially gardenesque in style, the old parts of the gardens at The Heights and Burswood use little lawn. Instead, they display 'the art of the gardener', as John Claudius Loudon put it. Interlocking gravel paths wind their way through dense shrubberies with pines and araucarias towering above. (Conifers often provided the dramatic silhouettes popu-

A wisteria-covered arbour (right) at Trelawny in the 1940s

Although the house at Trelawny, Ballarat, was altered soon after the photograph was taken in 1896 (see page 87), the garden has changed little. The young cypresses on the left now form an enormous arch, with space enough below them to store gardening equipment

lar at the time.) Swirling geometric shapes – ovals and circles in particular – are used repeatedly. These gardens, unlike those of the later nineteenth century, have little in the way of embellishment.

Although damaged in part, the garden at Trelawny in Ballarat, perhaps more than any other, captures the spirit of later nineteenth-century gardens of medium size. Such gardens once existed by the thousand in Melbourne and the larger country towns, but most have long since been subdivided. Trelawny has somehow managed to retain that elusive Victorian flavour conveyed so often by plans and photographs of the period. Gardens of this type tended to have a carriage loop as their principal feature. Often pedestrian entry was provided separately. The garden itself was a series of features frequently thrown together with little regard for the total effect. Typically

such gardens had a summer house (usually of a rustic nature), trelliswork fernery, fountain and pond. Terra cotta edging tiles and drains, together with decorative urns, adorned the gardens. Beds of annual flowers cut into lawns provided dazzling displays. These were all features common in the mansion gardens of the day and they gave to less grand dwellings, and their owners, an air of respectability and refinement. At their best such gardens were charming, but at their all-too-frequent worst they were discordant. In the first twenty years of the new century garden designers and owners endeavoured to rationalize the formal and informal styles that had often combined and competed disastrously in the previous two decades. The results for suburban gardens were mixed.

Most of the gardens in this section are private and therefore closed to the public; The Heights is open at specific times

Edged with miniature box, a curving path entices the visitor into the garden at Glenholme, Ballarat

Burswood, Portland

The *Portland Guardian* of 2 August 1855 tells us that the house being built in that year for the pioneer Edward Henty had 'that talented horticulturist Mr. Barnsby' to lay out its grounds. The stone house still stands, and the garden is still of considerable interest. It is impossible to say whether the garden now reflects Barnsby's plan, but the age of some of the trees would seem to indicate that they have been helping to give the garden its present form for a very long time, perhaps since the 1860s.

The garden is now dominated by a gently curving tree-lined drive. The western side follows a complex gardenesque pattern with a huge Norfolk Island Pine (*Araucaria heterophylla*) centred in an oval lawn. This lawn and many of the paths at Burswood are bordered with low, clipped hedges of golden privet and rosemary. There are much taller cypress hedges around some boundaries of the garden. On the eastern side is a twentieth-century rose garden set in another lawn. There is the remnant of an old orchard on the south side. This garden provides an appropriate setting for one of Victoria's most important old houses, though factories on the eastern side, the railway to the north, and recently an overpass on the north-west corner of the garden have made visual intrusions into it.

Burswood, Portland, in the 1860s, the mid-twentieth century and the 1970s. The carriage loop evident in all three photographs suggests some consistency in the general form of the garden over 120 years, but much of the detail has changed

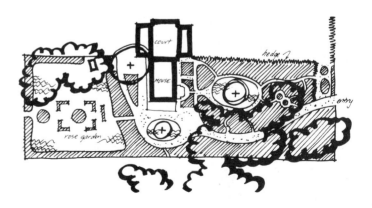

Burswood 1980

The Heights, Geelong

A prefabricated weatherboard house from Germany was constructed for Charles Ibbotson at The Heights in 1855, and the oldest parts of the garden most likely date from the same period. There are iron gates on the north-east corner, giving onto a curving, box-hedged driveway, while the main section of the garden is made up of gravel paths winding through dense shrubberies composed of such plants as *Duranta repens*, *Cotoneaster serotinus* and *Viburnum tinus*. Remnants of a prefabricated iron fence (of the type often called estate fencing) may still be seen.

Modifications made in the 1930s resulted in a new emphasis on natural plantings of flowers, especially perennials, and the introduction of picturesque gates and garden sheds, which are still in existence. An interesting old collection of bulbs includes *Tulipa saxatile*, *Convallaria majalis*, *Bletilla striata*, *Sisyrinchium striatum*, *Haemanthus coccineus* and *Cyclamen neapolitanum*.

A landmark in the area, the garden with its many fine trees – Norfolk Island Pine (*Araucaria heterophylla*), Pepper Tree (*Schinus molle*), Holm Oak (*Quercus ilex*), *Eucalyptus ficifolia* and exotic pines and cypresses among them – is beautifully sited on a hilltop with distant views to the You Yang ranges. Among the changes of recent years is the subdivision of an important cut-flower garden, which has been built over. Kept in excellent condition by its present owner, the National Trust of Australia (Victoria), the garden is a valuable component of an important complex of buildings. Assuming that the oldest part of the garden dates from the 1850s, this, like Burswood, is a particularly early example of domestic garden design.

Gravel paths and the shrubbery at left are believed to be part of the original garden plan at The Heights

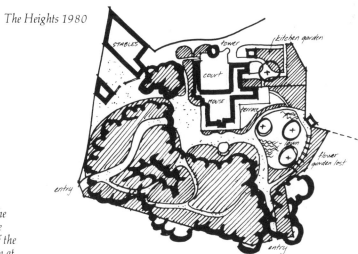

The Heights 1980

Glenholme, Ballarat

Surrounding a brick house built in 1871 and presumably dating from around that time, this garden is located in Webster Street – one of Ballarat's finest thoroughfares containing many historic buildings. The form of the garden is interesting and particularly pleasing, although there is no record of its having been designed by a professional. A former gold-mine puddling pond was put to attractive use as the site for a slightly sunken oval lawn. A winding path from the front gate is bordered with clipped box-hedging and there are a number of arbours and fussy path arrangements edged in rocks or box-hedging – true gardenesque elements. Several very good specimens of Giant Sequoia (*Sequoiadendron giganteum*) and a huge American Red Oak (probably *Quercus rubra*) dominate the planting.

Changes have been few in this garden, though a row of *Pinus radiata* has recently been removed along the driveway, some box-hedging has disappeared, and one small garden section at the rear has given place to a clothesline. This is, in fact, possibly the finest and most intact of Victorian 'suburban' gardens in the state, a garden enhanced by its relationship with a house that retains many of its original details and finishes both inside and out.

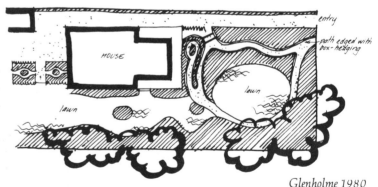

Glenholme 1980

Intricate gardens like that of Glenholme are now rare, for they need constant attention

Trelawny, Ballarat

Laid out in 1887 by Mark Dawe, an English relative of the family that still owns it, the Trelawny garden gives to an 1863 brick house a setting of peculiarly nineteenth-century character. A short, slightly curving asphalt driveway leads to the front door of the house via a circular roundabout of lawn with a Norfolk Island Pine (*Araucaria heterophylla*) – planted early this century – in the centre. This approach is no longer normally used by vehicles. A number of asphalt paths run through the garden, dividing it into sections of lawn and shrubbery. A cypress hedge nearly 40 metres long once bordered each side of a path leading to a side door of the house; another screened the stables behind it. All three sections of hedge have been removed, but two cypress archways believed to date from about 1890 remain features of the garden. The former very

elaborate fruit and kitchen gardens at Trelawny were subdivided for housing in the early 1950s (reducing the total area of the property from 1.2 to 0.4 hectares), but the general form of the pleasure garden is intact.

Part of what was once a circular driveway, which passes round a Norfolk Island pine at Trelawny

Trelawny in 1900 (left), with its new verandah and its name freshly inscribed above the front steps. Note the strip of grass around the flower bed: a common feature of gardens from this period, and still maintained here

Carn Brae, Hawthorn

A house designed by the well-known architect John Beswicke for his father Charles was built on this site in 1873. Reduced by Alfred Nicholas to its bluestone foundations but retaining a staircase and conservatory, it was rebuilt in 1921, and a large suburban garden was laid out around it. Many elements characteristic of the heavy and rather awkward, sombre style of the Edwardian period are apparent in it. There are a number of pergolas and, in particular, a large and elaborate one, in brickwork of two colours, adjacent to the front door. A conservatory attached to the house somehow lacks the delicacy of earlier structures of this kind. A massive fernery, comparable with the iron-framed one at Rippon Lea (which was built in 1896) and containing a running stream and waterfall, still stands at one side of the house. An area that once held the kitchen garden and flower garden, together with many glasshouses, has been subdivided and built over.

To many people this garden probably reflects the decline in taste of the period in which it was established. Nevertheless, with its front section entirely intact, it is of historic importance as the archetypal Edwardian garden.

Cadell, Echuca

The garden at Cadell, photographed in 1947, is another that has changed comparatively little. The architect A. J. Inches, who designed the house in 1900, was called in later to add the attic and other rooms. The garden's designer is not known

Two families linked by marriage have owned this property at various times ever since the house, designed by A. J. Inches, was built in about 1900. Dominating the garden are a circular carriage drive in front of the house, and many very large old trees of architectural form: there are three date palms, nine specimens of *Pinus radiata*, two Bunya Bunya Pines (*Araucaria*

bidwillii) standing 50 metres apart, and two Norfolk Island Pines (*A. heterophylla*), as well as a magnificent English Oak (*Quercus robur*) and four jacarandas.

The original picket fence survives, but the beautiful wooden gates had to be removed in the early 1970s. The wife of the present owner recalls that the 'original tennis court fence was made of rough tree poles and wire covered in climbing roses. One entered the court through a rustic rose arbour. My father [then the owner of the house] replaced the fence in the early 1920s with a cyclone fence, as the thorns made the search for tennis balls too difficult! Because of a better watering system [since the 1970s], some of those roses that had not been seen for over forty years have grown again on the fence'. There is now a swimming pool behind that tennis court, in an area that was earlier a rose garden.

Together with the house it surrounds, this Edwardian garden is a notable feature of the town of Echuca. Its collection of trees is especially fine for this area, and the garden conforms almost entirely with its original design.

*A wisteria-clad pergola
at the front entrance to
Carn Brae, Hawthorn*

*The delights of spring at
Glenholme, Ballarat:
ranunculi, bluebells,
ixias, forget-me-nots,
carnations and daffodils,
with wisteria beyond*

Front gardens

TENS OF THOUSANDS of small houses built throughout Victoria from the 1860s to the early years of the twentieth century once had front gardens of the 'villa' type. Typically the houses are set back from the street 4.5–7.5 metres. They generally have a symmetrical facade (though sometimes there is a bay to one side), and a verandah across the front. Owners of these gardens carved the small plot of land between house and street into almost as many different shapes as there were houses of this style, though there were many similarities. Keen gardeners would have found the shortage of front garden space frustrating. Indeed, said the *Victorian Farmers' Journal and Gardeners' Chronicle* in July 1860, 'Aiming at too much' was the 'prevailing error in villa gardens'. 'Suburban' gardens also showed many variations in form, but tended to be decidedly bigger than gardens such as these.

The front fence generally consisted of timber pickets with a gate in the centre. A clipped cypress, pittosporum or privet hedge up to 2 metres high often ran behind the fence, providing privacy and security. The rectangle of space remaining was then arranged into a geometric pattern of paths and garden beds. Circles, ovals, rectangles and squares were all used: gen-

Opposite: Charles Norton's early watercolour of the garden at Gwyllehurst, a villa in Wellington Parade, East Melbourne, belonging to his brother-in-law, the architect John Gill

Terra cotta tiles around quaintly shaped beds are frequently the main feature of terrace front gardens

erally, though not always, in a symmetrical arrangement. Lawn was practically never to be seen except in the more spacious and elaborate gardens.

Larger plants were generally pushed to the perimeter of the design, with flowers and smaller shrubs in the centre. Occasionally an urn or fountain, and more often a special plant, such as a cordyline or a camellia, stood in the centre of the garden as its focal point. Garden beds were most commonly delineated with terra cotta edging tiles, timber plinths or the long-living English Box (*Buxus sempervirens*), clipped from time to time. Climbing plants were trained over wire arbours crossing paths; they also cascaded from verandahs, which sheltered twisted and tiered wire plant-stands laden with ferns, begonias and other comparatively delicate plants.

Built in 1864, Gilsland is a Brighton villa whose front garden was well established by the time this photograph was taken in the 1880s. The same design and some of the same planting are apparent in the 1980s (page 94)

The garden at Rosebrook, near Horsham, is now largely grassed over, but the pattern shown in this 1872 painting is still discernible. Even in the remote Wimmera owners could take pleasure in an ornate little garden complete with strutting peacocks

Plans of Melbourne prepared from the 1890s onwards by the Melbourne and Metropolitan Board of Works to facilitate sewerage connections show the detail of numerous front gardens of this kind. Many of the houses survive, but in spite of – or perhaps because of a twentieth-century dislike for – their very distinctive designs, villa gardens have in the vast majority of cases long since disappeared. There could nevertheless be dozens more than the examples collected here.

All the gardens in this section are private and therefore closed to the public

Gwyllehurst photographed in 1860 (far left)

Geometric patterns in unending variety characterized the front gardens of Melbourne's villas around the turn of the century. Part of Power Street, Hawthorn

Two villa gardens at Brighton

A picket fence backed by cypress hedging screens the front garden at the Brighton villa called 'Gilsland', and the visitor enters it through heavy iron gates set to one side. This is a smallish garden, certainly established in its present form by the 1880s, and it makes a delightful forecourt to an interesting plastered brick house built in 1864. The layout of the garden may indeed be as old as the house.

Like so many villa gardens from the same period, this one is geometric in form, boasting flower and shrub beds bordered with miniature English box. Paths radiate from the centre of the verandah outside the front door, and there are no areas of lawn. Old-fashioned flowers proliferate – some of them, such as cinerarias, foxgloves and alyssum, self-sown for generations in the sandy soil. Other annuals regularly grown in Gilsland's front garden are antirrhinums, ranunculi, linaria and stocks. There are bulbs, helleborus and bergenias under the shrubs, which include three very old camellias. Wisteria climbs a veran-

A modern photograph of the Gilsland garden confirms its consistent shape over a century or more

Built twenty-three years later than Gilsland, this 1887 timber house at Brighton (far right) also has an interesting front garden that has changed little. Its giant New Zealand Cabbage Tree is conspicuous above a hedge of mixed species

dah post as it did in the early days of the garden. For thirty years it 'disappeared', however, and the owners were surprised and delighted to find a new plant growing in the old position – from long-dormant seed perhaps?

Old flagstones removed from the laundry have recently been used to pave the central part of the path system, and two tiny pools have been added to the largest bed. Some of the box-hedging in poor condition is being replanted.

THE SMALL GARDEN at the front of a timber villa built in 1887 at Brighton is another good example of a style that has almost died out in Victoria. There is a central gate and – as at Gilsland – symmetrical beds are bordered with box-hedging, a small proportion of which seems to be dying out.

Shrubs and flowers fill the beds, and a clipped hedge of pittosporum, coprosma and laurustinus behind a white picket fence hides the garden from the road. The composition is dominated by a large and multi-trunked specimen of New Zealand Cabbage Tree (*Cordyline australis*) in the middle of the central bed. Other plants of an essentially nineteenth-century character include roses, Easter daisies, abelia, rosemary, dahlias, guelder rose, red-hot pokers and the Californian Tree-poppy *Romneya trichocalyx*. The property still belongs to descendants of the original owner, and the layout of the garden is assumed to date from the late 1880s or the 1890s.

A villa garden in Hawthorn

In many ways a typical suburban villa garden from the late nineteenth century, this one is larger than usual. The slate-roofed timber villa, its broad verandah encrusted heavily with iron lace, has an old-world atmosphere that extends to and is reflected in its garden.

Heavy iron gates set back from the footpath at the centre of an elaborately detailed white picket fence lead into a circular carriage drive that gives the garden its main form. The outer edge of the asphalt drive is bordered with scalloped terra cotta edging tiles, some of which are original and some replacements. The circle of grass (about 10 metres in diameter) around which the drive passes has a tall old Norfolk Island Pine (*Araucaria heterophylla*) at the centre, with small trees planted alongside it in modern times for added privacy. A row of cypresses hanging more than halfway across the narrow street helps to make the garden conspicuous, as do the two immensely tall palms, a huge Silky Oak (*Grevillea robusta*) and a pencil

Detailing in the picket fence of this Hawthorn villa is unusual

Gilsland

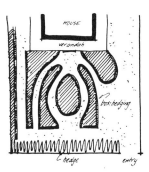

1887 Brighton villa

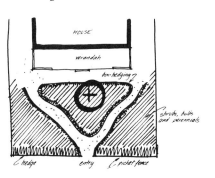

pine of similar vintage. There is a very large Lemon-scented Gum (*Eucalyptus citriodora*) beside the house, and two others behind it. The biggest of these gums has a trunk at least 70cm across. On either side of the turning circle stands an old guava (*Psidium* sp.), and the front steps of the house are flanked by camellia bushes. The various trees around the drive appear to have been arranged in such a way as to flower in succession throughout the year.

A villa garden at Kyneton

Dating probably from the 1880s or 1890s, this box-hedged garden lies in front of a weatherboard villa. Hedged beds, one circular and the other diamond-shaped, are separated by a central path. Hedging also extends around beds immediately in front of the verandah on each side of the front door, and between the main beds and the street. There are bulbs such as scillas and tulips planted within the circular bed and three rhododendrons, a peony and a Christmas lily in the diamond-shaped bed. Shrubs in the front garden include flowering currants, lilacs and japonica as well as some very old roses. There is a holly tree, a Japanese maple and a shady oak.

Box-hedging that survives from the nineteenth century is now scarce in Victoria, but a villa garden like this one, whose hedging is arranged asymmetrically, is rare indeed.

Dating from the nineteenth century, box-hedging is a feature of this villa front garden at Kyneton

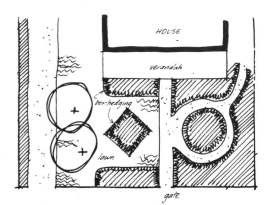

Kyneton

Villa gardens at St Arnaud, Maffra and Maryborough

Paths in the garden at St Arnaud are bordered with terra cotta tiles rather like those at Kawarau, Ballarat. The brick house was built before the turn of the century, and the form of the garden is thought to be unchanged from that time. There is a small croquet lawn to one side of the house but the garden is otherwise symmetrical, with gravel paths surrounding a central bed that is on an axis with the front gate. Specimens of White Cedar (*Melia azedarach*) standing one each side of the gate are probably the only remnants of the original planting, though the present-day roses, annuals and perennials are appropriate. Two garden beds immediately in front of the verandah, for some time given over to lawn, are being replanted with low shrubs by the present owners.

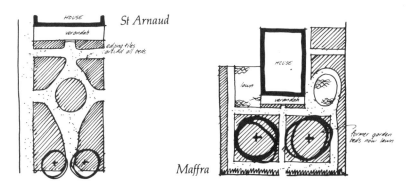

EMPHASIZING a symmetrical design with a pair of trees was a common practice in villa gardens. Two huge Norfolk Island Pines (*Araucaria heterophylla*) placed in the centre of the main beds dominate the small garden of a villa called 'Utingi' at Maffra. These trees have become a landmark in the town. The simple geometric form of the garden is known to have been similar early in the twentieth century, though much of the area now given over to lawn once consisted of beds of mixed flowers.

THE VILLA GARDEN at Maryborough cannot be said to have a distinguished design, but it is the only one recorded in Victoria as combining an asymmetrical layout with path-edgings of terra cotta tile. A clipped cypress hedge extends across the front boundary and the gate, placed in one corner, opens onto a path that curves to the front steps and the door in the centre of the house. Both this path and one that runs along the front of the house are bordered with tiles. House and garden layout probably date from the 1890s, but some of the original trees have been removed. Remaining plants include many of the old-fashioned kind. There are camellias, daphne and roses, with borders of lavender and bulbs such as jonquils and grape hyacinths.

Terra cotta tiles surround beds in the front garden of this villa at St Arnaud

Kawarau, Ballarat

Kawarau's late-Victorian timber house on brick foundations was built in 1903, and is heavily decorated on verandahs and ridges with cast iron. Scalloped terra cotta tiles rather than box hedges delineate the main garden path, which runs round a circular central area of lawn in the front garden. There is a small fountain in the middle of the lawn, which has a border of standard roses. The front gate is set back from the wooden picket fence (with golden privet hedge) and gives onto the encircling pathway, which passes under a modern wire arbour in connecting with a driveway that runs down the side of the house. The form of the garden is thought to be unaltered over the years.

There are no large trees here, and most of the plants are small shrubs, interspersed with annuals and perennials. Because no ancient trees bear witness to the age of the garden, one can only speculate as to the nature of the original planting: it may well have been similar to today's, for there are lilac, forsythia, azaleas, peony roses and camellias among the shrubs, and iris, daisies, lupins, foxgloves and forget-me-nots among the smaller plants at Kawarau. They help to make this an intricate little garden that perfectly complements the elaborate facade of the house.

*The front garden at
Kawarau*

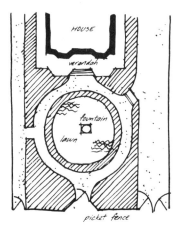

Smallest of all: gardens for terrace houses

As early as 1827 a change from short leases to perpetual ones encouraged Sydney landholders and entrepreneurs to crowd together as many families as possible onto one block of land. They did it by building terrace houses.

Terraces began to spring up in Melbourne just prior to the gold rushes of the 1850s, but it was the vast increase in population caused by gold fever that really led to the popularity of terrace housing in Melbourne. The first terraces were poorly built but soon more substantial rows were being constructed, until by the boom years of the 1880s splendid terraces were being built in great numbers, reflecting the affluence of the period, the prevalent passion for ornament, and the comfortable circumstances of those who inhabited them.

Being essentially space-saving, they left little room for gardens. Sometimes the front door opened directly off the street so that there was no garden at all. Others had a small plot, as wide as the house but generally no more than about 5 metres deep. The rear gardens were purely utilitarian – a space for drying clothes, for outbuildings and perhaps a few vegetables.

The main gardens generally had a front fence and side fences of timber pickets or wrought-iron palisade bars with cast-iron spears. A gate to one side led onto a straight path that ended at the verandah and front door. The rectangle of space left over was no doubt planted in as many different ways as there were terrace houses: little or none of that planting remains.

The style of these gardens probably changed very little between the 1850s and the end of the century. Loudon, in his *Suburban Gardener and Villa Companion* of 1838, had suggested a number of ways of treating small gardens and these were still evident in Melbourne in the 1880s and 1890s. Though it is not possible to know how the gardens were planted, one may make comparisons between those that have a distinctive form.

Royal Terrace in Nicholson Street, Fitzroy, is one of the earliest surviving terraces in Melbourne, having been completed in about 1856. It almost certainly had a fairly standard garden in a circular pattern and this was reconstructed, using some modern detailing, in 1981. Just around the corner, twenty-five years later, Barcelona Terrace in Brunswick Street was built for Estevan Parer. It consists of seven very elaborate boom-style terraces but the small front gardens are in exactly the same pattern as the Royal Terrace ones. Nearly all the detailing survives in each of the gardens at Barcelona Terrace, including the cast-iron fences, encaustic-tile paths, scalloped terra cotta edging tiles and the circular form of the garden. The tiled paths seem not to occur so much in the earliest gardens, though locally made 9 inch and 12 inch tiles, and 15 inch Chinese ones were available in 1862. Stone flags, such as those at Royal Terrace and Clarendon Terrace in East Melbourne (also about 1856) were certainly popular. These flag-

Formal garden elements on the smallest scale in a Fitzroy terrace

The circular bed was a common feature of nineteenth-century terrace house gardens, and it was generally filled with the choicest flowers and shrubs. A delicate tree such as the silver birch growing in this bed would have been uncommon; if a central plant were desired, it is more likely to have been a cordyline or special camellia

This pocket-handkerchief garden (far right) consists of nothing but a star-shaped bed within an elaborate iron fence

stones were of imported materials – Welsh slate and Arbroath, Caithness and York sandstones among them.

It is not certain when the terra cotta edging tiles were introduced, but they were certainly commonly available in Sydney when the *Illustrated Sydney News* of 26 October 1870 noted that 'at any of our pottery establishments and at most of our nursery and seed depots in Sydney, we can now obtain edging tiles of an immense variety of patterns. These, when sunk into the ground four or five inches, form a border at once elegant,

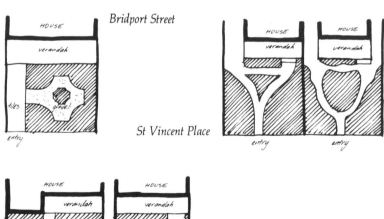

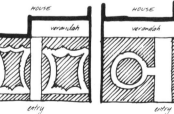

easy of arrangement and, we need hardly add, the most durable of all'. Henry Cawkwell of Malvern was a Victorian manufacturer of garden vases and edging tiles, as a catalogue from the Victorian Exhibition of 1875 testifies. He also had 'a fine exhibit of encaustic tiles' at the Melbourne International Exhibition of 1880–81, according to *Massina's Popular Guide*, which also commented on the 'important exhibit of various kinds of pottery, stoneware, and terra cotta' from Messrs Guthrie of Sandhurst.

With such standard detailing throughout the nineteenth century it is their form that is of most interest in terrace house gardens. Sadly, the shape of many of these gardens, provided by the pattern of the paths with their decorative edging tiles, has long since been lost and only a handful of intact examples survive. But they show amazing variety for what is generally a patch of soil of no more than 20 square metres.

The standard circular form is to be seen at Royal Terrace, Rushall Crescent and Barcelona Terrace in Fitzroy, at Bridport Street in Albert Park and at Bay View Terrace, in Grattan Street, Carlton. Other more complicated patterns in the shape of stars, crescents and scallops are to be seen in front of terraces at Scotchmer Street, Alfred Crescent and Rushall Crescent (in the same terrace as the circular one), Fitzroy, and at St Vincent Place, South Melbourne.

Generally, in a row of terraces the gardens are designed in pairs, each being a mirror image of its neighbour. Sometimes in larger terraces a central path divides the garden in two and each side is invariably the same shape as the other, as in a terrace at Mary Street, Richmond.

Occasionally additional decorative elements are used: in two of the Rushall Crescent gardens, for instance, the focus of the central bed is a cement urn placed on a large tiled pedestal.

All the gardens in this section are private and therefore closed to the public

A terra cotta vase on a pedestal faced with decorative glazed tiles in many patterns sits in a central bed that is the focal point of a terrace garden

Cottage gardens

IT MIGHT BE SAID that an historic cottage garden is a contradiction in terms. After all, are not cottage gardens the most ephemeral of creations, relying almost totally on short-lived plants for their special charm? Certainly Victoria's Historic Gardens Study uncovered very few extant cottage gardens that had been established before 1920, and even those slightly later ones around Edna Walling's cottages at Bickleigh Vale village, Mooroolbark, where the designer lived from the 1920s until 1967, are far from intact. On the other hand, a garden of this type may be established very quickly, because only the simplest of materials are required. It may, in fact, consist entirely of annual and perennial flowers that are in full bloom, and vegetables that are productive, within a few months of being planted. One of Victoria's loveliest cottage gardens, which surrounds a modern house belonging to the owner of Chateau Tahbilk winery at Tabilk, is barely twenty years old.

Cottage gardens are not necessarily associated with any particular era or style, but are simply a mixture of the functional and the decorative as seen by an individual owner. During the

This cottage garden at Vaughan is of the most unselfconscious kind

eighteenth century in Britain many of the plants that had been banished from aristocratic landscapes by William Kent and 'Capability' Brown were saved from extinction through their cultivation in cottage gardens. These gardens were later popularized, in the mid-nineteenth century, by painters such as Helen Allingham and William Coleman. Designers and writers like William Morris and William Robinson extolled their virtues. The former advised gardeners to 'fill up the flower growing space with things that are free and interesting in their growth, leaving Nature to do the desired complexity'.

Cottage gardens do tend to suggest a sense of gay abandon. They consist of a profusion of plants, all crowded together in a seemingly reckless manner – but the cottager always knows every one. Though plants tumble over each other – roses scrambling on hedges, gates, verandahs and arches – somehow in the disorder is a harmony of colour and form. And no matter how small the garden, there is always room for another cutting.

Occasionally clipped hedges and simple topiary are part of a cottage garden; often gravel or brick paths; almost never lawns; and rarely anything as formal or continuous as edging tiles. Victoria's old cottage gardens evolved in the best vernacular tradition. Any material at hand was used. At Mallacoota, on the east Gippsland coast, a pair of whalebones made an attractive arbour over an entrance gate. Along the coast shells were also readily available for edging paths. In gold country quartz did the same job – but with added sparkle.

Most of the cottage gardens that survive in Victoria have lost the complexity of their planting but the structure – where one existed – has had a better survival rate. Most commonly a straight central path divides the garden in two and there are sometimes triangular, square or circular beds. One Western District cottage garden still has a heart-shaped bed, placed inside the front gate in 1904 by its newly married owners. A split-paling or simple picket fence encloses such gardens, while wire or rough timber arbours arch over some of the paths.

Although native plants were sometimes brought from the bush into the early cottage gardens, their owners were much more inclined to fill them with treasures from the 'old country'. The British historian J. A. Froude wrote in *Oceana* (1886) of a garden near Ballarat:

We stopped for a few minutes at a roadside hotel, near the end of the embankment, to rest our horses. It was tidily kept and picturesquely situated. The little wicket gate was open. I strayed in and found myself in the garden of an English cottage, among cabbage-roses, pinks, sweet-williams, white phlox, columbines, white lilies and orange, syringas, laburnums, lilacs. Beneath the railings were beds of violet and periwinkle, and on a wall a monthly rose was intertwining with jessamine and honeysuckle. The emigrants who had made their home there had brought with them seeds and cuttings from the old home. They were 'singing the Lord's song in a strange land'.

The 'roadside hotel' may not have been as small as most cottages, but the nature of the garden was unmistakable.

Cottage gardens generally just happen. They may, of course, be given a helping hand, and Edna Walling did this for many of her Bickleigh Vale gardens between 1920 and 1950. Even these

A rose-covered wire arch at the entry to a Bealiba cottage

A cottage and its garden in Bickleigh Vale Road, Mooroolbark: the work of Edna Walling

were not really planned, but developed bit by bit. In their heyday they exemplified Walling's notion of the cottage garden, as she described it in *Cottage and Garden in Australia* (1947).

Always a cottage garden is visualised as being one that is packed with flowers, not masses of separate species in rows and beds of 'exhibition strains' of this and that, but all kinds jumbled up together, the tall sheltering the low, and the fragrant justifying their presence even when their colour and form may not; a veritable patchwork of colour . . . Always there is a little pathway of stone or bricks, always there is lavender, and herbs, and rosemary and climbing roses wherever support can be found for them.

All the gardens in this section are private and therefore closed to the public

Hillside, Beaufort, in about 1885: a garden full of treasures

Hillside, Beaufort

Probably built in the 1860s, and used as a post office until 1872, Hillside became the home of David and Rhoda Troy well before the 1890s. They had been married in 1869, and members of the family feel sure that the Troy children were born there. At about this time a vegetable patch and orchard were developing alongside the timber cottage, and a splendid collection of bulbs, roses, perennials and small shrubs filled the front garden.

Miss Ella Welsh, a granddaughter of the Troys, remembers the old home affectionately as far back as 1918. She speaks of the white and yellow jasmines growing on the conservatory, the climbing roses, verbena, fuchsia, erica, daphne, perennial phlox and guelder rose in the main garden, and the 'red japonica and masses of violets and mignonette bordering the front path'.

The present owner, who has lived at Hillside since 1939, says that all the plants mentioned by Miss Welsh are still to be found in their old positions, though a date palm that once stood in the centre of the white gravel path between gate and front door has been removed. An old boxthorn hedge screens the garden from the street. Other old-world plants in the garden today are lavender, ferns, spiraeas and berberis. Trees include two very large oaks, some wattles, and an elderberry, a linden tree, a laburnum and a mulberry.

It could be said that the ephemeral planting in *this* cottage garden is remarkably long-lived.

A cottage garden in Canterbury

The front garden of this timber cottage, built in 1893, is very small. There is a narrow brick path parallel with the front fence, and a central gate opens onto a tiled path that divides the garden into two sections. This part of the garden is full of old-fashioned flowers such as grape hyacinths, bluebells, lache-

Te Tua, Castlemaine

When the garden at Te Tua was first established by the present owner's father on a Castlemaine reef in 1900, he had to blast holes in the tightly packed shale before he could prepare his rosebeds. This gentleman was an enthusiastic gardener, importing his bulbs from Holland and his roses from Ireland. There have always been many roses in the garden. The cottage's cast-iron lace verandahs were once covered with them and there were originally several wire rose arbours along a path parallel with the front fence. A number of ramblers and bush roses still adorn the garden, and 'Ophelia', planted early this century and a favourite with its first owner, has been replanted recently.

The cottage was built in 1890 from the local sandstone – wheeled down the hill in a barrow – of a demolished Primitive Methodist church. The garden suits the cottage very well. It is largely made up of flower beds and brown gravel paths, and many of the beds are edged in clipped box: perhaps, suggests the present owner, to indicate 'where the soil ended and the rock started'! In fact, the nature of the ground seems very likely to have kept the form of this garden unchanged. A centrally placed, circular box-hedged bed is located on an axis with the gate and front door. It originally housed an orange tree surrounded with hyacinths, but now contains an Irish Strawberry Tree (*Arbutus unedo*), roses, penstemons and Easter daisy. Various 'cottage' flowers are planted at random in the garden – including lavender, carnations, polyanthus primrose, geraniums, shasta daisies and flag iris, with honeysuckle and tecoma on part of the verandah. There are proteas, a plumbago and a Spanish broom among the shrubs, and the biggest plant of all is a monster pepper tree. Some Australian plants including callistemons, hakeas and grevilleas have been added to dry parts of the garden in recent years.

nalias and freesias, and is dominated by several large camellia bushes. The garden behind the house appears to retain its nineteenth-century form, with a central path leading from the back door to the rear fence. A circular rock fishpond, vegetable garden and various outbuildings are to be found beside the path. There is a collection of ferns down one side of the house.

This garden provides an authentic setting for a small cottage that retains many of its original finishes inside and out; the form of both the simple front garden and the largely utilitarian back garden appears likely to have changed little over the last ninety years.

A cottage (left) in the Melbourne suburb of Canterbury; several enormous camellias form an arch across the tiled front path

Te Tua's planting extends beyond the gate, as commonly happens when the garden belongs to a cottage

Bickleigh Vale village

In contrast with the average suburban street, Bickleigh Vale Road (right) has all the qualities of an English lane

Edna Walling, who later created many cottage gardens, received basic training at Burnley Horticultural College. In this class photograph of 1917 she is typically wearing a hat and trousers (front row, second from right)

Around 1921 a young Englishwoman who had recently completed a course at the Burnley Horticultural College bought just over a hectare of rolling farmland at Mooroolbark, 33 kilometres east of Melbourne. The young woman was Edna Walling, who within a few years was well known in Victoria and beyond as a landscape designer of exceptional talent. Around the little English-style cottage that Walling built on her land she established a garden that helped to bring it into harmony with its surroundings – a principle of landscaping that marked her professional work throughout a long and distinguished career. The cottage was the forerunner of about sixteen others carefully constructed to harmonize with their environment. By purchasing 7.3 hectares adjacent to the first block, Edna Walling set her seal on a whole subdivision. Approved purchasers of land in what became known as Bickleigh Vale village were required to build cottages and gardens planned

by the vendor, who was destined to live there herself for more than forty-five years.

Nearly all of Edna Walling's cottages and their gardens remain at Bickleigh Vale village, though there have been many changes. Essentially 'English cottage' in style, the gardens typify Edna Walling's most relaxed design idiom. They are delicate gardens of an unstructured kind, relying more than most on keen and knowledgeable gardeners for survival. The foxgloves, forget-me-nots and erigeron that Edna Walling loved and planted everywhere will continue to self-sow, but so will the weeds that are liable to infiltrate such cottage informality. A number of the gardens at Bickleigh Vale village have been cut up for building blocks, and most of the cottages have been greatly enlarged. Nevertheless, these gardens make a unique collection. Closely associated with the most notable Australian garden designer of the twentieth century and immortalized in three of her books, they are a major component in an estate that is of immense interest to the history of town planning and residential design in Victoria.

Country estates

There is a fence being put up all round the house so as to form a garden in front. The fence is of upright posts with unbarked saplings laced in and out between them, close together. They are put close to keep out the fowls, and it makes a very pretty fence, especially when we get some vines and pumpkins growing over it. I have a small flower garden already in front of the house and some flowers do very well, but the soil is very hard and stony. Now Biddulph has employed the newly arrived Irishmen to dig up and trench it, and they are at present hard at work upon it. It is also to be manured from the stockyard. We are going to plant some bananas and orange-trees and vines in it; all the other fruit-trees are going down in the kitchen garden, which is at the foot of the hill by the creek that supplies us with water.

THUS WROTE Rachel Henning on 29 June 1863. She was describing her brother's homestead, Exmoor in Queensland, but a similar story might have been told thousands of times throughout Australia as new settlers pushed into virgin country, fenced their holdings and began to establish farms and grazing properties. Rachel Henning's garden was perhaps unusual in that it was under way before the homestead had a floor or the woolshed was built.

Opposite: Guilfoyle's domestic masterpiece, his paradise garden at Dalvui, Noorat, designed for Niel Black in 1898

The proud owners pose in their elaborate Hill End (N.S.W.) garden in 1872. They seem to have had a greater interest in gardening than in architecture

The garden of the first homestead at The Gums, Penshurst, seems to include some decorative planting as well as fruit trees, all enclosed within a split paling fence

Looking today at the tamed Victorian landscape with its well-established communications network and its many mature farm and station gardens, one can easily overlook the hardships and struggles of the pioneers and the careful nurturing these gardens received in their infancy.

Those first settlers who moved into new country with their sheep and cattle and a few other possessions were more concerned with survival than with the making of gardens. Their womenfolk may have had loftier ideas, but these often had to be curtailed until the first flush of wealth enabled such genteel pursuits as gardening for pleasure. So initially homestead gardens developed as almost entirely utilitarian affairs. Generally they followed a squared layout in front of the house and were enclosed in a fence strong enough to keep out animals. Since the chief purpose of the garden was to grow food, vegetables and fruit trees occupied most of the space. A few ornamental shrubs may have survived the first journey by bullock wagon. But seeds, safer and readily available in the main cities, were undoubtedly carried on many of the early expeditions. Even though food-growing was the only sort of gardening that really mattered at this stage, these treasures were planted close to the cottage for both protection and enjoyment, and in spite of their incongruity must have given the occupants a sense of

comfort and intimacy in their strange surroundings. But what we know today as the great homestead gardens of Victoria are not these early gardens. In fact, the garden at Green Hills, Tarraville, with its earthen paths around rectangular beds, is the only recorded survivor.

As the squatters consolidated their position and transport routes became better defined, as local towns and neighbours became established, as postal services developed and visitors arrived – in other words, as civilization of some sort reached these remotest of outposts – so too did gardens begin to flourish. The Western District of Victoria has the greatest concentration of large country gardens in the state, reflecting the wealth of landholders who by the mid-1860s each held an average of 8000 to 10000 hectares of freehold in this fertile part of Victoria. As early as 1857 the Manifold family owned 16000 hectares of freehold land and a further 24000 hectares leasehold. It is not surprising then that this family still owns three very significant properties with good gardens in 1982. Western District homestead gardens have survived better than others in the state partly because of a moderately cool climate and rich soils, and partly because of the relative stability of family ownership there.

The gardens that remain today are those surrounding the grand homesteads constructed in a wave that crossed Victoria from the late 1850s up to 1910, peaking in the 1870s and 1880s. By this time the wealth accumulated from their vast landholdings enabled settlers throughout Victoria to lavish fortunes on new houses. In the Western District the ring of chisel on bluestone could be heard far and wide. The garden no longer had to be largely utilitarian (vegetable patches and orchards remained, but were now usually well out of sight). Instead, like the house it surrounded, the garden was created to reward its owners for their past toil. It had to provide an appropriate setting for the mansion and, above all, to give pleasure and recreation to its owners. Croquet lawns, tennis courts, mown grass, walks, shrubberies, rockeries and flower gardens were all used extensively. But there was no uniformity of style. A carriage drive usually connected the approach, front

entrance and stable yard, but apart from this every garden was different.

Most Victorian gardens shielded the house from the surrounding countryside. The intention was probably to provide weather protection rather than to shut out a wild and foreign landscape, as is sometimes claimed. Indeed with their sense of 'the picturesque' people of the Victorian era probably enjoyed the wider landscape more fully than any subsequent generation. There are a number of Western District gardens that make brilliant use of their natural surroundings, the most notable being those of Titanga (Lismore), Merrang (Hexham), Meningoort (Camperdown) and Mawallok (Beaufort). At others the owners endeavoured to create idealized parklands. Mount Noorat's is a fine example but the grandest vision is that at Murndal, where the transformation of the landscape into an English parkland over a vast area was a conscious effort on the part of Samuel Pratt Winter to establish a heritage for his family – as was his commissioning of copies of paintings of his eighteenth-century forebears to decorate the homestead.

If there is some consistency in the pattern of development of these gardens it is to be found in a comparison of the earlier gardens with those that followed later in the nineteenth century and in the first decade of the twentieth. The earlier gardens had a tendency to be tight and compact in design (an obvious exception, for there is always at least one, is that at Bontharambo, which in the 1850s had swirling baroque paths encircling the house). Some of these gardens were swept away when the new homestead was extended. Merrang at Hexham, Stony Point at Darlington and The Union at Woolsthorpe are all examples of largish squared gardens being replaced by

Stony Point, Darlington, in the 1860s (above): a long way from anywhere, the large squared garden full of produce must have been a reassuring sight to hungry travellers. As the pastoralist prospered, the visitor to Stony Point could also feast his eyes on horticultural riches, as illustrated in 1910 (below). The food garden remained, but was relegated to a less conspicuous location

Murndal, photographed around the 1870s, never had a really large pleasure garden. Instead its owners – like William Kent – 'saw that all nature was a garden', and endeavoured to create an English landscape in the Australian countryside

lawns, driveways and gravelled walks. Mount Boninyong at Scotsburn has one of the most fascinating of homestead gardens since there the garden remained while the house changed. More commonly, however, the new mansion was sited some distance from the old house.

Later in the century there was something of a revival of the principles of the eighteenth-century landscape school, which William Kent had launched when 'he leaped the fence, and saw that all nature was a garden'. The nurseryman Thomas Shepherd had espoused these principles in his *Lectures on Landscape Gardening in Australia*, published in Sydney in 1836. The great champion of these notions for Victoria was William Guilfoyle, who mixed with them the current zest for variety and contrast. At Mooleric, Birregurra, his cordylines and palms punctuate the garden yet manage to harmonize with – even balance – the great sweeping lawn with its southern vista to the Otway Ranges.

Homestead gardens are by far the largest group of historic gardens to have survived in Victoria. There are a number of reasons for this. They have not been subject to the development pressures put on their city counterparts. Farm labour has often been available for gardens, and even today rural prosperity sometimes allows the employment of garden staff. Nor can the willingness of owners and families to work hard in these gardens be overlooked. But perhaps more important than any of these reasons has been the continuity of ownership of Victoria's homestead gardens, for longterm control by one family brings with it a measure of stability and a reluctance to change. Of the thirty or so homestead gardens described here, more than half have been under the continuous control of one family for periods of at least eighty years.

Whatever the reason, one of the great hidden treasures of Victoria must be its rich store of homestead gardens.

Most of the gardens in this section are private and therefore closed to the public; Werribee Park is open at specific times, while Bontharambo and Banongill (and possibly others) are open occasionally

Murndal, Hamilton

First taken up by Samuel Pratt Winter in 1837, the leasehold run that became the Murndal property in the rich Wannon River valley has been developed by five generations of the Winter Cooke family. The original stone hut dating from the 1840s became the nucleus of a house that was extended several times to become a substantial homestead.

It is believed that the garden in the immediate vicinity of the house was never significant, but scores of hectares surrounding the homestead constitute designed landscape in the tradition of the eighteenth-century English style: a scene that encompasses natural-looking groups of trees in what appears to be an extensive park, though some of it is grazing land. Avenues of trees lead out from the homestead and clumps of English trees in the paddocks are placed in prominent positions such as the crowns of hills. About 1 kilometre from the house there is a series of artificial lakes surrounded by willows, pines, cedars and monkey puzzle trees. The lakes used to be known to the Winter Cooke family as 'the garden dams'.

Margaret Kiddle says in *Men of Yesterday* (1961) that though

Samuel Pratt Winter took some pleasure in trying to acclimatize plants he had collected all over the world, he 'concentrated . . .chiefly on the trees and flowers known and loved in his [Irish] childhood'. Nostalgia for Britain is evident in the 'Coronation Avenue' (a new pair of trees is planted for each British coronation), 'Cowthorp Oak' (grown from an acorn of this tree, said to be the oldest oak in the world), and 'Richmond Park' (named after its London counterpart).

The grounds of Murndal provide an outstanding setting for a large house which, together with its contents, the various outbuildings and the landscape, is possibly Australia's closest approximation to an English manor and its precincts. The designed landscape is thought to be the largest of its type in Australia and is unknown elsewhere in Victoria. Many trees are over-mature, however, and some sections of the homestead garden have had to be abandoned.

One of a series of splendid dams descending the slopes above Murndal

Murndal's conservatory late in the nineteenth century

Wombat Park, Daylesford

Though the present garden at Wombat Park shows the general form established by Gavin Fleming of the firm Taylor & Sangster around a new homestead in about 1910, its outstanding feature is the collection of mature exotic trees dating from the 1850s. These were planted by the property's owner at that time, W. E. Stanbridge, M.L.C., who created what was known for decades as an outstanding garden. The *Daylesford Advocate* of 26 May 1885 provided a detailed description of 'The Hon. W. E. Stanbridge's Grounds'.

The writer remarked on the suitability of Daylesford's climate and soil for gardening, and called this the most impressive of the 'fine old gardens attached to residences that make no pretensions to architectural display'. Close to the house, and surrounded by tall native forest, there was a considerable area 'cleared and planted, and in this rather out-of-the-way place any one interested in arboriculture will find examples of exotic trees superior to any that can be seen in any private or public garden in Victoria'. Shrubs like laurustinus, guelder rose and

camellia were large and flourishing, and 'The numerous deciduous trees, with their bright green foliage, form a prominent and pleasing feature in the grounds. The oak, the elm, the plane, the beech, the chestnut, the walnut, are growing rapidly into timber'. Rare trees such as the Mexican Nut Pine (*Pinus cembroides*), planted by Stanbridge, are among those still standing. Trees of similar vintage at the Daylesford Botanic Gardens on neighbouring Wombat Hill complement those of Wombat Park.

Still owned by descendants of W. E. Stanbridge, the garden is entered through a long avenue of elms, and much of it now has the appearance of an arboretum. There are a number of old trees whose girth exceeds 3 metres. A splendid tapestry hedge, consisting of clipped specimens of shrubs with contrasting foliage and grown close together, borders the driveway as it approaches the house; it is a particularly good example and the only one known to exist in Victoria. Plants in the hedge include green, golden and silver hollies, laurustinus, Portuguese laurel, arbutus and pittosporum.

Trawalla, Beaufort

Less than two years after Trawalla was settled by the Kirkland family in 1839, Mrs Kirkland recorded that their primitive hut had 'a little flower garden enclosed in front . . . and we had now plenty of vegetables'. There were also, not long afterwards, 'young gooseberry, currant, and raspberry bushes'. Large and sophisticated gardens like the one that developed at Trawalla later in the nineteenth century (and long after the brief sojourn of the Kirklands) must often have begun in some such simple way, but very early accounts are rarely available.

Early in the twentieth century Trawalla belonged to Admiral Bridges, who – according to *Victoria's Representative Men at Home* (1904) – had near the house 'a collection of flowers, shrubs, &c., which have been gathered from the four quarters of the globe'.

The rose garden at
Trawalla in 1915 (left);
in more recent times
(below) the gravel paths
have been grassed over
and the palms, grown to
enormous size, removed

The garden now has a number of major components, including a sweeping front lawn, a rose garden, a pergola (covered mainly by an ornamental grape), shrubberies and kitchen garden. Attached to the 1891 homestead is a very fine working conservatory. At the rear of the house lies an extensive woodland colonized by bluebells, jonquils and daffodils. The majority of trees in the woodland are oaks. About 11 hectares of land around the house are fenced off from stock, with perhaps 1.5 hectares closely cultivated.

The garden is an important part of this very large homestead complex and is thought to be little changed since the 1890s, except that the rose garden has been simplified and reduced in size in recent years. The palm trees that were once planted among the rose bushes have been removed.

Glenara, Bulla

The Italianate house at Glenara was built for pastoralist Walter Clark in 1857, and presumably the garden was laid out soon after. At any rate it was well established by the time it was painted by Eugène von Guérard in 1867, and its old form can be discerned today: the original 10 hectares have, however, shrunk to a little over 3.

The garden has a spectacular site sloping down to large outcrops of granite along the Maribyrnong River. Old trees between the house and river include a number of conifers. To the west of the house is an Italianate terrace whose balustrades and urns are finely detailed. The terrace is flanked by a staircase on either side leading to what was once an elaborate path system, now largely overgrown. A bridge across the gully on the south side gives access to a small hill on top of which is

a rustic bluestone lookout tower, a particularly impressive structure. The planting in this area is predominantly native. A large daffodil collection assembled by Alister Clark, who bred the famous pink daffodil, has naturalized along the banks of the river. Mr Clark was also a rosarian – said by Dr A. S. Thomas to have 'done more for the rose than any other Australian'. In the 1960s Ellis Stones modified the garden slightly in widening the driveway. He also designed a swimming pool and largely native section of the garden that together form a link between the house and an old building that was once the property's winery.

Glenara's is one of the earliest domestic gardens in Victoria that still shows its original pattern. Though parts of the garden have been overrun with periwinkle, and the areas nearest the house receive most of the attention, house and garden still make a striking combination.

Eugène von Guérard's preliminary pencil sketch for his well-known oil painting of Glenara. Comparison with the Nettleton photograph on page 31 confirms the accuracy of this drawing

116

This pen and wash sketch of Bontharambo's 1843 slab hut was drawn from the tower of its new mansion, erected in 1858. The simple squared layout of the garden is typical of early utilitarian gardens

The broad paths in Glenara's garden – painted by Eugène von Guérard in 1867 – were edged with mown grass, and trees below the house were planted in rows; but across the foot-bridge in the foreground, the formal garden merged with a wilder natural landscape

Meningoort, Camperdown, painted in 1861 by Eugène von Guérard from behind the house. The earliest trees planted in the straight avenue leading up to the homestead are believed to have been wattles

The bridge (far left) across the river at Glenara, Bulla, gives onto a winding gravel path that terminates at the bluestone lookout tower. Alister Clark developed this pink daffodil (left) at Glenara, where bulbs have naturalized along the river banks

Many large gardens are divided into compartments, but a formal avenue such as this at Trawalla, Beaufort, is rare. Beneath the oaks the ground is clothed with daffodils and bluebells

The great floral parterre
at Werribee Park,
Werribee, in process of
being re-formed in 1979

A beautiful old garden
seat at Bontharambo,
Wangaratta

The box-hedged rose
garden established at
Delatite, Mansfield, in
the 1950s

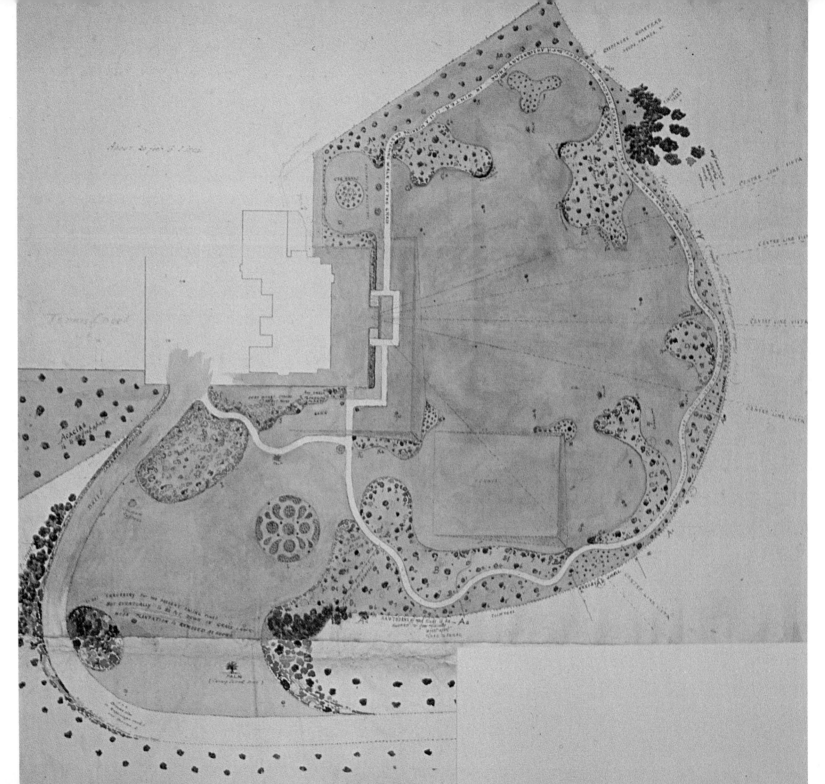

William Guilfoyle's plan of the garden at Mawal-lok, Beaufort (1909). The now mature garden has confirmed the designer's wisdom in endeavouring to create vistas from the terrace. The plan shows arabesque shrub beds, characteristic of Guilfoyle's style, giving a large space an interesting form

*Meningoort before 1867
(far left), around 1901
(left), and in 1981
(below): the house has
been greatly extended, but
the turning circle in front
is discernible in all three
photographs, as in von
Guérard's 1861 painting
on page 117*

Meningoort, Camperdown

When the garden at Meningoort was painted by Eugene von Guérard in 1861, its structure was much as it is today. Since the original bluestone homestead had by then been built nine years, it seems likely that the garden dates from somewhere around 1852. The house was enlarged in 1887.

This is perhaps the boldest piece of garden design in Victoria. An avenue of blue gums leads straight to the front door of the homestead. A large, unembellished carriage circle conducts the visitor to a flight of stairs that opens onto a terrace, from which another flight leads to the house. These elements are all on the main axis, creating a strikingly grand approach. They are also in line with Mount Meningoort (the house is situated on the side of this mountain) and Mount Leura some 16 kilometres away. The terrace extends into the landscape on either side of the house, and park-like grazing land, planted with Moreton Bay figs, cypresses, pines, monkey puzzle trees, elms, oaks and pink-flowering gums, surrounds the entire approach to the homestead. Old trees near the house include hollies and Irish yews. Excluding the turning circle, the original garden would have covered about 0.2 hectares.

The garden's association with one family (which first settled the area in 1842), and with an important house that retains

much of its original internal decoration, adds to its significance. Much of the detail has disappeared, however (including a floral parterre from the terrace in front of and on either side of the house), and a large kitchen garden and orchard have been abandoned.

Merrang, Hexham

The garden at Merrang possibly dates, in part, from 1859 when the house was first built, but its present form is more likely to derive from 1865 when the house was greatly extended and the large retaining wall, a form of ha-ha, was built. This wall is a major feature of the garden, allowing distant views from the front of the house across an orchard to the southern landscape and giving the house a relationship with the surrounding countryside that is unusual in Victoria. There are dry-stone walls of particularly fine construction dividing the garden and its immediate surroundings into different compartments. The property is entered through a large parkland designed in about 1875, with a picturesque lodge at the en-

Merrang in 1863 (below), two years before its ha-ha was constructed and (right) in 1888, with the ha-ha wall visible between the house and a hawthorn hedge

trance. Part of the garden has been abandoned in recent years, and the terraces in a paddock are a reminder of the once-large kitchen garden. From its original size of about 2.4 hectares, the garden has in fact been reduced by two-thirds.

Bontharambo, Wangaratta

The Reverend Joseph Docker, who originally came to Australia as a colonial chaplain in 1828, had been a farmer and grazier in New South Wales for several years when, inspired by Major Thomas Mitchell's explorations, he journeyed with his family and all his belongings from Windsor to the Bontharambo Plains in the north-east of Victoria. He took up a considerable tract of land in 1838, living first in a slab hut, then a more spacious house, and eventually a fine two-storey homestead designed by Thomas Watts and built in 1858. It was, in a sense, a house built on gold, for the Dockers made a fortune selling meat to miners of the Beechworth fields in the 1850s.

The design of the garden for Bontharambo's grounds was apparently the result of a public competition, the garden seeming to approximate most closely to the plan submitted by a John Hotson. On a grandiose scale almost unparalleled in Victoria, it included an extensive parkland. There is certainly a large area of parkland at Bontharambo today, and it is entered through a cast-iron gate at the end of a 2.4 kilometre drive lined with elms, kurrajongs, ashes and camphor laurels. In the park a series of curving rides are laid out, eventually arriving at the house.

The formal garden has largely disappeared but the citrus grove still stands on one side of the house, below a severe stone and brick terrace. A fernery once attached to one of the arcaded verandahs has been removed. The remains of a standard rectilinear utilitarian garden can still be seen in front of a surviving early cottage. In spite of the losses, the basic structure of the garden remains, a garden whose grandeur still complements that of the great house at Bontharambo.

Delatite, Mansfield

While only the outline of a bark outstation established in the late 1830s by the Hunter brothers is still visible on the Delatite property, the homesteads that followed were much more substantial. One block from George Chenery's group of buildings constructed in the 1860s of bricks from Mansfield still stands alongside of the present house, dating from 1890.

A small garden was laid out in the Chenerys' time, between their house and the stables and in an area that became the front of the new house; an orchard was set out on the eastern side, towards the Delatite River. Several trees, including three magnificent pear trees, remain from that planting and are part of the modern garden of 1.25 hectares.

The drive of *Pinus radiata*, planted in about 1898 under the direction of the then manager, Mr Edward Macartney, was used for the first time in 1901 when his funeral cortege passed through it.

To the wife of Geoffrey Ritchie, who moved to the property in 1903, is attributed the design of the fine garden that developed in the early years of the century at Delatite. Mrs Ritchie used the existing orchard trees, the slope down to the river,

An early twentieth-century view towards the Delatite River at the bottom of the Delatite garden. The pear tree heavily in bloom, and shading a rustic garden seat, probably dates from the 1860s or 1870s

123

and the river itself as the bare bones of the garden, which she fleshed out with curving flower beds, extensive lawns and a background of trees and shrubs: a plan that has not changed substantially. Elms were planted in an 'English bluebell wood' and a new orchard was carpeted with daffodils. So great was Mrs Ritchie's devotion to her garden that one of the gardeners was heard to express the fear that if he fell over on the job she would dig him in as compost!

Another talented garden-maker, Mrs Ritchie's daughter-in-law Sylvia (together with her husband's cousin Miss May Fisher, who had trained at Burnley Horticultural College), modified, improved and maintained the garden from 1936 on wards. During this time the box-hedged rose garden - perhaps the best example of the style in Victoria - was laid out (in 1952–53), and many more shrubs and trees were planted.

The delicate garden on this property, reminiscent in style of the naturalistic landscapes of the English designers Gertrude Jekyll and William Robinson, makes a splendid setting for the old homestead and its older adjunct, while the main drive, on an axis with the front door, adds a degree of grandeur. Though many of the minor elements and the detailed planting have changed over the years, the main structure of the garden dates from the early twentieth century, and a small amount of the planting from the 1860s.

The Laurels, Learmonth

Leaving the county of Hereford, England, in 1852, William Vaughan unsuccessfully sought gold in Victoria before deciding to resume the occupation he knew best – farming. By 1854 he was the owner of the property that became The Laurels, later to pass to his granddaughter, the present owner. Vaughan built the original homestead (together with the district's first flour mill) in 1857, and it was greatly extended subsequently.

The garden is roughly 1 hectare in extent, excluding the orchard, and is thought to have been begun at a very early

Opposite: The old pear tree at Delatite, seen from the other direction

The circular box-hedged rose garden at The Laurels now contains other shrubs and flowers in addition to a few old roses

The rose garden

box-hedging

stage, with its general pattern dating from the 1870s. One of the early gardeners at The Laurels was a ticket-of-leave man who had once been a lawyer in London. Some of the unusual trees and shrubs on the property are said to have been planted by this man on the advice of Dr Ferdinand Mueller, for many years Director of the Melbourne Botanic Gardens. There is still an old specimen of the Chinese Weeping Cypress (*Cupressus funebris*) in the garden, and a Monkey Puzzle Tree (*Araucaria araucana*).

The most notable feature of the garden is the original circular box-hedged garden, once devoted to roses but now containing shrubs that nevertheless include four old roses, two being 'Cécile Brunner' and 'Souvenir de la Malmaison'. There are other old roses in the garden and two rose arches. Along the drive, the shrubs that give the property its name are clipped each spring, while others that remain untrimmed have become quite large specimens. A section once devoted to berry fruits is now planted with trees, and the vegetable garden has become smaller over the years. The old croquet lawn has recently had a sycamore planted in the middle of it. Though a grapevine walk has been lost through the collapse of its wooden supports, some of the original vines still cover the western verandah of the house. This old garden, in spite of such small changes, is largely intact.

125

Mount Boninyong, Scotsburn

Although the present homestead at Mount Boninyong was not built until 1884, it seems that its garden is the same one that surrounded an earlier slab homestead on the same site. It is therefore possible that the garden may date from at least the 1850s or 1860s. (Mount Boninyong was first settled by the Scott family in 1839.) The main garden, about 70 metres long and 40 metres deep, was laid out immediately in front of the house and consists of a concentric semicircular path system. Some parts are bordered with box-hedging, others with small rocks, and others again with a simple, thick terra cotta edging tile. This section of the garden is planted with flowers and shrubs that include many camellias, rhododendrons and azaleas. There are also two specimens of *Magnolia grandiflora*. A ter-

raced lawn to the side of the house is hedged with pittosporum and surrounded in part by an iron fence that was brought from Scotland by the family while the house was being built in 1884: the lawn was used at the time for croquet. Clipped pittosporum and privet hedges divide the more utilitarian parts of the garden (containing vegetables and fruit trees, and more extensive than the front garden) behind the house. The garden is entered from the main road through a set of elaborate timber gates set on dressed bluestone piers. An outer, less formal section of the garden that consists of a parkland of cedars, cypresses and oaks has been fenced off for grazing.

Mount Boninyong's garden may well be one of the oldest surviving domestic gardens in Victoria. The design is of a type common in the mid-nineteenth century, but this is the only known example surviving intact.

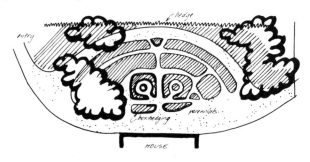

Barunah Plains, Hesse

The sheeprun that later became known as Barunah Plains was taken up in the 1840s, and the pioneering Russell family, which owned the property from 1851 onwards, maintained control of it until the 1970s.

In a letter to William Lewis on 27 May 1853, Alexander Russell had one or two interesting comments to make on the Barunah Plains garden and its elusive nature at the time.

I got a complete drenching that day I left the Plains . . . Tom [Russell] – the confounded fellow – would not let me away until I saw his garden, so that it was eleven O'clock before I got started . . . Can you tell me, Willie, where the garden at the Plains is situated? – while Tom was sowing his Paddock he told me to take a look at his garden. I walked good three miles about the place, but feint head I saw deserving the name of one . . .

James Russell, son of George Russell of Golf Hill, Shelford, built the house at Barunah Plains in 1866 to the design of the architectural firm Davidson & Henderson, enlarging it in 1886. An unknown garden designer made good use of the setting of the fine bluestone building, providing delightful walks along the Warrambine Creek on its southern side. Features typical of a large nineteenth-century country garden were established and still survive at Barunah Plains: a sunken croquet lawn (no longer used for croquet), tennis court, rose gardens, orchard, kitchen garden and various shrubberies incorporating small trees, shrubs of all kinds, and perennials. Tall old trees include pines, eucalypts, monkey puzzle trees and cypresses.

There have been few changes in the garden's layout since at least the 1890s. An area of nearly 3 hectares is still devoted to formal garden, and less formal sections together with parkland cover another 2 hectares or so. The garden is part of a complex that includes stables, woolshed, cottages and other outbuildings, with the homestead as its focal point. The present owner is working towards restoration and extension of the garden, and has planted thousands of new trees, mostly Australian species, in shelterbelts around the property. Part of the garden reached by crossing a bridge over the creek had its tangle of elm suckers and boxthorn bulldozed in 1980 in the attempt to restore its original character of lawn and trees.

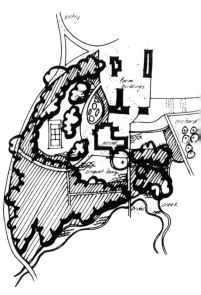

Barunah Plains 1980

Recently restored, this old gate marks one of the entrances to Barunah Plains

Mount Noorat, Noorat

In *Men of Yesterday* (1961) Margaret Kiddle writes of the great bluestone house built in the early 1870s for the Western District's distinguished pioneer Niel Black. Its position, on rising ground and with distant views to the east, was selected with great care, and 'Long before building began. . .[Black] had levelled the ground and planted a background of trees so that his homestead should have its proper setting'. The garden at Mount Noorat was given a good start. On 12 March 1892 the *Australasian* published an illustrated description of Mount Noorat:

A great plantation of conifers (right) made a backdrop for Mount Noorat

Deciduous trees planted in groups at Mount Noorat

The garden is in a saucer-shaped hollow about two acres in extent, and the soil is excellently suited for the purpose. . . Almost all kinds of trees and flowers thrive luxuriantly, the growth of most of the plantations having been exceptionally rapid. The plantations, &c., round the house are about 35 acres in extent, and they are varied in character. As is very often the case in Victoria, the Pinus insignis [*P. radiata*] has been very largely used to form the main body of the plantations, but there are deciduous trees in abundance as well. . . The walks are nearly all bordered with English primroses, which grow in the utmost luxuriance. . .

Though the main house was demolished in 1941, and the grounds are now in a derelict condition, there is still a fine collection of trees at Mount Noorat in those '35 acres' that surrounded the house. In addition, Mount Noorat has one of the best private parklands in Victoria – 60 hectares of exotic trees planted in clumps and in a perimeter belt, indicating some understanding of eighteenth-century English landscape principles. The whole garden was once one of the grandest in the Western District, and there are still traces of old features. It is

approached through a long avenue of elms, which terminates
at a fine gateway. Further along an inner avenue is a Gothic
lodge designed, like the demolished mansion, by Charles Webb.
Behind the site of the old house are the remains of a once-
large fruit and vegetable garden and a shrubbery, together
with the ruins of many glasshouses and other ancillary buildings. A semicircular ha-ha wall, still standing, was designed to
allow views from the front of the house into the parkland.

The grounds of Mount Noorat make a significant contribution to the outstanding landscape of the Noorat area, which
includes two other properties associated with the Black family:
Glenormiston, owned by Niel Black till late in the 1860s, and
Dalvui, on which his youngest son Niel early in the twentieth
century built a mansion around which William Guilfoyle designed his finest surviving private garden.

Noorilim, Murchison East

Comparable in scale and form with that at Werribee Park,
Noorilim's garden of nearly 3 hectares, though essentially simple, is one of the largest in Victoria. Like Werribee Park's
garden, it gives to an important country mansion a setting of
suitable proportions and character.

The large and impressive homestead was built in about 1870
for the Winter family, and the garden dates from the same
period. A long driveway, with shrubberies partly concealing the
view ahead, sweeps up to the house (most of the shrubberies
have been replanted in recent years, though some old olives
remain). A lawn of about 2 hectares extends from the front
door of the house; a new lake covering 0.4 hectares has been
constructed in this area, and will supply water for the whole
garden. The perimeter of the lawn is planted with old trees
that include elms, spruces, cedars, pines, pepper trees, silky

oaks, kurrajongs, Irish strawberry trees, and osage orange; there are also a bunya bunya pine, monkey puzzle tree and magnificent Moreton Bay fig.

The garden was neglected and grazed for many years and some of the detail may have been lost, but it is being restored by its present owners: new beds and a rose garden have been formed close to the house, replanting is in progress, and the fenceline has been moved back to its original position.

Titanga, Lismore

This garden began in about 1872, the year in which Alexander Buchanan built his long, low bluestone house among the local banksias, acacias and sheoaks. A 535 millimetre rainfall and the belief that underground and dam water in the area was too brackish for gardens dictated the establishment of hardy, drought-resistant plants, and it was not until 1938 that dam water was found to be satisfactory and piped for garden use. Buchanan made the most of the site's natural assets, placing his house on a ridge from which the view extended across a plain to several extinct volcanoes – including Mount Elephant, 10 kilometres away – and to Lake Tooliorook.

A fenced garden of about 1 hectare was laid out, mainly beside and at the rear of the house. The trees, shrubs and flower beds of the garden were intersected with paths broad enough to be used by maintenance vehicles. (Much of the terra cotta tiling bordering these beds is still in place.) After the First World War a rundown orchard became the site for a tennis court, and once water was available for the garden, a small

Titanga is approached through an extensive parkland planted as an arboretum of Australian trees. The richness of this planting (far left) is in marked contrast to the relatively sparse vegetation of the early days (opposite)

Titanga's formal garden in its early stages (left), long before it gained the enclosed and intimate quality apparent below

lawn with lily pond was established, and plants that would not have survived in the original garden were added.

This part of the windswept Western District of Victoria originally carried few trees, but the Titanga property seems to have been in the hands of assiduous tree-planters right from the start. Alexander Buchanan put in many kilometres of windbreak trees, mostly blue gums and sugar gums, as well as dotting the home paddock with specimens. J. L. Currie, who bought the property in 1886, extended the shelterbelt planting greatly, and in 1918 the present owners' father began the extensive planting of eucalypts in the home paddock that had reached two hundred species by 1947. This parkland covers a large area between the front gate (with its picturesque Gothic lodge) and the homestead 1.75 kilometres along the drive. Young native trees continue to be planted at Titanga in the 1980s.

The layout of the garden is little changed over the years and is a major component of this important homestead complex. In its association mainly with the back of the house, the design of the formal section is unusual. The relationship – eighteenth-century in concept – of the front of the house to open parkland is unique in Victoria.

Apart from one small patch of lawn, the garden is entirely
devoted to shrubberies. A rusticated summer house has recently collapsed. The garden contains many interesting plants, such
as a rose ('Marie van Houtte') one hundred years old and a
number of trees at least eighty years old – cedars, palms and
lilly-pillies, and two specimens of *Magnolia grandiflora*.

Greystones, Rowsley

This garden of 1 to 1.5 hectares was presumably laid out when
the two-storey house was constructed in about 1875. It was
certainly well established and attracting attention by early
1889, when J. Johnstone wrote an account for the *Bacchus
Marsh Express* of a rewarding visit to Greystones, at that time
'Mr Greene's gardens'.

The long, winding and densely planted driveway of today
was arresting then: 'Moving slowly along the twining drive we
noticed on both sides many of the choice ornamental trees; the
Wellingtonia gigantea (mammoth tree of California) was there,
in its glory; the Araucaria's looked most beautiful, while the
elms are growing with great luxuriance.' Johnstone wrote of
the vegetable and fruit gardens: 'The kitchen garden is square,
and well laid out; the walks are edged with suitable edging
plants; the apple trees are loaded with fruit . . . ' The orchard
was regrettably popular with parrots (a 'growing evil'). Toma-
toes trained on trellises were carrying a heavy crop: 'in fact the
garden is well cropped, and nowhere in Australia have I seen a
better kept garden.' In 1889 there were in the grounds a
summer house and a 'well erected shade house'; a fernery
adjoining the house had 'tree ferns growing up spreading over
the rocky mounds, while some of the choice creepers twining
round the pillars were in a mass of white blossom'. Johnstone
was also impressed by the rock garden, the flowers (including
some carpet bedding) and the shrubs.

The garden at Greystones is surrounded by a stone wall and
a large lawn extends in front of the house, but the main

Eeyeuk, Terang

The symmetrical, looped path system immediately in front of
the house at Eeyeuk is different in form but similar in concept
to that at Mount Boninyong, Scotsburn. Here walkways are
wide enough to accommodate a car. These paths were once
lined with box-hedging, but only small sections of it remain.
The garden, about 100 metres by 100 metres in area, is
thought to have been laid out when the two-storeyed bluestone homestead was completed in 1875 for Alexander Dennis.

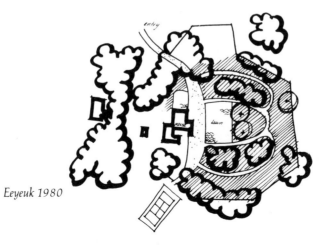

Eeyeuk 1980

garden falls down a steep hill to one side. A series of terraces incorporates two formal rose gardens, one set in lawn and the other in paths of brickwork. The rockery is unusually large and still a feature of the garden, and the shrubbery is intersected by many interesting paths.

Eynesbury, Melton

The large bluestone house at Eynesbury was constructed in the early 1870s for Samuel Staughton, and wings were added in the 1880s. The date of the garden's commencement is unknown but it was presumably associated with one of the main periods of building. A circular carriage drive dominates the front of the house, and the main front garden is surrounded by a semicircular ha-ha wall. This is a true ha-ha because (unlike most in Victoria, which are really retaining walls) it has a ditch at its base. It is possibly Victoria's best example of this device for keeping animals out of the garden without using a fence. The one that was built near the 1857 homestead at Werribee Park is of similar scale and design. Between the ha-ha and the driveway is a path following the line of the wall, with spoke-like paths providing views into the landscape. The garden is assumed to be in its original form.

The original homestead at Werribee Park photographed from the mansion in about 1915: the semicircular shape of the garden and the ha-ha wall that encloses it are both very similar to those of nearby Eynesbury

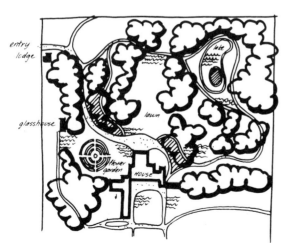

Werribee Park 1980

Werribee Park, Werribee

Though the style of the garden at Werribee Park might be said to be Guilfoylean, and some have attributed its design to William Guilfoyle, there seems to be no evidence to support the claim.

The Werribee Park mansion, of bluestone faced with free-stone, was built for Thomas and Andrew Chirnside between 1874 and 1877, and an area of 10 hectares was set aside for a park and garden. Large quantities of black soil from Point Cook (which also belonged to the Chirnsides) were delivered for the benefit of the garden at about the time the building was completed. The two-storeyed Italianate house of sixty rooms was enlarged during its years (from 1923) as Corpus Christi College, a seminary for Catholic priests. Remodelling of

the garden was begun by students in 1924 or 1925. They initially concentrated on 2 or 3 hectares that had been fenced off and become neglected (the rest of the garden was in good condition at the time). Paths were gravelled, flower beds were established, and the old horse trained to pull a mower was set to work. The area included the Chirnsides' lake, which had never held water for long. An attempt to refill the lake in December 1926 ended as a fiasco; nearly a metre deep after several days of labour, the water took only one day to disappear.

Entered via an impressive set of gates and a small lodge, the garden is very large in scale and yet simple in design, comprising sweeping lawns, shrubberies, paths and the lake, which was filled again in 1981 and seems likely to continue to hold water. There is a grotto on an island in the lake. Early photographs of the garden indicate that there were once extensive flower beds near the house, and a new parterre has been cut into one lawn on an elaborate pattern similar to the old one.

Many fine mature trees stand in the grounds – on the lawns and in more informal areas of grassland – and a reconstructed glasshouse is in use. There are more than 350 species of trees, including four kinds of oak, four of cypress, and three of *Araucaria*. A short section of bluestone ha-ha wall on one boundary of the 1857 homestead, which still stands on the property, is unusual in Victoria in incorporating a ditch rather than being essentially a retaining wall (the style of the ha-ha at Eynesbury, Melton, is similar). The Werribee Park garden is being restored by the Victorian Government, owner of the property since 1973.

The architecture of the house may be far from ordinary, but the planting in this simple garden (right) would once have been familiar to thousands of cottage-dwellers in Victoria

Belmont's small dam (far right) is a charming and unusual element in the garden

The garden at Belmont is entered through a lych gate — a feature rare among Victoria's domestic gardens

Belmont, Beaufort

James Frazer Watkin, grandfather of the present owner of Belmont, laid out its garden in about 1870 when the house was built, or possibly when it was enlarged in about 1880. In its early years the garden was much bigger (4 or 5 hectares reduced to 0.2) and more elaborate than it is now, with an extensive orchard and a very large and fine timber-lattice fernery similar in style to the original one in the Ballarat Botanical Gardens. Like the Ballarat building, this has long since disappeared. There were many more paths, some with creeper-covered arbours and arches crossing them.

Entered through a lych gate, the garden has a large dam close to the house as its main focus. There is the atmosphere of a cottage garden about the grounds, with their close-planted camellias, rhododendrons and magnolias, their roses and dahlias. Nevertheless, Belmont has many fine tall trees, including oaks, pines, cedars, blackwoods, cypresses and lightwoods. Diminished in size, and with its old driveway overgrown, this garden has certainly been altered over the years. But it sets off a particularly interesting timber house, and the lych gate – a rare enough feature – is exceptionally fine.

Renny Hill, Camperdown

The list of Western District gardens thought – but not proved – to have been designed by William Guilfoyle includes Renny Hill, Camperdown. It is considered possible that William Taylor, builder of the homestead in 1876, arranged for Guilfoyle to design its garden, since he was responsible for having him lay out the Camperdown Botanic Gardens a dozen years later. A gravel driveway almost encircles the house, and is a dominating feature of the 0.4 hectare garden. The north side is the

main pleasure garden and typically Guilfoylean, featuring arabesque beds and tall palm trees. A large kitchen garden on the south side is still productive, and the cast-iron verandah is covered with wisteria. This garden is among a minority of Western District gardens that does not have the benefit of a permanent water supply.

Renny Hill (above): even in 1910 the dominating palm was well covered with ivy, though it has grown much taller since (left). The iron 'estate fencing' at the side of the house was commonly found around the larger nineteenth-century gardens, especially in the country

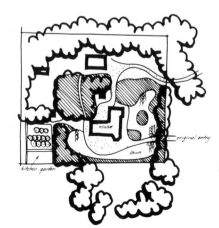

Renny Hill 1980

137

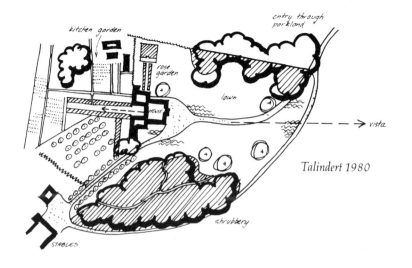

kitchen garden

entry through parkland

rose garden

lawn

house

vista

Talindert 1980

shrubbery

STABLES

Talindert, Camperdown

Family tradition has it that this too is a Guilfoyle-designed garden, but there is no documentary evidence available. William Guilfoyle was, however, known to have been acquainted with the Manifold family.

The huge house at Talindert was built by James Manifold, M.L.C., in 1890 and enlarged in 1907. The garden, of more than 1 hectare, is approached from an extensive parkland of deciduous trees, the drive sweeping around a hill and onto an axis with the front door of the house. A large lawn and shrubberies extend on both sides. There is a kitchen garden with ancillary structures, including a working vinehouse of glass, behind the house; the vegetable garden is divided from the orchard by a long herbaceous border designed by the late Lady Manifold early in the 1950s. She also planted a rose garden to the north of the house and divided it from the adjoining paddock with a sculptured 'living fence' of dense green ivy trained over a framework of chicken wire. A major vista extends from the front of the house across the lawns into the landscape to the east. Another fine vista looks from the south side of the house along an avenue of white flowering cherries to an attractive stable building.

Though a row of palm trees has been removed alongside of the entry drive, and a number of beds for annuals have been grassed over, this garden remains in largely original condition. Its park and grand approach are rare in Victoria and comparable with those at nearby Meningoort; they contrast interestingly with the rectilinear pattern of the kitchen garden.

The decorative ivy screen dividing Talindert's large vegetable garden from a formal rose garden, seen across the bole of an ancient peppercorn tree

Dalvui, Noorat

Unlike Renny Hill and Talindert, Dalvui has ample documentation for its claims as a Guilfoyle garden. On 1 August 1898 William Guilfoyle wrote to Niel Black, owner of Dalvui and third son of the pioneer pastoralist of the same name:

I am sending you the plan by rail today... The space marked out, is really capable of being made into a very beautiful place, and my object in colouring the plan was, principally, for the purpose of indicating the positions where, in my opinion, red, yellow and variegated leafage should be amongst the greenery.

A carefully thought out list of the principal trees and large shrubs suitable for the locality is appended. I should advise you however, to *add* to that list, any kinds that may be doing well at Mt Noorat and Glenormiston [nearby properties also associated with the Black family] and other places, because you may be almost certain that they will thrive in your place also...

About the kind of tree suitable for your long drive or avenue, I am at this moment uncertain what to recommend.

Guilfoyle did, however, remark on the suitability of oaks (*Quercus lusitanica* or *Q. robur*) and elms for drives. The trees actually planted in the outer drive were poplars and, within the gates, silver birches. The same letter advised Black to obtain the services of a gardener who would carry out the plan intelligently. Guilfoyle had practical hints on tree-planting to offer ('go in for deep tillage everywhere') and recommended turning a stony ridge into a rockery embellished with clambering and succulent plants.

Guilfoyle's overall garden plan for Dalvui does not seem to have survived, though there is a plan for the orchard: this shows the varieties recommended as well as positions for the trees.

By the time the Queen Anne house designed by Usher & Kemp had been built in 1908, parts of the garden were well established, but Niel Black drowned at sea when the *Waratah* sank in 1909; the property was then bought by the Palmer family, which owned it until 1974. The Palmers got an established Guilfoyle garden sooner than expected. At the time of

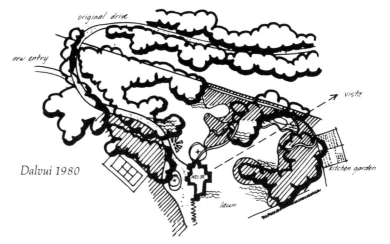

Dalvui 1980

The pond at the bottom of Dalvui's garden, shown here in its early stages. Spiky plants around areas of water seem to have been part of William Guilfoyle's design idiom

139

acquiring Dalvui they had engaged the designer to plan a garden for their property The Bend at nearby Terang.

Dalvui's 2 hectare garden, a true English paradise in the Australian countryside, is one of Victoria's masterpieces of planting and garden design. Except that it lacks palm trees, it is typical of Guilfoyle's style; the avenue of silver birches is splendid, the rockery large and well formed, and the shrubberies thickly planted; a great lawn sweeps from the house to a large pond. There is a recent swimming pool (well concealed from the main views), but the garden is otherwise assumed to conform with its 1898 structure.

Viewed from the air, Dalvui's turreted Queen Anne house, sweeping lawns and curving shrubberies

Looking across the Dalvui lawn to the drive of birches

Mooleric, Birregurra

Mooleric's homestead was built for the Hon. James Strachan in 1871. The property passed to the Armytages in 1880 and then to the Ramsays in 1899. A two-storey bluestone wing was added to the house in 1923.

It was through the close friendship of Mrs Isabella Ramsay with William Guilfoyle that the Director of Melbourne's Botanic Gardens came to design the garden at Mooleric in 1903. Writing to Mrs Ramsay in 1904, he remarked on the usefulness of curving lines in landscape work: 'one can twist them anywhere to suit, or to save the cutting out of a tree.' Paths, shrubberies and the drive at Mooleric bear witness to Guilfoyle's love of the arabesque, which was indeed one of the hallmarks of his style. He continued to take an interest in what he is said to have called his 'best small private garden' until his death in 1912.

The garden, of something like 0.4 hectares, is certainly an outstanding example of Guilfoyle's mature landscape design. A winding drive giving glimpses into different sections of the garden leads to a gravel forecourt in front of the house. The main garden consists of sweeping lawns bordered by dense shrubberies of a mixed nature.

Palms and other plants of strongly architectural character are located in key positions – where, for instance, they can be seen through the gap between two patches of shrubbery. A perimeter path leads through wire arbours set in rockeries on either side of the entrance drive. From the drawing room a southern vista extends across the main lawn, over low shrubs to a view of the distant Otway Ranges. A kitchen garden of just under 0.5 hectares is partly maintained.

In addition to some original drawings for the garden, there are letters from Guilfoyle and sketches of arbours and outbuildings – some of which were never constructed – among

An early view of the approach to the homestead at Mooleric (below left)

William Guilfoyle's plan and planting suggestions for the pond still to be seen at Mooleric

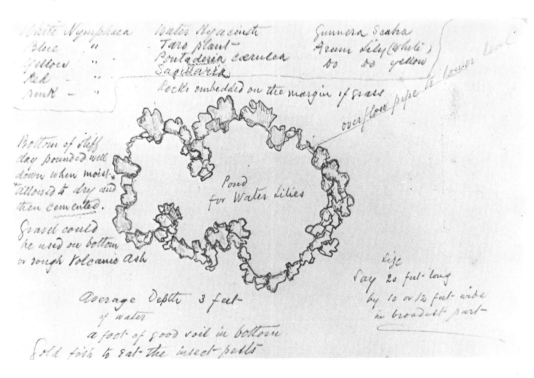

the Andrew Ramsay Papers. A number of flower beds cut into the lawns have been removed in recent years, but the general form and planting at Mooleric remain remarkably intact. The garden at nearby Turkeith, owned by the same family, is considered likely to have also been designed by Guilfoyle.

Guilfoyle drew this summer house plan for Mooleric, but the building was never constructed

One of Guilfoyle's sketch plans (far right) for Mooleric's grounds

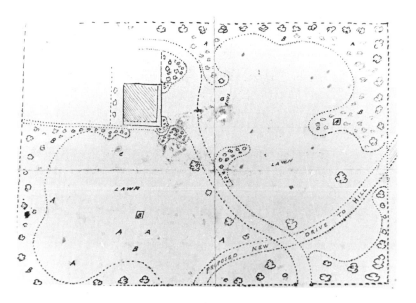

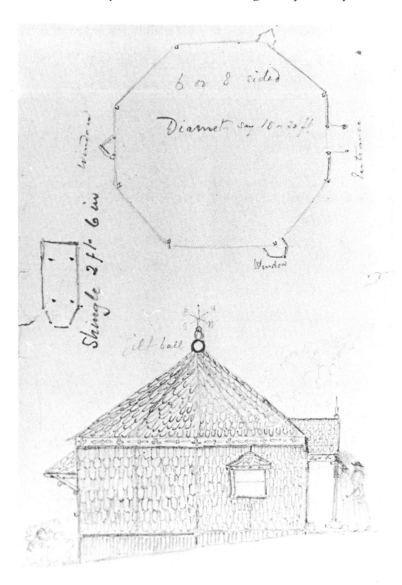

Banongill, Skipton

No plans or letters survive to support the Fairbairn family's belief that William Guilfoyle designed part of Banongill's garden early in the twentieth century, but in the opinion of Guilfoyle's biographer, R. T. M. Pescott, the family is right: he considers that it represents a typical Guilfoyle garden. The huge lawn sweeping on a broad front from the house down to the creek is characteristic of Guilfoyle's style, as are the several palms on the lawn. The original comparatively simple homestead, built in 1853 by William Anderson, was incorporated in a much larger house erected alongside of Mount Emu Creek early in the twentieth century. Mrs E. M. Wheatley (formerly Fairbairn), who was born in 1892, remembers her mother's disappointment when a number of large cherry plums were cut down to enable the extensions. She believes that it was at this point that Guilfoyle was called in to redesign the front garden (formerly the side), and that he laid down the extensive north lawn, planned the pergola, and set out the drive that

This 1904 photograph documents the clearing of cherry plums that had been alongside of the old Banongill homestead (at right-hand end of building). Extensions to the house changed the side garden into the front garden, and the Fairbairn family believes William Guilfoyle to have redesigned this area

swings past the front of the house and around the original tennis court to the rear.

The Fairbairns lived at Banongill from 1895 to 1975 and in the 1930s began to collect and grow the daffodils for which the garden is famous and which have been allowed to spread along the banks of the creek. Other naturalized bulbs are iris, cyclamen and scilla. The garden now extends over more than 5.5 hectares and is one of Victoria's very largest private pleasure gardens. The spacious lawn with its palms has changed little over the years. On one side it is bordered by a broad path curving along a shrubbery, and on the other by the very long wisteria-covered pergola. The area taken up by the first tennis court became a Japanese garden in the late 1950s.

Among the trees are numerous varieties of cypress, birch, poplar, ash, maple, eucalypt, wattle and oak. Shrubs include buddleia, hawthorn, prunus, grevillea, persimmon, lilac, crabapple, laurustinus, osage orange, roses and camellias. In addition to the naturalized bulbs there are lily of the valley and tuberoses growing at Banongill. Two or three terrace beds are sown down to annuals each year, and there are also annuals that self-sow to some extent; all the other flowers, however, are perennials.

Banongill in 1911, its sweeping new lawn well established, and trees and shrubs developing

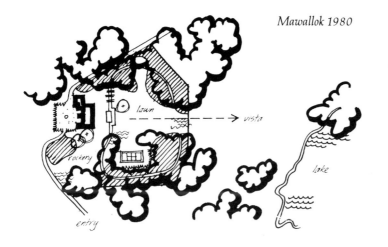

Mawallok 1980

Mawallok, Beaufort

Not far from Banongill lies Mawallok. Acquired in 1847 by Alexander Russell and Co., Mawallok remained in the hands of the Russell family until 1980. The property is situated in excellent wool-growing country and is well known for the quality of its pastures, its fine wool and its cattle.

William Guilfoyle was responsible for the design of the 2.8 hectare garden, which includes a typically sweeping lawn on which sentinel-like palm trees once stood. The lower right-hand corner of the 1909 plan, where the signature would normally have appeared, is missing, however. It would not have been surprising if the plan had been drawn up by another draughtsman under Guilfoyle's supervision: in 1909 he was under considerable pressure from ill health (and also, to some

This early view of the Mawallok garden shows a post-and-wire fence keeping the grazing sheep out of the garden; a ha-ha wall served the same purpose from about 1937 – with even less interruption to the vista

degree, from public criticism), and he resigned as Director of the Melbourne Botanic Gardens in September of that year.

At about the same time the young Melbourne engineer John Monash (who, as General Sir John Monash, was to command the Australian Army Corps in 1918) was commissioned to extend the existing small dam into a lake deriving from the area's splendid natural springs. This water supply ensured that the garden need never suffer drought damage. It is said that three thousand drayloads of soil were carted in for the garden at Mawallok, and large numbers of exotic trees (including many conifers) were planted throughout the property.

A ha-ha wall constructed in about 1937 between the garden proper and a six-hole golf course below it has allowed the view from house to lake to be completely unimpeded. The palm trees included in the plan by Guilfoyle were removed in about 1935. The narrow and curving path that once formed a walk right round the lawn is now broken, but the original rockery persists. The garden's northern vista remains its dominating feature: a view that covers extensive lawns edged with magnificent trees and shrubs, and carries the eye across the lake to far-off Mount Cole.

Six homestead gardens modified in the twentieth century

Gardens naturally change over time and it is not always easy to determine whether or not the changes have compromised the original intention. These six gardens have been altered more than other homestead gardens described here but they still reflect something of their original form and character.

The homestead garden at Mount William, Willaura, begun in the 1870s, is one of the larger ones in Victoria. Its 2 hectares are laid out in different compartments including a cypress-hedged kitchen garden and rose garden. Cypress hedges planted by the present owner's father after he bought the property in 1919, and still trimmed twice a year, are a feature of this garden, helping to enclose the spaces and reinforce the compartmentalized design. The centrepiece of the garden is a huge, flat, rectangular lawn containing a long pool and pergola on its central axis.

Another very large garden – almost 3 hectares in extent – is that of Seven Creeks, Euroa. The first homestead, now much

extended, was built in 1852 and beautifully sited on the bank of Seven Creeks. Most of the development of the garden occurred between 1913 and 1972. A rose garden here is surrounded with box-hedging, and the rest of the grounds consist of sweeping lawns, shrubberies and fine trees.

Murrindindi Station at Yea, like Mount William, has a cypress-hedged rose garden, which is entered through arches cut in the hedge and topped with triangular pediments. This dominant feature of the garden was created after 1881, when Daniel McLeish bought the property. Other features of interest include a large reflecting pond, an especially long pergola, and a considerable amount of box-hedging.

Another garden with a large pergola is The Union near Woolsthorpe in the Western District. The house was built in 1857, and parts of the garden date from the 1880s or earlier. The pergola, now completely engulfed by its original wisteria, is the only surviving element of what was once an elaborate flower garden divided into beds and paths. These were originally edged with redgum plinths together with one border of scalloped terra cotta edging tiles. The complicated geometric

arrangement has now been replaced by lawn, as have two beds once shaped in the form of a heart and a club.

Woolongoon, Mortlake, has a garden that has been continually changed but generally conforms with a layout developed between 1911 and 1920. A fine shrubbery has paths edged with miniature box. Of particular interest are a rusticated summer house, an excellent kitchen garden, and an oak planted by the Poet Laureate John Masefield in 1934.

Bolobek, at the base of Mount Macedon, enjoys the good soil and cool climate of its neighbouring, but more elevated, hill station gardens. It is perhaps the most magical garden in Victoria, combining the best features of an Edwardian garden with a new pattern and planting begun in 1969. Many of the magnificent trees have been retained, including an avenue of poplars and one of lindens, which now form major axes in the garden. Bolobek is essentially a rectilinear garden with strong axes, vistas and cross-vistas. This geometry is reinforced by

Opposite: The Union, Woolsthorpe, in the 1880s

Though the house had a new Edwardian facade and twin gabled wings, The Union's garden in 1909 (left) was little changed in style from the 1880s

By 1982 (above) the small beds at The Union had long since been grassed over; the only remaining feature of the old garden is the pergola on the left, still bearing its original wisteria

A corner of the garden at Bolobek. The rose is 'Iceberg'

Opposite: The Cruden Farm drive, lined with magnificent lemon-scented gums

a walled rose garden, pergolas, clipped hedges, and a long, low, modern house. Several less formal areas provide a foil for the geometry, however, and the planting is of the most exquisite delicacy.

Cruden Farm, Langwarrin

Parts of the garden at Cruden Farm were designed by Edna Walling in 1929–30 for Mr and Mrs Keith Murdoch, later Sir Keith and Dame Elisabeth, around a two-storeyed timber house (designed by Harold Desbrowe Annear) into which an existing cottage had been incorporated. White columns reaching the full height of the facade may have inspired the choice of the Lemon-scented Gum (*Eucalyptus citriodora*) – with its tall trunks soft pink in summer and white in winter – to line the gently curving drive: the relationship between the two elements

is striking. In front of the house the avenue opens onto a turning circle, the grassy centre of which is planted with a couple of lofty elms and an oak. The closely cultivated parts of the grounds probably amount to an area of about 0.8 hectares.

To one side of the driveway are two walled gardens designed by Edna Walling and built from stone quarried on the site. They are closely integrated with outbuildings constructed at about the same time from similar stone. Walling planted the larger garden with standard crab-apples and espaliered fruit trees and the smaller with roses, but none of this planting proved satisfactory. The upper garden was turned over to herbaceous plants when the fruiting species failed after only a few years, and a long and narrow lawn leading to an ornamental pond is now bordered on both sides with perennials and small shrubs. The smaller walled garden was always too hot for roses and they were moved to a better site in 1980. This area has now been paved with old bricks, and semicircular stone steps from the larger garden lead down to a pear-shaped swimming pool. These steps and another Walling-designed set nearby are an attractive feature reminiscent of the work of Gertrude Jekyll. Foliage plants in tubs are spaced along the walls. Thus the contents of both enclosures have changed almost entirely since they were first laid out.

On the north-eastern side of the house are pleasant walks between small trees, shrubs and perennials, beyond which an extensive and largely uncluttered lawn allows long views into the grazing paddocks of the farm – originally 36 hectares in size and now expanded to about 54 hectares. Except for a few surviving trees, this part of the garden shows no sign of the rather formal layout planned by Edna Walling: a bushfire damaged it badly in 1945. Large trees in the grounds include birches, eucalypts, various oaks, and a camphor laurel that is the only garden tree dating from before 1928.

Cruden Farm's fine garden is of historical interest in that some of its structure was the work of Edna Walling; but it may be said to reflect rather more accurately the taste and gardening skills – developed over the past fifty years – of its owner, Dame Elisabeth Murdoch.

Mountain refuges

IN THE Cameron Highlands of Malaysia can be found a quaint 'English pub' full of glazed chintz and floral linens and surrounded by a flourishing garden of hollyhocks, foxgloves and hydrangeas. Around it, in the cool mountain air, are the summer homes of this country's wealthy inhabitants. In India during the Raj almost the entire British administration moved from Calcutta to Simla and Darjeeling for the hot season in order to conduct the country's affairs in comfort. Wives and families rested in such hill stations throughout the summer.

Australian colonists too sought to escape the scorching sum-

Opposite: Pampas grass, a chinoiserie bridge and exotic trees were all part of the misty tranquillity of Mount Macedon, seen here at the height of its fame as a haven for weary Melburnians of ample means

Simla in India, the prototype for summer retreats around the world

151

mer heat. Victoria's Dandenong Ranges, the Mount Lofty Ranges of South Australia, Mount Wilson in New South Wales, Kalamunda in Western Australia, Mount Wellington in Tasmania and Toowoomba in Queensland are all areas to which the wealthy have traditionally retreated, but Mount Macedon, with about thirty properties surviving from the nineteenth century, remains the most extensive.

In 1904 *The Cyclopedia of Victoria* described the houses of Mount Macedon as 'a family sanatorium . . . delicate people and children desiccated and withered by the hot air of the city and suburbs during the months of December, January and February, soon reacquired their bloom and freshness and lost their languor and lassitude'. The hill station gardens of the Dandenong Ranges have largely been swallowed up by the urban sprawl. Mount Macedon, however, is 65 kilometres north-west of Melbourne, just out of reach of this malady. Even today it evokes images of tennis players in long white trousers, of croquet, bush picnics, elegant house parties, balls, hunting trophies – and above all, of gardens.

In the early 1870s parcels of land ranging in size from 4

hectares became available at Mount Macedon. By road or rail this land was readily accessible from the city, and men of means – attracted by the picturesque scenery, the summer coolness, and the horticultural promise of the rich soil – bought and built there.

One of the earliest was the stock and station agent Charles Ryan, of whom his granddaughter Maie Casey wrote in her 1962 book *An Australian Story 1837–1907*:

We have heard of the fervour with which he threw himself into his Macedon adventure. After buying twenty-three acres of land below the summit of the mount he began to construct his house and garden together in consultation with W. R. Guilfoyle who had become Director of the Melbourne Botanical Gardens in 1873 . . . Already both men were thinking of the trees and shrubs they had known in other countries that could be blended into the Australian scene. Over the period of their association flora from all over the world – Japan, India, America, and many other places – were imported by Charles Ryan for Macedon and by W. R. Guilfoyle for Melbourne. These plants were nursed, experimented with, increased and exchanged.

Thus, the lovely garden and the house above it grew.

In 1898 this property, Derriweit Heights, was lost to Charles Ryan through the economic catastrophes of that decade; in 1970 it was lost to Victorian garden history through subdivision.

Another Mount Macedon residence that has vanished is the 'Government Cottage', which was sold as a private house in 1934 and burnt down in 1954. J. A. Froude wrote in *Oceana* (1886) of a visit to the cottage as a guest of the Governor of Victoria, Sir Henry Loch:

round the house, oaks and elms, cypress and deodara seemed at home and happy; filbert-trees were bending with fruit too abundant for them to ripen, while the grounds were blazing with roses and geraniums and gladiolus. The Australian plain spread out far below our feet, the horizon forty miles away; the reddish-green of the near eucalyptus softening off into the transparent blue of distance . . . The situation is so beautiful and so healthy that it is a favourite with the wealthy Melbourne gentlemen. Seven hundred feet above us the accomplished Sir George Verdon [the owner of Alton] has built himself a most handsome mansion surrounded by well-timbered grounds which he has inclosed and planted.

In the winter, which he spends in Melbourne, this highland home of his is sometimes swathed in snow. In summer the heat of the sun is tempered by the fresh keen air of the mountain . . .

Sir George had made a point of blending his exotic plantings at Alton with the forest surrounding his property. Thus, as 'Wanderer' observed in 1894, 'the English oak and the Australian blackwood will be found growing side by side, and agreeing wonderfully, both as regards form and colour'. Plants identified at Alton in 1978 by Dr J. H. Willis include the conifers Douglas Fir (*Pseudotsuga menziesii*), Giant Redwood (*Sequoiadendron giganteum*), Oriental Spruce (*Picea orientalis*), Deodar Cedar (*Cedrus deodara*) and European Larch (*Larix decidua*) – 'surely', says Dr Willis in his report, 'the best private collection of large conifers anywhere in Victoria'. The numerous species of autumn-colouring trees include a splendid Weeping Beech (*Fagus sylvatica* 'Pendula'). There are some interesting trees from New Zealand at Alton, among them Rewa-rewa (*Knightia excelsa*), Red Beech (*Nothofagus fusca*) and N.Z. Olive (*Gymnelaea montana*). There is still a 'pleasing harmony . . . between the introduced vegetation and

surrounding native bushland'. Alton remains an outstanding garden, though its kitchen garden and many glasshouses no longer survive. The main pleasure garden consists almost entirely of slate paths winding their way down a steep hill between a dazzling array of plants.

The vice-regal presence at Mount Macedon from 1884 encouraged settlement by the élite of Melbourne and lent a sense of occasion to the social gatherings on 'the Mount'. 'Cottages' – many of them actually large houses – sprang up on the cool southern slopes. They were built in a variety of styles – half-timbered, picturesque, cottage ornée, bungalow and hunting lodge. Their names perhaps give a clue to their derivations – Kirami, Kuranda, Tanahmerah, Bungl'hi and Darjeeling.

That these properties were developed at a time when the passion for gardening under Queen Victoria's reign was at its height perhaps helps to account for their size and virtuosity. The decision by the famous Victorian nurserymen Taylor &

A stone pavilion adjacent to a croquet lawn at Alton overlooks the garden as it falls away from the upper terraces

Sangster to establish a branch of their Melbourne firm at Mount Macedon in 1876 must have contributed to the richness of the plant material that still survives in the gardens. John Smith & Sons had begun a nursery at nearby Riddells Creek in 1863, and the Government Nursery at Macedon was established in the 1880s. A string of wealthy owners, boom conditions, an ample water supply, and deep rich soils on a south-facing slope – all these factors conspired to bring about a gardening bonanza at Mount Macedon.

Between forty and fifty major gardens were established – some as much as 12 hectares in extent. They featured large glasshouses, lakes and ponds, formal terraces, summer houses and walks that generally descended from the richly cultivated and manicured parts of the garden to fern-shaded walks along the creeks which ran through most properties. Owners and head gardeners were equally enthusiastic in competing at the annual horticultural shows. Crateloads of plant treasures from all corners of the earth arrived. By 1887 Taylor & Sangster's catalogue boasted 120 varieties of rhododendron, and when the famous British nurseryman J. H. Veitch visited Mount Macedon in 1893, he 'expressed surprise at the great variety and wonderful growth of our conifers'.

Another garden that 'Wanderer' remarked on in the 1890s was that of Duneira, first taken up in 1872 by S. H. Officer:

It is only a few years since Mr Reid purchased the property [in 1890], and though it is one of the best, if not actually the best site on the Mount, it was then little better than a wilderness. Mr Reid has spared neither trouble nor expense, and the result is that quite a transformation has been effected. After passing the lodge at the main entrance, a broad serpentine drive leads up to the house, and from there the grounds are laid out in broad sloping lawns, surmounted with choice borders and fringed with trees, which, however, do not interfere to any great extent with the view. There is, of course, no lack of flowers, which grow luxuriantly on the Mount, but the great feature of 'Duneira' is the lawns . . .

Still an impressive feature, the lawns are now rivalled by many of the plants that presumably were placed by Reid. The elm-lined driveway smothered in forget-me-nots in spring, the

sculptural groups of rhododendrons, and the great drifts of primroses under the trees are all part of this fine garden, which has been cherished by a number of different owners in the twentieth century.

The garden at Ard Choille, designed for William MacGregor by Taylor & Sangster, was laid out before 1895. MacGregor had been briefly a member of the Legislative Assembly of New South Wales and for several years Chairman of B.H.P. A feature of the landscaping was a string of lakes stocked with trout and carp, but Ard Choille also boasted lawns, terraced gardens, and large numbers of exotic conifers and deciduous trees. The present nameplate spells the name of the property 'Ard Cheille', which – says local historian H. B. Hutton – is closer to its pronunciation.

Ard Choille, though a very important historic garden, is beyond the boundary of an area of about 176 hectares classified in 1978 by the National Trust of Australia (Victoria). Those within it include Durrol and Greystanes (both designed by Edna Walling), Alton, Duneira, Ard Rudah, Cameron Lodge, Forest Glade, Cheniston, Camelot, Huntly Burn and Hascombe. Some of the gardens in the classified zone are in very good condition, some are seeing a renaissance under new owners, and others are neglected to one degree or another. All are notable for their fine specimens of exotic trees and shrubs, some of them rare species. The Trust considers that the Mount Macedon gardens 'represent one of the most important collections of nineteenth century gardens in Australia. Their importance is not so much in the individual design of each garden but rather as a total collection. Botanically and horticulturally the gardens are also of importance and in addition they reflect the prevailing social attitudes and aspirations of the late nineteenth century'.

All the gardens in this section are private and therefore normally closed to the public; a number of them are open occasionally

Opposite: One of a series of lakes at Ard Choille, whose original owner would hardly recognize his property in its derelict state; the garden nevertheless still has great appeal

Six gardens by Edna Walling

AROUND THE TURN of the century in Britain the landscape designer Gertrude Jekyll managed to synthesize two opposing styles of garden design – the formal and the natural – into an harmonious style. She did this by creating gardens with a strong architectural structure of terraces, balustrades and pergolas and then softening the outline with plants that climbed and spread and scrambled in all directions. From the 1920s, Edna Walling planned many gardens of a similar kind in Australia, as well as the cottage-style gardens already described. She planned a total of several hundred gardens in Victoria, but relatively few survive as witness to the talents of this great garden designer.

All the gardens in this section are private and therefore closed to the public

Yathong, Benalla

The garden at Yathong, designed by Edna Walling in 1928 for Mrs H. Ledger around a house whose nucleus was built in about 1905, is one of Walling's earliest known surviving gardens. More than 0.2 hectares in area, it displays an emphasis on architectural structure that is typical of her more formal designs, and it may be contrasted with the nearby garden of Wooleen, which is much more informal. Both of these gardens in the township of Benalla are essentially 'suburban'.

The main lawn, which was planned to double as a tennis court (with removable nets), is divided from the terrace and side garden by a low stone wall, partly topped with a wisteria-clad colonnade that gives increased depth and enticingly framed vistas to the garden. As in many Walling designs there is a 'wild garden' of massed trees and shrubs – birches, crab-apples and a Chinese elm still among them today.

A colonnade divides the garden at Yathong, Benalla, into two parts as well as framing views beyond

Mawarra, Sherbrooke

Like Folly Farm, whose garden Edna Walling designed somewhat later, Mawarra is located in the Dandenong Ranges. It has far more in common with the sophisticated hill station gardens at Mount Macedon, however, than with the rural informality of Folly Farm.

Walling designed this garden for the Misses Marshall and their sister Mrs A. W. McMillan in 1928–29. About 1.5 hectares in area, it is situated on a steep hill in rich, loamy soil. The design, reflecting Walling's interest in Italian gardens, is based on a classic Italian Renaissance pattern, with the main axis plunging down the hill and with terraces of varying character at right angles to the axis, running across the slope. The garden has a strongly architectural form that incorporates massive flights of stairs, ramps, pergolas and geometric ponds; all of these were built by E. H. Hammond, who did a great deal of Edna Walling's construction work. The whole is softened by a very delicate planting scheme: there are babies' tears between the steps and on the curving walls, foxgloves in unexpected corners, and bulbs clumped around the base of randomly planted birches.

Mawarra's garden is perhaps the best surviving example of Edna Walling's work. Sections of the garden were not completed according to Walling's plan and several alterations have been made, but the dominant form and character are hers. Indeed,

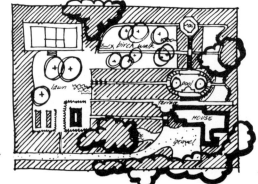

Mawarra 1980

her ideas have been carried through with great integrity, and the detailing of rockwork is particularly good. The now mature planting has mellowed the architectural forms, as the designer envisaged. In concept and execution the garden is one of Australia's outstanding designs of the twentieth century.

Folly Farm, Olinda

Part of a 4 hectare property in the Dandenong Ranges, this is very much an informal country garden, though the owner commissioned Edna Walling to design it after seeing one of her most formal city gardens, that of Dr Ringland Anderson in Toorak. The rambling timber house on the property was originally a tiny weekend cottage built in 1911. Edna Walling designed the main part of the garden for Dr Leonard Cox, a distinguished scholar of Oriental art, in the mid-1930s. Her design for the driveway followed several years later. These areas make up two distinct sections; natural parkland forms another.

The 0.2 hectare main garden, which comprises a central lawn with scalloped shrubberies on all sides, has several rock outcrops built by Ellis Stones. Hollies and cotoneasters have self-sown and become something of a problem in this section. Walling 'naturalized' the drive from a straight avenue to a winding lane with dense planting on both sides. Dr Cox himself designed the extensive parkland (0.4 hectares) for which Edna Walling had suggested the concept. It consists of a large, sloping lawn with a copse made up of many trees and shrubs, including clumps of birches, self-sown natives such as blackwoods, and a number of apple trees. A ferny sunken patch in this area is known to the family as Dingley Dell, a name thought to have been given it by Edna Walling.

The garden is one of the best of the surviving Walling gardens designed in a natural manner; it is a masterpiece of planting textures and forms, relying little on colour for its effect.

Ardgarten, Grassdale

It is nearly a hundred years since this grazing property was first taken up by members of the family that still owns it. The slate-roofed homestead was erected in 1857, a few years after the land was first taken up, although the building has been extended a couple of times since then.

Edna Walling designed the garden in about 1935, combining a terrace of strikingly geometric form with a more natural garden beyond it, the total covering about 0.4 hectares. The terrace was designed and constructed with great skill. Though the lower part of the original driveway has become overgrown, the part nearer the house is still in use and the plan is otherwise intact.

A specimen of *Magnolia grandiflora* that was planted well before the 1930s is still flourishing to the west of the house, and there is a very old mulberry tree near the terrace. Many of the trees and shrubs planted by Edna Walling remain at Ardgarten. Among them are a tall Prickly Paperbark (*Melaleuca styphelioides*), three specimens of Blue Spruce (*Picea pungens glauca*) and two of the Aspen (*Populus tremula*), one of Walling's favourites. As in most Edna Walling gardens of this period there are also silver birches. Trees planted on an extensive lawn that was originally intended (but never used) for a grass tennis court include a pinoak and a form of weeping elm. Near the house is a thicket of cotoneasters, with camellias in a sheltered position along the eastern wall.

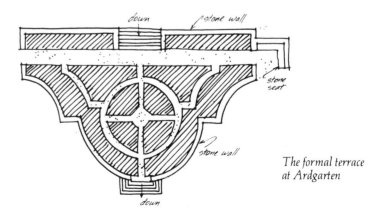

The formal terrace at Ardgarten

Looking through the front gate into the garden at Wooleen

comprises Australian plants such as mintbushes, callistemons and lemon-scented tea-trees. Both of these parts of the garden overlook Lake Benalla; the site of the more recent 'wild garden' was originally planned as a drying area. The layout is otherwise little changed.

There is a Walling-designed garden seat and set of concrete mushrooms (one a birdbath) in the Wooleen garden. A rock outcrop here was both designed and constructed by Ellis Stones in the 1960s. The garden contains a collection of more than 155 varieties of camellia.

Boortkoi, Hexham

No doubt this station, first taken up in about 1859, had some sort of garden right from the start. But the present garden, of about 1 hectare, was designed by Edna Walling in the 1930s round the old bluestone homestead. It is divided into several distinct parts, including a geometric rose garden and lawn; these are both enclosed within semicircular stone retaining walls. The formal areas lead into a large, sloping 'natural garden' along a creek. Here boulders provide the steps, in contrast with the dressed stonework of the more formal part; there are flowering apples and fruiting quinces, together with mulberries, almonds, cherry plums and species of *Crataegus* in this section. A large pergola laden with blue wisteria and built of white plaster columns topped by a superstructure of saplings runs parallel with the creek.

Boortkoi's is one of the few big country gardens whose design by Edna Walling was largely carried out. It demonstrates her talent for happily relating formal and informal elements. The strong geometric forms are softened by a casual planting arrangement, and the garden takes great advantage of its beautiful site.

Few alterations have been made to this garden. The informal section was grazed for a number of years but is now being restored.

Wooleen, Benalla

Designed ten years later than the larger grounds of neighbouring Yathong, this garden, like Folly Farm's, is an excellent example of Edna Walling's more natural style, even though it is classified here as 'suburban' (it is between 0.15 and 0.2 hectares in area). From the front gate, carefully placed specimen trees (a maple, Chinese elm and silver birches) along the main vista give the garden a sense of depth. The 'wild garden' planned by Edna Walling has become a more open shrubbery of rhododendrons and azaleas, and a newer version of the wilderness

This 'wild' part of the garden at Yathong is in marked contrast to the more formal areas

Designed in the 1930s, the garden at Boortkoi showed Edna Walling working in a formal vein that is very much apparent in her plan

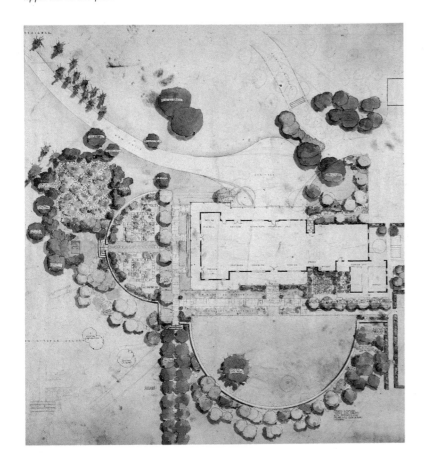

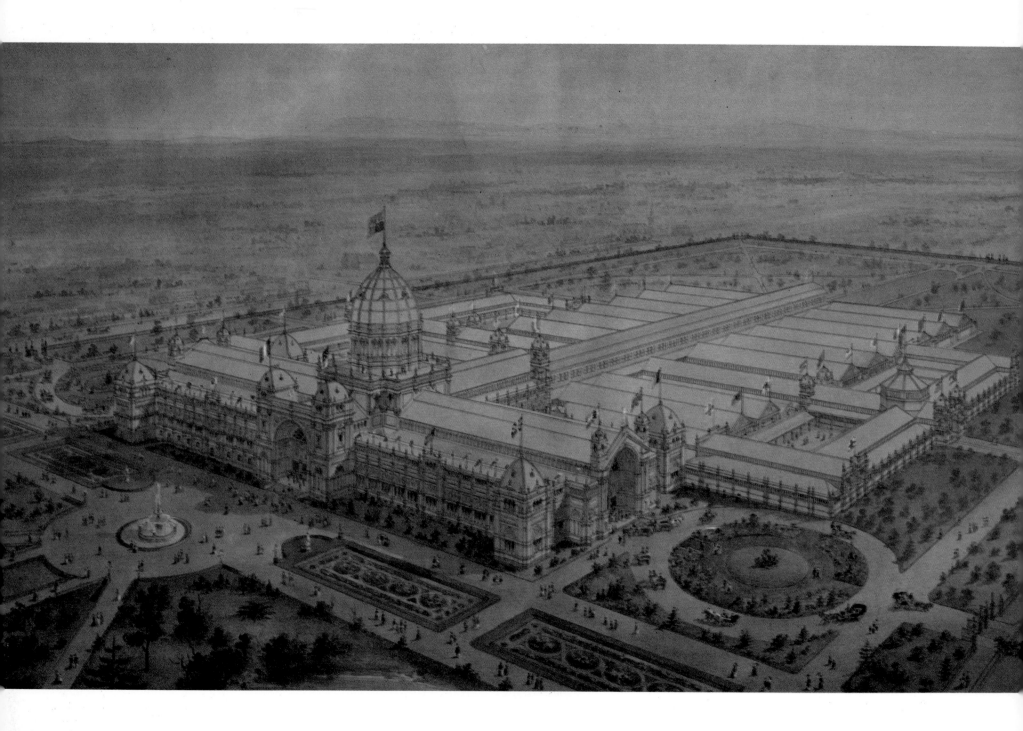

Public gardens

WHILE THE civic leaders of many towns and cities throughout Victoria included botanic gardens in plans for their growing urban areas they also, to some extent, made provision for reserves devoted more singlemindedly to beauty and recreation.

These took many forms. Camperdown in the Western District has elms planted in wide median strips and in a number of noble avenues. One of the manifestations of Bendigo's astonishing wealth was the Conservatory Gardens, which matched in horticultural terms all the exuberance of its public and private buildings. Together with several statues and beds of annuals cut into lawn, the Victorian conservatory that gives this small park its name is enclosed within a highly decorative cast-iron fence and gates. Immediately east and north of the city of Melbourne a number of dignified squares were laid out when Andrew Clarke succeeded Robert Hoddle as Surveyor-General in 1853 – Curtain, Argyle, Lincoln, University, Macarthur and Murchison Squares, as well as St Vincent Place in South Melbourne.

Opposite: A bird's-eye view of Melbourne's Exhibition Building and its garden layout at the time of the Great Exhibition of 1880–81

In the heart of Bendigo and adjacent to the leafy informality of Rosalind Park, the Conservatory Gardens still conspicuously retain the flavour of public gardens of the nineteenth century

The pond in the Treasury Gardens has shown at least two quite distinct faces during the twentieth century. It is thought to have masqueraded as part of a Japanese garden until around 1934

At a meeting of the Victorian Gardeners' Mutual Improvement Society in July 1860 there was lively discussion on the important question of planting public reserves. One proposition put to the meeting was that parks 'should be planted on the principle of park planting known and practised in Britain as far as those are applicable to our climate and circumstances'. The elm, poplar and oak were considered to be deciduous trees that were both suitable and available, but a majority of members agreed – surprisingly enough – that 'very many of the native trees of Victoria are peculiarly adapted for park planting, and should be used as far as possible'. Large numbers of blue gums and smaller numbers of other natives were certainly planted in parks in the nineteenth century, but the exotics finally won the day.

The greatest surviving public gardens in Victoria, and indeed in Australia, are those that encircle Melbourne: the Domain, and the Alexandra, Carlton, Fitzroy, Treasury and Flagstaff Gardens. Such parks have always given people breathing-space, a soothing environment for exercise and relaxation. Now that these gardens are mature, it is easy to overlook the battles that took place to preserve their sanctity. Not all were won, but enough to make Melbourne's gardens in the 1980s one of its most impressive features. Anthony Trollope, writing of them in his book *Australia and New Zealand*, published in 1873, was not enthusiastic about their appearance but acknowledged their recreational value:

It is the width of the streets chiefly which gives to the city its appearance of magnificence; – that, and the devotion of very large spaces within the city to public gardens. These gardens are not in themselves well kept. They are not lovely, as are those of Sydney in a super-excellent degree. Some of them are profusely ornamented with bad statues. None of them, whatever may be their botanical value, are good gardens. But they are large and numerous, and give an air of wholesomeness and space to the whole city. They afford green walls to the citizens, and bring much of the health and some of the pleasures of the country home to them all.

Melbourne was fortunate to have at its disposal designers like James Sinclair, William Guilfoyle and his brother John, and Charles Bogue Luffmann – men who, however fussily they may have embellished their creations, gave them a lasting nobility in design and planting. Despite the intrusions into the Fitzroy Gardens – a model village, playgrounds, Cook's Cottage and so on – the integrity of those gardens has survived because of the dominant avenue plantings. The Treasury Gardens, across Lansdowne Street from the Fitzroy Gardens, are only about one quarter of their size, but are similarly conspicuous for the lofty trees that give the impression of a forest at the city's fringe. Their designer in 1867 was Clement Hodgkinson, then Assistant Commissioner of Lands and Survey.

Of particular interest in some of these gardens are the remnants of bedding-out practices of the late nineteenth century. The multi-coloured borders along the main path in the Fitzroy Gardens and the parterre on the south side of the Exhibition Building in the Carlton Gardens provide tantalizing glimpses of a skill that has almost vanished.

A different kind of public garden was popular with Melburnians in the nineteenth century, though an early example, the Cremorne Gardens in Richmond, suffered financial difficulties almost from their inception. Founded by James Ellis of London's Cremorne Gardens, they were bought by the actor and entrepreneur George Coppin in 1856. These were pleasure gardens, consisting of 4 hectares of ornamental planting among which were set out attractions that included a theatre, menagerie, artificial lake, maze, pavilion for dancing, fountains, grottoes and bowling alleys. The Cremorne Gardens closed early in 1863.

All the gardens in this section are open to the public

One of the main pathways through the Fitzroy Gardens: it is these avenues of mature elms that give the gardens their special quality

The Flagstaff Gardens

These gardens have the most interesting historical associations of any of Victoria's public gardens, the site being first used, in the 1830s, as a cemetery for early settlers. In 1840 a signalling station with a flagstaff was erected on what to that point had been known as Burial Hill and was soon to be called Flagstaff Hill instead: an excellent view of Port Phillip Bay was obtainable from the higher parts of the hill, though only glimpses of it can be had in the 1980s. The year 1850 was a landmark in Victoria's history, and it was on Flagstaff Hill that the colony's separation from New South Wales was proclaimed on 11 November.

Popular with Melbourne's residents for many years as a place to stroll at leisure, 7 hectares of the hill were reserved for the Flagstaff Gardens in 1873. By 1891, however, the grounds needed redesigning, and John Guilfoyle, a younger brother of William Guilfoyle, and the newly appointed Curator of Metropolitan Parks and Gardens, was given the job. The *Garden Gazette* of August 1903 described Guilfoyle's work as a 'complete transformation':

The area around the pioneers' memorial as pictured in 1903, when picket fences rather obtrusively segmented the gardens

The Flagstaff Gardens in the 1970s (far right)

Opposite left: John Guilfoyle's 'beds and borders' at the Flagstaff Gardens in 1903

The Fitzroy Gardens

The Fitzroy Gardens were originally laid out under their early name of Fitz Roy Square by Edward La Trobe Bateman in 1857, becoming the Fitzroy Gardens five years later. Though Bateman later designed several private gardens of the Western District in a pleasantly natural style, historian Dr John Foster of the University of Melbourne has stated that he 'conceived his squares, not in the tradition of eighteenth century land-scape with its sweeping perspectives and enticing illusions, but as an ornamental extension of the nineteenth century city itself'. Bateman conspicuously failed to take advantage of the slopes and watercourse that were features of the 25 hectare

Detail of Kearney's map of 1855 showing Fitzroy Square, later known as the Fitzroy Gardens

Trees were thinned out where necessary or advisable, and beds and borders of flowers sprang into existence; a Rosary was also established, which proves to be a very popular feature when the plants are in bloom.

Numerous fine specimens of Palms and other foliage plants are to be met with in the gardens, and the borders contain a choice selection of herbaceous plants, the whole being in a state of cultivation creditable alike to the curator and the small body of men working under him.

Located on the edge of the Melbourne Central Business District, the gardens still offer a major area of open space close to the heart of the city. An extensive concrete crib wall dating from the 1960s and covered with creepers, herbaceous plants and shrubs fronts onto King Street. The other boundaries are La Trobe Street, William Street and Dudley Street. The gardens now consist of a pleasantly sloping parkland, with lawns, avenues of trees and ribbon borders of annual flowers. There are many beds of roses. Large trees planted in the lawns include elms, oaks, ashes, poplars, pines, spotted gums and a few palms. Though they have seen many changes, the form of the Flagstaff Gardens probably dates from the 1890s.

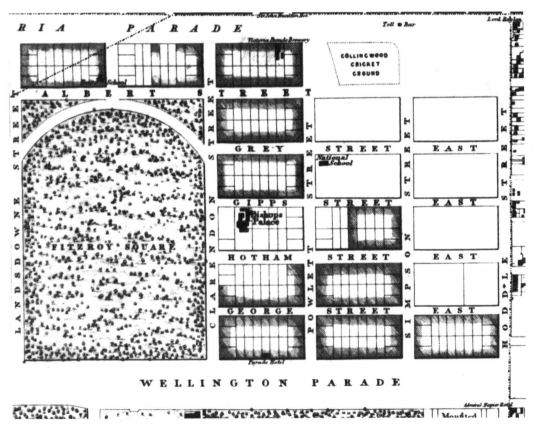

167

site – bordered by Lansdowne Street, Wellington Parade, Clarendon Street and Albert Street – and his plan was decidedly formal and geometric.

According to Andrew Garran's *Picturesque Atlas of Australasia* (1886), the square in 1860 was 'an unenclosed and dreary waste, destitute of herbage, and sparsely sprinkled with aged gum trees'. Garran gives credit for the subsequent transformation of the Fitzroy Gardens to Clement Hodgkinson, but it is generally considered that the first curator, James Sinclair, deserves most of it. Sinclair had come to the gardens in 1858 with a high reputation in Europe and a number of horticultural publications to his name. He was certainly a much more experienced landscape designer than Edward La Trobe Bateman. Sinclair advocated in his writings a natural style of landscape, and he set out to soften Bateman's angularities and make effective use of the land at his disposal. Sinclair planted the avenue of elms along Hotham Walk, as well as many oaks, pines, cypresses and Moreton Bay figs that are still standing. He also planted large numbers of blue gums, which were all removed after his death in 1881, when the committee of

management and subsequent curators endeavoured to please popular taste by adding lawns and flower beds in the late-Victorian manner.

Iron fences enclosed many of the lawn and garden areas in the early gardens and statues of classical figures stood in the grounds: a number of them came from the Cremorne Gardens in the Victorian suburb of Richmond when the famous pleasure gardens closed in 1863. By 1934 almost all the statuary, often disfigured by members of the public and repeatedly restored, had been disposed of.

Now the gardens largely consist of natural-looking parkland, though there is a spectacular and ever-changing display of bedding-out maintained on either side of one of the long central walks. Some of the finest avenues of trees in Victoria are to be found in the Fitzroy Gardens. Indeed, they are almost without parallel in the whole of Australia. The cottage designed by F. M. White and built in 1866 for James Sinclair still stands, but a number of new elements have been added since the early 1930s. These include playgrounds, a model village, and the reconstructed Cook's Cottage, whose recreated

eighteenth-century-style garden is of special interest. Though some of these additions have seemed alien and undesirable, the Fitzroy Gardens maintain an honourable place in the group of gardens surrounding Melbourne's centre, and merge particularly well with the Treasury Gardens on the far side of Lansdowne Street. With their general form and planting very much as designed by James Sinclair, the Fitzroy Gardens must rank among Australia's most beautiful urban parks.

The Carlton Gardens

In 1857, when Edward La Trobe Bateman drew up a landscape plan for the Fitzroy Gardens, he also designed the Carlton Gardens, now often called the Exhibition Gardens. Right from the start, however, the 25 hectares at Carlton suffered a variety of setbacks. There were clashes of interest: the desire of people from neighbouring suburbs, for example, to continue to run goats on the area within Nicholson Street, Carlton Street, Rathdowne Street and Victoria Street that the Melbourne City Council wished to landscape. There was vandalism (some of it perpetrated by former goat-owners, perhaps), with many thousands of plants being stolen or destroyed during the early years of the gardens. The historian Dr John Foster considers that William Hyndman, the council's gardener in the 1860s, must bear some of the blame for the poor condition of the gardens in 1873, when Clement Hodgkinson, by this time Inspector-General of Gardens, Parks and Reserves, produced a development plan for them. Hodgkinson's plan, a modification of Bateman's involving, among other things, considerable re-planting and a simplified path system, was never completely carried out; but it certainly helped to give the Carlton Gardens their present form.

In the meantime the gardens had survived another conflict of interests that came close to allowing a road to cross them from Queensberry Street to Gertrude Street. However, the central part of the gardens disappeared during the construction in 1879–80 of extensive buildings designed by Reed & Barnes to house the Great Exhibition of 1880. It is thought that Taylor & Sangster designed the floral parterres on the south side of the building after its completion; these enterprising nurserymen undoubtedly contributed to the landscaping, as an 1887 catalogue published by them testifies:

We have laid out and planted many of the largest gardens in Victoria, and our successful re-arrangement of the Melbourne International Exhibition grounds is well known to the general public.

Not everyone saw the alterations in the same light as their

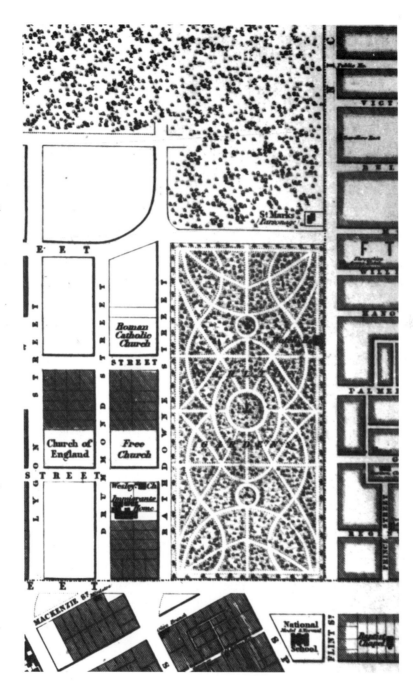

Opposite: The Carlton Gardens, photographed in about 1875 and probably looking in a north-westerly direction. The road in the foreground appears to lie within the gardens

Since La Trobe Bateman did not provide a plan for the Carlton Gardens until 1857, the complex path system indicated in Kearney's map of 1855 must be regarded as a romantic projection into the future. His depiction of Fitzroy Square (page 167) is realistic by comparison

171

designers. In September 1880 *Melbourne Punch* had poked fun a couple of times at the large fountain under construction ('The Dean has objected to the four urchins dancing the Can-can round the top. A contract is out to clothe them in Geelong tweed.'), and in December passed judgement on the land-scaping:

The way the grounds are laid out round the building puts one in mind of so many jam tarts or loud-patterned hearthrugs fastened together. But they suit the fountain admirably, and the fountain suits them. Indeed, we think the laying out of the grounds and the fountain one of the chief 'exhibitions' of the Carlton show.

William Guilfoyle's brother John worked on the gardens in about 1890, just before he was appointed Curator of Metropol-itan Parks and Gardens. Nevertheless the central and northern sections of the gardens seemed already doomed as landscape, and unsympathetic auxiliary buildings, huge car-parking areas and sundry municipal misalliances have swamped these areas completely over the years.

Only the southern section of the Carlton Gardens really survives. It was, as John Foster has said, 'favoured by its city aspect and the splendid backdrop of the Exhibition facade' and 'remains one of the few genuinely nineteenth century public gardens in Melbourne'. This part of the gardens is dominated by several major vistas to the fountain built in 1880 and to the main entrance of the Exhibition Building. There are many fine trees and avenues, and two large ponds with islands in them; bedding-out is still practised in some of the original parterres, though their scale is greatly reduced: much of the area once occupied by parterres is now given over to lawn and shrubberies. In 1980 a carpark on the eastern side of the main building was removed and a new garden with a Victorian flavour (and including a parterre) was laid out. Other carparks continue to impair the relationship between the Exhibition Building and its gardens, but the main structure of the southern parts survives, as do many of the early elms, oaks and plane trees.

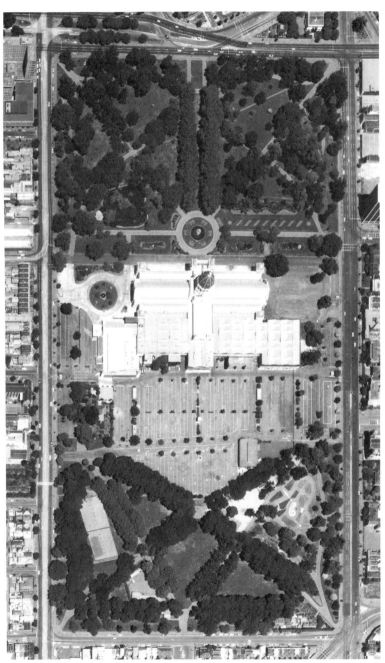

Opposite: One of the lakes (left) and the 1880 fountain (above)

A 1979 version of Melbourne Punch's jam tarts (far left)

Melbourne's Carlton Gardens from the air (left). In contrast to the elaborate garden front conspicuous in the painting on page 162, the southern side of the Exhibition Building now displays only remnants of earlier flower beds. North of the building, the area once occupied by temporary exhibition pavilions is dominated by vast carparks

Burnley Gardens, Richmond

It has been assumed that lavish plans for Burnley Gardens, drawn up by Alfred Lynch in 1861, were never implemented. Nor do other early plans in existence match the present layout.

Opened in 1863, the gardens were used by the Horticultural Society of Victoria for the experimental growing of fruit trees – trials that were of considerable importance to commercial and private fruit-growing. The area also included, from the beginning, pleasure gardens accessible to the public every day of the week.

Passing into the hands of the Department of Agriculture in 1891, Burnley Gardens became the site of the School of Horticulture. John Patrick, Lecturer in Amenity Horticulture at Burnley College, considers that the principal appointed to the college in 1897 was a key figure in the shaping of the gardens. C. Bogue Luffmann was a man of strong personality and decided views on gardening – both of which are evident in his 1903 book *The Principles of Gardening for Australia*. The growing of flowers, said Luffmann, was not gardening: such plants were 'mere details' in the landscape. In a notable reaction against the Victorian passion for individuality in plant colour and form, he declared: 'it is a painful fact that as plant-growing grows in

A palm, sequoia, jacaranda and bunya bunya are conspicuous in this photograph of Burnley Gardens taken in 1919. So are the garden stakes and plant labels

Students at the college in 1899, dressed to kill, are supposedly learning the finer points of horticulture (right and far right)

174

popularity, the art of gardening declines.' Luffmann put his theories into practice at Burnley, and the gardens were described early in the twentieth century as 'enchanting'. John Patrick believes that Luffmann's trees and part of his ground-plan persist at Burnley.

The well-known garden designer Millie Gibson, who had been a lecturer at Burnley College from 1918–22, and returned as a part-timer in 1947, also did some design work at Burnley. She landscaped the area around the building begun in 1945–46 for the School of Primary Agriculture and Horticulture (now the main building of the horticultural college), screening and softening its rawness.

The range of plants at Burnley Gardens – appropriately in what for nearly a century has been an institution teaching horticulture – is very wide: there are many eucalypts as well as deciduous and evergreen exotics in the grounds. Ornamental plantings cover more than 4 hectares, and there are about 3 hectares of fruit trees and experimental plots.

Burnley Gardens have frequently had a small army of workers, paid or unpaid (above)

Two provincial public gardens of the 1870s

The Beechworth Town Hall Gardens were 'temporarily reserved' and gazetted late in 1874, after the Secretary for Lands had checked with the Secretary for Mines that 'mining interests' would not be injured thereby: a query of some importance with regard to gold-mining towns like Beechworth. Another note among records of the Department of Crown Lands and Survey is dated September 1874 and says: 'The land is lying waste at present.'

Once granted permission to establish the gardens, the Beechworth United Shire Council was quick to deal with its piece of waste ground: a plaque records that 'These gardens were laid out in 1875 when many of the present trees were the gift of Baron von Mueller famous Australian botanist'. A large, open-sided pavilion forms the focus of the gardens, which cover about 0.4 hectares and are essentially composed of lawn and trees. *The Cyclopedia of Victoria* (1905) called the gardens 'a small recreation ground containing many fine trees and shrubs', and remarked on the use of the pavilion by a band on summer

The Beechworth Town Hall Gardens in 1907 were much more formal than they are today; the fountain (minus its top tier) and the summer house (with galvanized iron instead of shingles) survive

1935, the Phillips Gardens at Maryborough have a lake at the centre of an elaborate path system. The area of the gardens is about 1 hectare, and they are now essentially 'municipal' rather than 'botanical'. The lake was originally a dam on the main lead of the goldfields at Maryborough, and was bought by the council in 1860 for £70 as a source of water for firemen and horses. When the Goldfields Reservoir was commenced in 1862 use of the dam was gradually discontinued until it became part of the gardens. Records of the Department of Crown Lands and Survey include a letter dated October 1872 from the Town Clerk of Maryborough to the Commissioner of Lands and Survey asking that the land known as the municipal dam reserve be 'permanently reserved for botanical purposes'. The council could then 'plant along the course of the main drain to avoid the unsightliness which marks it at present'. By April of 1874 the dam had been cleaned out (by prison labour) and some ornamentation of the area had been done. The gardens were not actually gazetted until 1879.

There have been many changes here, but parts of the original pattern, including the lake and some of the paths, have survived. Large trees include a Lemon-scented Gum (*Eucalyptus citriodora*), Camphor Laurel (*Cinnamomum camphora*), several Plane Trees (*Platanus* sp.) and a stand of English Oak (*Quercus robur*).

evenings. A number of urns near the Beechworth Town Hall may be the remains of a once more decorative layout. The Town Hall Gardens are an important element in Ford Street, the principal thoroughfare of this historic town. Among their close neighbours are several significant buildings, including the shire hall, Burke Museum, gaol, Lands Office and Forests Office.

DESIGNED BY the Town Surveyor in 1876, and known as the Maryborough Botanical Gardens until named after Henry Neville Phillips, Town Clerk of Maryborough from 1888 to

Original plan of the Maryborough Botanical Gardens, later known as the Phillips Gardens

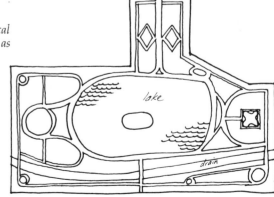

176

Central Park, Malvern

In his *History of Malvern* (1935), J. B. Cooper says that in May 1906 the Malvern Council considered the purchase of land at the corner of Burke Road and Wattletree Road for a park. There is more to the story than that, however.

Philip Leahy, Special Projects Officer for the City of Malvern, relates in an unpublished paper (1982) that before the council took steps to acquire the land, it had already served a useful purpose as part of the Melbourne Golf Club's first course. Established in 1891, and obtaining the prefix 'Royal' in 1895, the club had investigated several possible sites for links when Sir Matthew Davies, M.L.A., facilitated its 'permissive occupancy' of an extensive area that had been subdivided for housing in 1885 but not yet built on. Stretching from Wattletree Road as far south as Waverley Road, the 'Caulfield' course lay on undulating ground, and though the vegetation might have been expected to include indigenous species, only 'dark pines' and 'straggling clumps of gorse' were mentioned in a *Leader* article that reported the club's opening day in July 1891.

During the next decade houses crept nearer and nearer to the golf-course, and the Royal Melbourne Golf Club moved to Sandringham in 1901. A number of ex-members, who formed the nucleus of the Metropolitan Golf Club, continued to use the Caulfield links until at least 1906, and in 1907 the Malvern Council paid £5000 for seventy-five building blocks and a private road that made up the 7.5 hectares of Central Park.

No longer crossed by the sixth and seventh fairways, the gardens soon began to take shape. Cows that had grazed the golf-links were a threat to the many trees planted in about 1911, and a fence surrounded the area until 1918 (and at various other times in the park's history). By this time there were a fine timber kiosk (costing £1100 in 1911) and band rotunda in the park – neither of which is still standing. The steel, glass and concrete conservatory completed in 1927 at a cost of £3500 is a feature of Central Park in the 1980s, displaying colourful plants like begonias and coleus as well as ferns and other greenery, just as it did when first opened. The Curator's Report of 1928–29 described it as

something of which the citizens of Malvern may be justly proud. Three excellent exhibitions have already been made, the first comprising tuberous-rooted Begonias on the South side, and Coleus on the North side . . . The centre has been kept filled with Palms, Ferns, Aspidistras, fibrous-rooted Begonias, intermingled with tropical plants. Sunday afternoon appears to be the favourite visiting time, and the fact that as many as 2000 visitors have been counted on a single afternoon speaks volumes . . . The surrounding lawns and beds have been completed and planted with trees, shrubs and herbaceous plants, which enhance the beauty of the design.

The author of the report was F. L. Reeves, who claimed credit for this part of the gardens: 'With advancing years the full scheme will assume the character originally conceived by me, and I venture the opinion that it will then be voted one of Malvern's most beautiful assets.'

Earlier in Reeves's time the southern part of the park had been taken in hand. His report for 1921–22 documents the formation of curving avenues that are among the park's modern attractions: the metalling of the drives and the planting of

Planting the first trees along the western boundary of Central Park, Malvern, in about 1911. Councillor Alex McKinley is holding the spade

elms on either side are recorded. Trees planted in about 1919 – 185 specimens of Kurrajong (*Brachychiton populneus*) intended as memorials to Malvern soldiers killed in the First World War – were not thriving, and it was intended that they should be lifted and better soil provided for them. (More than 14 000 drayloads of soil were carted into the park in the next couple of years.) By 1925 many of these trees, whose 'growth had left much to be desired' in their original positions, were transplanted along Kingston Street, the park's western boundary. The fact that only about fifteen kurrajongs remain in 1982 suggests that they were not an ideal choice. Many trees besides the kurrajongs had been planted in memory of the fallen, however. Joe Hunter, who came to Central Park as a gardener in 1940 and stayed for forty years, remembers brass plates bearing soldiers' names on posts beside golden poplars, cypresses, palms and other trees.

At the end of his term as Mayor, Councillor H. G. Wilmot

in 1928 gave the council a large marble fountain for Central Park, and it was set up in a sunken area near the conservatory. But both this fountain and a drinking fountain presented by Oliver Gilpin in 1929 had within a few years been badly damaged by vandals. Reeves had plant thefts as well as vandalism to report in 1931–32, but he declared nevertheless that the gardens were looking well.

Central Park still looks well. Near the conservatory with its opulent displays are bedding-out areas, some of them bordered with iron hoops. As in so many public gardens, however, floral displays are greatly reduced here from the days when Joe Hunter and his colleagues, like the gardeners who preceded them, raised flower seedlings of every kind and colour. The trees dotted throughout the lawns include eucalypts, silver birches, pinoaks and golden poplars, and a short row of very large golden poplars forms a splendid backdrop to the sports oval that has always been part of the grounds.

With elms lining the drives half grown, and planting around the 1927 conservatory well established, Central Park around the 1930s was a pleasant place. At this time a feature of the planting was a parterre forming the words 'To the Unknown Warrior'

The spirit of an Edwardian garden survives at Central Park, Malvern (above), with its bedding-out, iron hoops, and spectacular floral and foliage displays in the conservatory

Ribbon planting at the Fitzroy Gardens is maintained under a longstanding tradition; a brilliant effect is achieved here with foxgloves, antirrhinums, and violas in yellow, purple and white. The avenues have a mood and a light of their own

Fit for a mansion

F ROM THE mid-nineteenth century on, gardens ranging in size up to 12 hectares were laid out around most of the large houses built in Melbourne and some of the major country towns. These mansion gardens began to spring up especially in Toorak and St Kilda, developing later in suburbs like Caulfield, Kew and Malvern. They were the gardens of the rich – professional men (except for the doctors, who generally lived at their city consulting rooms), administrators and merchants. In a few cases such as that of Charles Armytage, who acquired Como, South Yarra, in 1864, prospering squatters bought city mansions in which to live for at least part of the year, although more often they leased their town houses.

Both Kearney's 1855 maps of Melbourne and the detailed plans drawn by the Melbourne and Metropolitan Board of

Hilton House, Hawthorn: all the ostentation that money could buy

Opposite: The Rippon Lea conservatory viewed from the drawing-room in 1982

Works in the late nineteenth and early twentieth centuries (prior to sewerage connections) give a clear impression of the number and extent of these gardens, which covered hundreds of hectares in Melbourne's middle-belt suburbs.

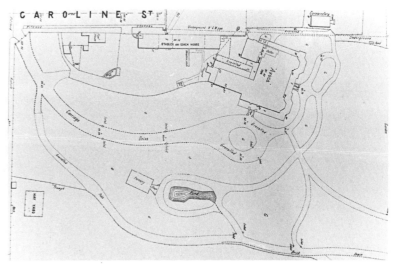

The inauguration in 1857 of Melbourne's first reticulated water supply, from the Yan Yean reservoir, must have been a factor of some importance in the establishment and maintenance of extensive gardens around the city. Not that the Yan Yean supply was always satisfactorily reliable and pure, but it was a substantial step forward. The minutes of a meeting of the Victorian Horticultural Improvement Society early in 1863 spoke of Mr David Johnston's fine display of roses and gladioli, 'shewing what Yan Yean will do in the hottest weather'.

Like the houses they surrounded, mansion gardens differed enormously in size and style. Some, such as those at Raheen

The M.M.B.W. map of Avoca, South Yarra (right), is an excellent guide to the mansion's garden components early in the twentieth century

The goddess Diana had ample opportunity to contrast her privileged position in the grounds of Hilton House, Hawthorn, with that of less affluent neighbours

and Burke Hall in Kew and Stonnington in Malvern, favoured Renaissance motifs, with balustraded terraces capped with vases and urns, all set in a formal, rectilinear design. Others such as the gardens of Hilton House in Hawthorn and Fortuna in Bendigo were grotesquely eccentric: Henry Henty even had a Burmese temple in his garden at Tarring, Kew. There was every variety in between. But in nearly all cases they were featuristic – often extremely so. Whether these features were tied together in a rectilinear pattern such as that shown in the painting by William Tibbits of an Abbotsford house (1884), or whether they were loosely scattered in a more natural arrangement as at Rippon Lea, they all nevertheless drew from a large and similar repertoire.

Of course more than just a house and garden was involved. Rather, they were miniature estates with all the accompanying outbuildings – servants' quarters, stables, manure pits, fowl runs and pigeon house. The more decorative structures were to be found in the garden proper – aviary, conservatory, fernery, summer house and lodge, together with vases, urns, pedestals, arbours, ponds and fountains. These were all features designed to add interest and diversity to the garden.

These gardens were the pleasure grounds of local society

and the cause of considerable rivalry and competition among their owners. They were exhaustively described in the popular press of the day, reporters offering the most critical analysis where they felt it was justified.

The mansion garden was divided into several parts. Invariably the utilitarian areas were placed out of sight, and they often included a vegetable garden, orangery, hothouse, orchard, picking garden (for cut flowers), paddocks and drying ground. The entry drive generally dominated the main part of the garden, and around it and the mansion were disposed parterres, shrubberies, croquet lawn, flower and rose garden, lawns and borders. Neatly clipped hedges of cypress, pittosporum, hawthorn and sometimes Osage Orange (*Maclura pomifera*) often separated these different spaces.

Generally the planting in the mansion garden was dominated by large evergreen trees and shrubs. Favourites for driveways and perimeter screening included pines, cypresses, pittosporums, araucarias, cedars and Irish strawberry trees. The more decorative planting was dazzling in its variety. Many owners had a passionate interest in horticulture and their gardens provided an opportunity to show off their abilities. This they were often encouraged in by their head gardeners, many of

This Melbourne house, long unidentified, was painted by William Tibbits in 1884. It is now known to be The Rest at Abbotsford, then owned by R. Goldsborough. Its garden can be said to possess everything a gentleman of that period might desire: an arbour, conservatory, flower garden, fountain, urns, and an onion-domed summer house

South of the mansion at Rippon Lea in 1880 was a gardenesque collection of flower beds and paths

Opposite left: 'Tea with Mrs Tait' outside a relatively simple summer house

arranged in a picturesque or artistic manner . . . are dignified with the title of museum grottoes . . . it is octagonal in shape, about ten feet across . . . The subjects used in the decoration number fully fifty mosses and lichens, about a dozen cones and other seed vessels, besides various other materials of vegetable origin, while the flat dome of the roof is covered with shells, also arranged in figures, and surrounding a representation of a starfish in the centre.

Sadly, but not surprisingly, the summer house has disappeared, though another fantastically ornamented structure – a true grotto, this one on which a gardener called Webley is said to have worked survives at Werribee Park. Some gardens changed as fashions changed, while lawnmowers, readily and cheaply available by the mid-1870s, greatly extended the possibilities of garden design. Both these factors may have played a part in the considerable alterations made at Rippon Lea, Elsternwick, a dozen or so years after the commencement of this garden. As originally laid out in the 1860s it was a complex series of interlocking geometric shapes comprising mostly paths and gar-

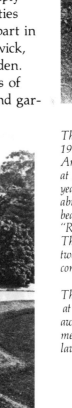

whom had been trained in the great gardens and nurseries of Britain. Hugh Glass, in his immense garden at Flemington House (later Travancore) built a special hothouse for the *Victoria regia* lily. Owners went to no end of trouble to obtain the best and most spectacular results. The Hon. Edward Henty diverted the sewage from the Alfred Hospital into his garden at Offington in St Kilda Road. According to the *Leader* of 3 June 1876, his stove (heated glasshouse) contained 'one of the most interesting and select collections . . . in the colony; many of them have been imported direct from England, some from the Pacific Islands, a lot of Orchids from Java, and others from various places, forming a list numerous enough for a respectable English nurseryman's catalogue'.

Others took the passion for variety and decoration to extremes. The horticultural notes in the *Leader* often reported such cases enthusiastically, as on 15 April 1882:

Mr. Renwick, Garrell, Glen Eira-road, has recently had a summer house decorated in a highly artistic manner by Mr. Webley, nurseryman, gardener, and garden decorator, Malvern. Such erections . . .

The Garden Gazette of 1902 described Mr Anderson, head gardener at Rippon Lea for some years, as a man 'to whose ability and care the beautiful grounds of "Rippon Lea" owe much'. There were sometimes twenty men under his control

The old croquet lawn, at right, was swept away during establishment of the great west lawn about 1883

den beds. After 1880 it was remodelled in a more natural style reminiscent of William Guilfoyle's work at Melbourne's Botanic Gardens, its great western lawn a new and important element in the design.

Only a handful of Victoria's mansion gardens remain today, although there are many contemporary descriptions and photographs. Where the house has survived it is all too often jammed in on all sides by other houses. Fortunately the gardens at Como and Rippon Lea – both regarded in their heyday as outstanding – have survived to some degree, and are now cared for by the National Trust.

Most of the gardens in this section are private and therefore closed to the public; Como, Buda, Rippon Lea and Fortuna are open at specific times

Opposite: Como very early in the 1860s

Como's gates (below) fronted Toorak Road until moved to their present position in Como Avenue; within the garden (below right) box-hedging lined many paths

Como, South Yarra

James Sinclair, the noted nineteenth-century gardener and garden-writer, included Como among the 'principal gardens round Melbourne' of which he described two hundred in his book *The Beauties of Victoria in 1856*. Como, wrote Sinclair, possessed

Sloping lawns, made gay, green and pleasing by art and Nature; gravel and wood-land, hill and dale, river and lake, are all here, adding grandeur to a substantial mansion and suitable appendages, with a pair of iron gates and their accompaniments fit at all times to keep up Victoria's dignity. Many are the rare exotic trees newly planted, and many more tall growing, making this without doubt one of the prettiest seats on the Yarra.

The two-storey mansion at that time was the property of John Brown, a merchant and master builder, and the garden Sinclair describes must predate the 'approach and principal part' said by the *Australasian* of 17 March 1866 to have been 'laid out and

planted' in 1857 by William Sangster. (The first part of the house had been begun by Judge Edward Williams in 1847, and Kearney's map of 1855 confirms the early existence of a garden on the site.) Sangster was a leading horticulturist and designer, who went into partnership as a nurseryman with William Taylor on leaving Como in 1866.

The large orchards, ornamental plantations and gardens at Como in the 1860s covered about 6 hectares – part of a 20 hectare property between Toorak Road and the River Yarra. The comprehensive description of the Como garden provided by the *Australasian* makes it clear that soil was a problem. Before planting began, trenching and draining were essential. A shelterbelt of blue gums had been planted in about 1857 to protect the area from south-westerly winds. The writer mentions a lawn on the eastern side of the house, flower beds, a croquet lawn, a terrace and a fountain. Buffalo grass was said to be thriving; the 'lawn grasses' had died right out. Box-hedged walks, some of which also remain, were tidily surfaced

An old photograph verifies the dominance of conifers depicted by William Tibbits in Como's garden

with gravel found on the property. Articles in subsequent issues praised the orchard and remarked on the relative growth of various trees and shrubs at Como: the specimens of Norfolk Island Pine (*Araucaria heterophylla*), Bunya Bunya Pine (*A. bidwillii*), Cluster Pine (*Pinus pinaster*) and Stone Pine (*P. pinea*) were doing well; Canary Islands Pine (*P. canariensis*) and Scots Pine (*P. sylvestris*) were not. The most satisfactory of the deciduous trees on such unsatisfactory soil was the English Oak, *Quercus robur*.

In these early days, says Dr John Foster in *Historic Houses of Australia* (1974), the house and garden 'were the centre of a hospitality legendary for its extravagance'. But in 1864 Como Brown's fortunes declined and the property was sold to Charles Henry Armytage (son of a pioneer pastoralist) in whose family Como remained for ninety-five years. Charles Armytage died in 1876 and after the death of his widow in 1909 the estate was sold, under strict covenants that largely ensured that subsequent development around the house was appropriate.

Some 2 hectares, with the house, remained the property of three Armytage sisters until sold to the National Trust (as its Victorian headquarters) in 1959. In that year a committee of management was set up. Its chairman, Professor John Turner, has described the changes in Como's garden since that date, together with the thinking behind them:

The well-designed and mature garden around the old house itself presented. . .few problems. Many of the fine trees, including a magnificent Moreton Bay fig, mature Araucarias and other conifers, the camellias and larger rhododendrons, were still in good heart, and the major requirement was the improvement of the lawns and their borders, the modernisation of the reticulated water supply and the fertilisation of the soils. Finding it impossible to regrass some of the more shaded areas, we covered them with dense beds of ivy, which was a favourite plant of the Victorians; we believe that these dark stretches of ivy add dignity to the subdued landscaping of the old garden, and they certainly simplify the maintenance . . . The Committee was faced with much more difficult problems when they moved out from the house to the large and neglected vegetable garden, and the large grassed horse paddock and other peripheral areas where no real landscape gardening had ever been attempted

Not all of the garden visible in this painting belongs to Government House, Melbourne. William Tibbits painted it from across the Botanic Gardens lake in 1878

Como, by William Tibbits, painted in 1875

The rustic bridge, summer house and lake at Rippon Lea (left)

At Buda, Castlemaine: a tennis pavilion converted into a plant-house (above), and an aviary

...we decided to landscape the remaining neglected parts of the property as one easily maintained garden; and to do so, as far as possible, along the lines of what might have been expected if the house had remained under continuous private ownership.

Some of the changes – the enrichment of the beds with more herbaceous species, the repaving of the old courtyard, the replacement of *Oxalis* by bluebells under the elms – were the responsibility of the committee, advised by its professional members, Eric Hammond, Grace Fraser and the head gardener Chris van Riemsdyk. But the landscaping of the neglected old vegetable gardens was done by John Stevens, and across the main drive Ellis Stones created one of his characteristic rock gardens bordering a new pool planted with aquatic species.

Only in the large open paddock along Williams Road, outside the garden proper, has the committee introduced some Australian eucalypts and heathland shrubs, although it should be pointed out that some of the finest trees of the old garden are the Moreton Bay fig, the araucarias and the kauri of semi-tropical Australia. But on the whole Como is a garden of the Victorian era, with some eighty tree species and many shrubs and herbs from all parts of the world. The fountain garden, the croquet lawn, and the borders of the main drive are still essentially as they were originally designed, and on two sides the main gardens and house are still sheltered and defined by a hedge of massive mature trees of the Monterey Cypress (*Cupressus macrocarpa*).

Buda, Castlemaine

The large garden at Buda was created by Ernest Leviny, a Hungarian silversmith and goldsmith, in or about the 1860s. The single-storey Italianate mansion of rendered brick now consists of thirteen rooms, but was originally a six-roomed bungalow ('Delhi Villa') built by a colonel of the Indian army. Leviny increased the size of the garden to about 2 hectares, over half of which was laid out in a generally rectilinear fashion.

Gates at Buda

The balance was kept 'wild', to encourage growth of the local wildflowers in spring.

Dr Ferdinand Mueller, then Government Botanist and Director of the Melbourne Botanic Gardens, was a friend of Leviny and is known to have stayed in the house on a number of occasions. It is possible that he influenced the design and planting of the garden. He certainly provided seed for some of the trees. Interesting features include an aviary designed by Leviny, using cast iron from the local Thompson's Foundry, and a tennis pavilion – both excellent and rare examples of nineteenth-century garden buildings. The entrance gate is also of interest, being of a particularly intricate design, and the massive clipped cypress hedge planted by Leviny in front of the house is probably the largest in Victoria.

In about 1918 the tennis court was converted into a formal garden designed by Miss Dorothy Leviny, who used the tennis pavilion as a fernery and added a fountain and sundial to the front garden. There are now built-up beds of bulbs, perennials and shrubs (including peony roses, camellias, buddleias, lilac and lavender), while trees planted by Leviny have become fine mature specimens. There is a large English oak near the tennis pavilion, as well as specimens of Bunya Bunya Pine (*Araucaria*

Opposite: A view of Rippon Lea from the 'nursery lawn' in about 1902. The ballroom and conservatory are on the left

By 1875 Rippon Lea's rose garden (below) was well established. The espaliard of vines (right) at Rippon Lea was at the centre of its vast orchard and kitchen garden. Eight paths, dividing the area into sections, ended here

bidwillii), persimmon (*Diospyros* sp.) and Golden Rain Tree (*Koelreuteria paniculata*).

Buda is one of the few large nineteenth-century suburban-style gardens in Victoria to retain its original form together with its peculiarly nineteenth-century character.

Rippon Lea, Elsternwick

The *Australasian* of 25 December 1875 summarized the earliest stages of Rippon Lea's garden:

The grounds have been planted by the present proprietor, who commenced operations some seven or eight years ago, laying out the place upon a much smaller scale than the present, great additions having been made recently. The main approach is from Hotham-street, by a well-formed winding drive, with fine bold curves . . . On either side are borders planted with a good selection of miscellaneous trees and shrubs, which have made fine growth, many of them now forming good specimens.

The 'present proprietor' was Frederick Sargood, whose father had established a highly profitable drapery business in Victoria in the 1850s. The younger Sargood had built a two-storey brick house in 1868 on what was at the time an 11 hectare block of land.

Ruth Sanderson, in a research paper on the development of Rippon Lea's garden, has documented the complex series of changes through which it passed between 1868 and 1972, the year in which the property came into the hands of the National Trust. Her researches have not established the identity of the garden's designer or designers, but she says that 'The

The bridge and lake at Rippon Lea in 1980 (far left), bearing a striking resemblance to those of Broad Green Lodge, Surrey (left), in 1878. Frederick Sargood's father had returned to England and moved into this country estate in 1858, and Sargood may have noted some of its features for future reference when visiting England in 1861

Opposite: With the lookout tower, grotto and waterfall newly constructed, the enlarged lake became an even more exciting part of the garden in the 1880s

possibility that Frederick Sargood planned his own garden is not to be dismissed'.

During and after Sargood's absence overseas from 1880 to 1882, considerable changes were made to both house and garden, the professionalism of the landscaping alterations suggesting the involvement of a designer other than the owner, capable and enthusiastic though he was. In this second phase, the gardenesque elements of the earlier garden were largely removed in favour of the more natural, picturesque style popularized by William Guilfoyle in the Botanic Gardens. This did not mean the loss of what Ruth Sanderson calls the 'richness and diversity of High Victorian planting'. The great western lawn, established then, enabled 'a circulation pattern which linked the major elements of the pleasure garden. . . At each change of direction, interest and curiosity were aroused'. The lake was greatly enlarged and its every possibility exploited for such lakeside features as a grotto, waterfall, and mound with lookout tower. The large, externally buttressed fernery of 1880 was succeeded by an even larger iron-framed fernery built in 1896 and still standing: this was designed by Lloyd Tayler and

Fitts, using components cast by George Smith's Sun Foundry, Glasgow.

Frederick Sargood, knighted in 1890, was a wealthy man of diverse interests. Rippon Lea's garden was well known as one of Melbourne's grandest, a sumptuous setting for the Sargoods' many garden parties and fetes. Some were no doubt held at night, for – says the *Garden Gazette* of July 1902 – Rippon Lea was electrically lit throughout, and a 'veritable fairyland' after dark.

It is the garden remodelled after 1880 that essentially survives at Rippon Lea today. The major elements include a curving drive lined with oaks, the extensive lawn to the west of the house, the lake, grotto and fernery, a conservatory, and a number of rustic garden buildings – the lookout tower, an archery pavilion and several summer houses among them. Provision for irrigation and drainage was made very early in the life of the garden, and a later system incorporating pipes for distributing liquid manure as well as water to the plants was equally complex and efficient; electric pumps have replaced the windmills of earlier days, but much of the scheme still operates. A swimming pool and surrounding pergola and summer houses in the 'Hollywood' style were added in the 1930s.

Now reduced to just over 5 hectares, Rippon Lea probably still has Australia's best private urban garden in the 'grand manner'. Its collection of rustic garden buildings is outstanding, and the fernery is one of the largest ever to be constructed in a private garden.

Rippon Lea 1980

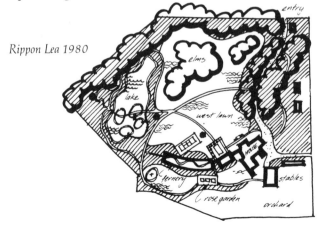

Government House, Melbourne

A public competition failing to bring forth from its twenty or more entries a suitable plan for the landscaping of the Domain and the new Government House grounds, the Government of Victoria in 1873 accepted a simplified version of the unsolicited design offered it by Joseph Sayce of Caulfield, a gentleman said by the *Australasian* of 28 June 1873 to be 'long and favourably known as an amateur horticulturist possessing both taste and skill in garden ornamentation'. For three months of 1873 Sayce, engaged as temporary curator, worked on the implementation of his plan while the building of Government House proceeded. Then, at the end of June, what Sayce called 'the parsimony that... suddenly affected the Ministerial mind' brought his involvement to an end and put the development of the grounds under the control of the new curator of the 'Botanical and Domain Gardens', William Guilfoyle.

Appointed on 23 July 1873, Guilfoyle wasted no time in inspecting progress on the landscaping and suggesting modifications to Sayce's design – simultaneously making wide-ranging alterations at the Botanic Gardens. In his first report to Clement Hodgkinson, Inspector-General of Gardens, Parks and Reserves, Guilfoyle criticized Sayce's choice of the slowgrowing Monkey Puzzle Tree (*Araucaria araucana*) and Giant Sequoia (*Sequoiadendron giganteum*) for an avenue leading to Government House. He also urged, among other things, more generous curves for part of the drive.

In a report on Gardens and Parks to parliament in the following month, Hodgkinson agreed with 'a large proportion' of Guilfoyle's proposals, but did not recommend 'the alteration proposed by him in the private drive formed by Mr. Sayce, as the cost of such alteration would be incommensurate with the advantages to be derived from it'. Nevertheless Guilfoyle's report to parliament in May 1874 mentions his recurving of the drive, which enabled it to 'enter with a bold sweep the expanse of gravel which, in my opinion, should be created in front of Government House'. Guilfoyle also claimed that his prediction about unsatisfactory growth in the monkey puzzle and giant

Government House in 1880 (opposite) and 1982 (above)

197

sequoia trees had proved accurate, and advised breaking up the formal rows with various conifers already well established elsewhere in the Domain. Guilfoyle had successfully transplanted many sizeable trees in the Botanic Gardens by this time, but it was some months earlier still that Joseph Sayce was writing of 'the tree-lifters which I have had specially constructed' for transplanting 'trees of considerable size' from one position to another in the Domain; they had all apparently taken kindly to the move. It has been speculated that Guilfoyle learnt something of landscaping from Sayce; did he also adopt Sayce's technique for the shifting of large trees?

In spite of Guilfoyle's amendments, the garden at Government House remains essentially faithful to Joseph Sayce's plan. There are sweeping lawns on the western side and formal terraces to the north. A large kitchen garden is located behind the mansion.

Though the design remains intact, considerable replanting has been necessary since 1976, following the over-maturity and decline of various species since the Second World War. The 11 hectare garden at Government House, Melbourne, provides an appropriate setting for what is possibly Australia's grandest house.

Astolat, Camberwell

A photograph taken in 1916 from the eastern balcony at Astolat shows lightly timbered grazing country beyond the side fence, with not a single house in sight. By that time, however, the garden in front of the two-storey mansion (built in 1882 by the Derham family) was well established in its present form, with one eucalypt surviving from the natural vegetation of the site. This tree was very large by 1946, when its propensity to

Government House and some of its early planting, seen across the modern rose garden

198

drop limbs from time to time brought about its removal. The stump – up to 75 cm across in places – still stands, covered with ivy, at the northern end of Astolat's beautiful oval lawn. A long, winding driveway opens out into a turning circle around this lawn, which provides the mansion with a spacious forecourt. For many years now the lawn has been planted with fine grasses, but it was originally of buffalo grass.

From the street, the mansion and a tennis court complete with Victorian tennis pavilion are hidden by trees and dense shrubberies. Only a short segment survives of a narrow band of mown lawn that once ran along the outer edges of the drive. Although a large willow that overhung the tennis pavilion and a Moreton Bay Fig (*Ficus macrophylla*) in the same quarter of the garden have both disappeared, there are many fine mature trees still standing. They include a magnificent specimen of the New Zealand Kauri (*Agathis australis*), several wide-spreading English Oaks (*Quercus robur*), a giant *Liquidambar styraciflua*, a couple of Bunya Bunya Pines (*Araucaria bidwillii*), and single specimens of Silky Oak (*Grevillea robusta*), Firewheel Tree (*Stenocarpus sinuatus*) and *Jacaranda mimosifolia*. From their size, all seem likely to have been established when the garden was fairly new. Among the shrubs are a number of rhododendrons planted early in the twentieth century, as well as camellias, spiraeas and lavender. A productive vegetable garden is maintained near a rear corner of the house.

Though the land on which Astolat stands was originally twice its present size, the grounds have been nearly a hectare in extent since early in the century. Together with tall trees in adjoining properties, such an extensive and well-planted garden gives the mansion privacy as well as a splendid framework.

Opposite right: Astolat in 1903 had no flower beds fringing this part of the oval lawn, and the drive, now asphalted, seemed to be composed of coarse sand

Seen from the front steps of the house, the tall trees on the road boundary make a handsome barrier (above left)

Astolat's charming Victorian tennis pavilion (above right)

Fortuna's gradual metamorphosis from gold-mine (about 1902, right) to landscaped mansion (about 1930, below) is apparent in these two photographs

Pompeii in the Antipodes (far right): the Italian water garden installed by George Lansell at Fortuna

Fortuna, Bendigo

Fortuna's garden was created by the 'Quartz King', George Lansell, between the 1870s and his death in 1906. It is located on the site of the fabulously rich 180 Mine, and developed gradually as parts of the property became redundant for gold-mining. A single-storey villa stood alongside the mine when Lansell bought it in the early 1870s, but this was incorporated into a mansion that grew to thirty rooms. Attached is a particularly fine conservatory with etched-glass walls.

One of the garden's unusual features is an Italian water garden, complete with fountains, statue, niches and Roman column. Many of these items were imported from Italy – an example of the extravagant eclecticism made possible by gold. The present lake, roughly triangular and once the largest of six on the property, was originally a settling pond used in the mining operation.

The total area of the property is now 6.7 hectares, though it is believed to have been greater at one time. There are many old trees at Fortuna. A double row of fourteen tall palms lines one side of the lake, with a dozen or so poplars behind them. Pepper trees and Norfolk Island pines abound, the latter lining half of another side of the lake. One or more specimens each of pine, cypress, eucalypt, redwood, fig, oak, pyramid tree, weeping willow, bunya bunya, camellia and pittosporum are dotted about the grounds. Part of the garden has now been built over but George Lansell's surviving trees and shrubs, and many others planted since 1942, are being cared for by its owners since that date, the Department of Defence, whose Army Survey Regiment is now located at Fortuna.

Miegunyah, Toorak

The original house on this site dates from 1856, and some of the largest trees do too. There have, however, been many changes to both house and garden since that time. Soon after purchasing the property in 1910, Russell Grimwade (later Sir Russell) increased its size to more than 1 hectare by securing four blocks from an adjacent subdivision. Later on, the rambling single-storey house became a much more imposing two-storey structure, whose design was mostly the work of Harold Desbrowe Annear. The inventor, industrialist and benefactor occupied Miegunyah until he died in 1955, and on the death of Lady Grimwade in 1973 the property was bequeathed to Melbourne University.

The present form of the garden was largely established by its owners of sixty years, though Edna Walling, Ellis Stones, and later John Stevens were involved in development of parts of it.

A sweeping lawn planted with specimen trees dominates the garden. There are a very large, very old Moreton Bay Fig (*Ficus macrophylla*), two huge Chinese Elms (*Ulmus parvifolia*), two English Elms (*U. procera*) and ten oaks among these trees. The garden has four other and contrasting sections: a small kitchen

The garden front at Miegunyah

garden, a sunken box-hedged rose garden thought to be the copy of an unknown garden in England, a birch copse (once the site of a tennis court), and a small arboretum, maintained in an informal style and consisting only of Australian plants. In spring the birch grove is carpeted with daffodils in the English manner. An attractive shrub at the edge of this part of the garden is *Malus ioensis*. The arboretum reflects Sir Russell's interest in and research into the genus *Eucalyptus*, about which he wrote a book first published in 1920.

Surrounding a house of some historical interest, the garden at Miegunyah is one of the few remaining well-maintained large private gardens in Melbourne.

Marathon, Mount Eliza

Built for Lieutenant-Colonel H. W. Grimwade by the fashionable architect Walter Butler, house and garden were completed in 1914. The property originally covered 13.5 hectares but is now reduced to a little over 1.5. A rose garden, an orchard with espaliered walk, a kitchen garden and a number of glasshouses were placed at some distance from the house and have long since disappeared. However, the main ornamental garden survives in its entirety.

The house is a typical large Butler house with a rambling, gabled, asymmetrical design. Although Butler believed a garden should be an architectural extension of the house it surrounded, he gave the garden at Marathon a very formal, symmetrical design. It has a splendid site on a clifftop overlooking Port Phillip Bay. Butler's interest in connecting house and garden is evident in a large verandah room that is part of the house but completely open to the garden.

Comparable in concept with Edna Walling's great garden Mawarra, this garden descends a steep hill in front of the house in a series of large level terraces, each with its own individual character. The first, a narrow terrace of lawn, descends to a large balustraded croquet lawn partly enclosed by unusual trellis screens draped with white wisteria. Below this the next terrace is divided into two separate flower gardens, one centred on a circular fountain and the other on a sundial.

The last terrace, which includes a Korean 'guardian', has an Oriental flavour, a large rectangular pond being planted with papyrus and having at one time been adorned with a Japanese lantern. A small rill, a semicircular wall niche and a fountain are strongly reminiscent of some of the gardens of Gertrude Jekyll and Edwin Lutyens in England. Indeed the form of the pond is almost a copy of part of their great garden at Hestercombe in Somerset.

Although there is a central axis to this garden it is played down in favour of a set of parallel paths and stairs on either side. A large pergola on the seaward side of the croquet lawn frames enticing views from the garden to Port Phillip Bay, but helps to enclose the garden visually. On the land side is the 'Green Alley', a spring garden containing camellias, azaleas and a large variety of flowering bulbs.

Cranlana, Toorak

The garden at Cranlana was laid out in 1932 for the highly successful retailer Sidney Myer, following his acquisition of a piece of land that brought the total size of the property up to its present 1.5 hectares. The designer was the architect Harold Desbrowe Annear, who died soon after planning the garden and thus was not involved in the house alterations that subsequently turned a villa into a mansion. This is his only authenticated landscape design.

The main part of the northern garden is Italianate in style, with a large stone-walled sunken garden, on two levels, extending from near the front of the house. There are graduating rows of annuals around the edges of the higher garden, and a pond with central fountain in the lower. For many years the beds lining these walls held an ever-changing display of thousands of annuals in ribbon borders; the area has now been planted mostly with shrubs such as dogwoods, rhododendrons and camellias. Statuary, urns, seats and fountains in the sunken garden were chosen by Sidney Myer and his wife (later Dame Merlyn Myer) during a visit to France.

Beyond the sunken garden, on the northern perimeter of the garden and running east-west, is the Long Walk, a path of

crazy paving extending more than 80 metres with Italian statues (dated 1885) at each end. Other parts of the garden are less formal than these areas, and include an extensive lawn on the southern side of the drive.

Magnificent iron gates and pediment at the entrance to Cranlana were designed by Desbrowe Annear and hand-wrought in Melbourne by Caslake's. The straight drive dividing the garden into two parts is lined with Bhutan Cypress (*Cupressus torulosa*).

The oldest trees on the property are four English Oaks (*Quercus robur*) and a giant Cedar of Lebanon (*Cedrus libanii*) – both established before 1920. Other fine trees include a Tulip Tree (*Liriodendron tulipiferum*), a Coral Tree (*Erythrina* sp.), a splendid Copper Beech (*Fagus sylvatica* 'Cuprea'), and pinoaks and weeping elms. There are picking and kitchen gardens (not used much today) and a large working conservatory where orchids are a speciality.

The sunken garden at Cranlana (below left), as photographed for the 2 April 1934 issue of the Australian Home Beautiful. Many specimens of 'Lambertiana' cypress were planted in this area, but only four survived. Otherwise, the garden in 1982 (left) remains essentially the same

Part III
Going, going...

WHEN James Sinclair wrote his rather quaint little book *The Beauties of Victoria in 1856*, he was able to describe two hundred outstanding gardens in Melbourne, though he could have included many more without touching on anything other than mansion and suburban gardens around the city. And Victoria was only twenty-two years old at the time! Over the following forty-odd years, which carried the colony into the twentieth century, the number of its significant gardens would have multiplied many hundreds of times.

But what remains of the gardens that flourished in 1856? Perhaps it is remarkable that a single one of Sinclair's gardens is recognizable after 130 years: Como in South Yarra – 'between the Yarra river and the Gardiner's Creek Road' (now Toorak Road) – was included in Sinclair's book and, for all its changes, still has a lovely garden with a few of its original features intact. A few gardens besides Como's date back, in some respect or other, to the 1850s. And most of the ninety or so historic gardens examined here, first established in the nineteenth century, are notable for retaining something of their original layout and planting. No doubt there are more than this

Part of the Carlton Gardens in 1979

Opposite: Como in 1982, its axis – focusing on the fountain – basically unchanged

number tucked away in the countryside or hiding in obscure suburban streets. There are tens of thousands of streets in Melbourne alone and they have not been systematically searched by any means: many more suburban, cottage, villa and terrace house gardens remain undiscovered. Much more is known about the larger establishments – botanic, public, mansion and homestead gardens – although inevitably a few important ones will have escaped the net.

Added to these ninety gardens are a further eighty or so which, though largely lost, still retain some part or parts of historic interest. Woodlands near Ararat, for instance, now bears little resemblance to its appearance in 1869 when it was painted by Eugène von Guérard. Most of the garden has been fenced off, but there are some magnificent surviving trees, a number of fountains, vast terraces almost unmatched

Camnethan Homestead, near Smeaton, in its prime: an elaborate garden, immaculately kept

in Victoria, and a wonderful surviving latticework fernery complete with pots and the various devices for hanging them. Woodlands was evidently still impressive in 1891 when the Governor of Victoria, Lord Hopetoun, inspected it with a view to purchasing the property as his country residence.

Camnethan Homestead near Smeaton, although on a much smaller scale, is likewise set in a garden full of reminders of past glory. Its present condition would not have drawn even a glance had it not been for several nineteenth-century photographs depicting it as one of the most elaborate small gardens known to have existed in Victoria. In the derelict area surrounding the house are plant-stands of twisted wire, arbours, and the remains of timber screens and pergolas.

Ercildoune at Burrumbeet is another. Its vast garden was probably started in 1839 when the Learmonth brothers completed the first stage of their Scottish-style baronial mansion. What is left includes several lakes, a walled garden of 0.4 hectares, the vestiges of a large box-hedged parterre, and a marble well-top brought from Egypt. Much of the detail has gone but the form of the garden is still evident, giving clues enough to the scale and complexity of this once-grand place. It is essential that while something remains of gardens such as this, they should be recorded. Then even if they are eventually lost, their plants and layout will still be known.

Since modern gardens of quality are far from rare in Victoria, need we concern ourselves with old ones? Are they more beautiful, more exciting than those established in recent decades? Why, in short, do historic gardens matter?

Historic gardens are important because they make up a strand in the fabric of our past, helping our understanding just as old buildings, costumes and furniture do. An old garden dominated by a pair of bunya bunya pines and an ancient row of cypresses speaks to us of a nineteenth-century passion for dark-foliaged trees of striking form. The remains of summer houses and broad terraces are redolent of a former age when families took their leisure in gardens and lavish parties were held in them by the wealthy. Old kitchen gardens, perhaps only faintly outlined, remind an overfed generation that the

Cumnethan Homestead in 1979 (left)

The beautiful garden at Bolobek, Macedon (right)

Fersfield, Gisborne (below): protected to some degree by legislation invoked by the Shire of Gisborne

earliest settlers in the remotest areas had to grow their own food or starve. Plans and records showing dozens of varieties of the various fruits in private orchards reflect a preoccupation with horticultural achievement – with the lure of propagation and species-improvement. Studying historic gardens can provide an insight into our social, horticultural and scientific background. And if there are retained not only old photographs, paintings and descriptions but also a core of actual gardens, our understanding must be all the richer.

While old gardens are not necessarily more attractive than comparatively new ones, there is nothing in a young garden that can match the dignity of huge and ancient trees. Probably no one today (except perhaps in a restoration project) would choose to set up such a complex pattern of paths and drives as was common a century ago. Yet surviving examples invariably look much more appropriate around a building of similar age than would a modern landscape. And when an old garden still possesses fine trees, a design that is characteristic of an earlier time, and the authentic flavour of that period, it is a fascinating relic of the past, something to be saved if at all possible.

Victoria's most significant historic gardens, totalling around ninety, are far fewer than the state's buildings of comparable importance. Although many have been lost, the National Trust in Victoria can still designate nearly three thousand buildings as worthy of conservation, and this list grows each month. Even the Historic Buildings Preservation Council, which has the statutory powers to prevent the demolition of historic buildings, and which is much more selective in adding to its list than is the National Trust, has over five hundred buildings on its books. Other artefacts from our past are treasured in the La Trobe Collection of the State Library of Victoria, which has a steadily expanding stock of letters, diaries, photographs, paintings and rare books.

All these are priceless records, and nobody would wilfully allow their destruction. Attempts to demolish or alter an important historic building now inevitably meet with a barrage of opposition, and it would be a bold man or woman who would dare suggest touching up a Buvelot or von Guérard painting to 'improve' it. But historic gardens often seem to attract another response – one of indifference, which is condemning more of them every year. True, buildings and documents are easier to conserve than a garden, which has that very special ability to grow, and therefore eventually must die. Gardens are so transitory, indeed, that they may disappear quite quickly. One would have imagined that the garden designer Ellis Stones (1896–1975), whose best work was done in the 1960s and 1970s, would have left many examples of his craft, even though the gardens were almost formless. Yet in 1982 a writer on his life and work can find no more than a few gardens that still bear his stamp.

There are many reasons why our list of historic gardens stands at only ninety-odd. Owners of the larger urban ones increasingly in the twentieth century found skilled labour scarce and expensive, and as cities expanded the land they occupied became prime real estate. (Perhaps social upheavals and economic pressures after the First World War brought the most noticeable changes of this kind.) Rates inevitably increased and one by one the great urban estates were forced to subdivide. The present street pattern in some suburbs, especially Toorak, still reflects the earlier use of this land. Winding

Prime real estate in the twentieth century, Leura in Toorak was described critically in the Leader of 22 April 1876: 'The lawn slopes directly from the edge of the drive... Unfortunately it has been divided by a walk leading to the kitchen garden, which greatly impairs its appearance; and, to make matters worse, the walk, instead of running straight, is twisted into a curve ...'

Opposite: Forget-me-nots and spring-flowering bulbs along the drive at Duneira, Mount Macedon. This fine garden has had continuous care from successive owners

cul-de-sacs were often originally the driveways to one house, where now dozens of buildings are dotted along the street. Illawarra Crescent (once the drive for Illawarra) and the curving portion of Kensington Road (once the entry to Grantham) are two such cases. Subdivision did not, of course, reduce the number of gardens in a suburb. Rather, it added considerably to it. But very often every trace of one kind of historic garden, the large and elaborate pleasure garden of the rich, was swept away.

Complacency and lack of interest have been partly responsible for the losses. The plight of the state's historic gardens, or the nation's for that matter, has never been much in the minds of the people, even among groups concerned about our heritage. Owners and their friends and family have often mourned the destruction of a favourite garden, or part of a garden, but mostly they have not thought of it as a loss to the state. (Nor did they worry much about their old buildings until a new consciousness sprang up in the 1960s.)

The old bougainvillea rest house and its replacement at the Royal Botanic Gardens, Melbourne

As with most things, gardens changed according to fashion, and in doing so sometimes deprived or almost deprived succeeding generations of any experience of a particular phase or feature. In the late nineteenth century, for example, ribbon planting – the planting out of annual flowers in ribbon-like strips of various colour on the long borders flanking drives and paths – was the height of fashion. On 4 March 1876 the *Weekly Times* described the garden at Findon in Kew, the home of the Hon. Henry Miller:

On nearing the house a narrow border of riband bordering is seen. This extends along the front of the house and consists of a dark-foliaged Coleus for the back, Flower of the Day Pelargonium for the middle and Blue Lobelia for the front, and edged with Chamomile. Planted at regular intervals in the above bordering are some fine strong plants of the Abutilon Thompsonii, the large golden-spotted leaves of which form a striking contrast to the dark foliage of the Coleus . . . On one side of a straight and long walk is another example of riband bordering, comprised of Lobelia next edge, then Pelargonium (Flower of the Day) next that Zinnias, and lastly a backing of tall Dahlias nicely furnished with bloom.

A few municipal gardens still display bedding-out and ribbon planting – the main east-west walk through the Fitzroy Gardens is perhaps the most elaborate still maintained. Laid out with a precision requiring tapes, rulers and templates, such beds could once have been seen on a similar scale in hundreds of private and public gardens. This form of intensive gardening has all but disappeared. Many now regard it as vulgar, unfashionable, and a waste of money. But how interesting it is to be able to see at first hand a spectacle that was once so universally popular.

Planting fashions have also changed in another respect. The Maranoa Gardens in Balwyn, commenced in 1926 and devoted to the cultivation of native plants, is a sort of historic garden even now. It was unfashionable when ribbon planting was still being practised. But now the tables have turned and native plants are all the vogue. One wonders how often the historic features of gardens have been swamped in the past few years by the eucalypt and its native accomplices, which have themselves ushered in a new phase of Australia's garden history.

Not all changes in fashion have harmed historic gardens, however. The present interest in ferns, shadehouses, conservatories and wire-basket planting has perhaps returned something of an earlier spirit and detail to some Victorian gardens.

Certain garden features have been lost through nothing other than old age. Nineteenth-century garden buildings were generally of fragile construction and quickly became dilapidated without continual maintenance. Of the thousands of lattice summer houses once found in Victorian gardens there can only be a bare handful left.

With a decline in the horticultural enthusiasm of late-Victorian times, there was often a diminution in the size of gardens and a simplification of their layout and planting. Other gardens were simply abandoned. Sometimes the house was destroyed, as at Mount Noorat, Noorat, or simply vacated as was the case at Ercildoune, Burrumbeet, and Narrapumelap at Wickliffe. On some large country properties surrounded by enormous gardens – such as Woodlands at Ararat, Glen Alvie near Colac and Glenara at Bulla – parts were simply fenced off to be grazed.

Mismanagement, too, has robbed some gardens of their intrinsic historic significance. The local botanic gardens or public park seems to be the first choice of councils for the site of the service club wishing well, a new bowling green, the centennial statue, an historic cottage or the much-needed public toilets. Perhaps these elements are not so bad in themselves, but often the very number of them begins to overwhelm the character of a garden and destroy its integrity. The Fitzroy Gardens in Melbourne and the Ballarat Botanical Gardens, both fine gardens of immense significance, are coming close to losing their special character through such excrescences.

All these factors have contributed to the relatively small tally of historic gardens in Victoria. The ninety gardens that are considered to be particularly worth preserving come in all sizes and shapes – from the tiny terrace oblongs to the broad landscape of the Royal Botanic Gardens. It is not, however, the small gardens with their limited maintenance requirements or

the publicly funded gardens with their annual budgets that are at greatest risk, though many could do with additional funds or an objective appraisal of their future development. Nor are important larger gardens such as Rippon Lea, Como and The Heights under threat – cared for as they are by the National Trust. Some of the others belong to institutions or private citizens who have the knowledge, incentive and wherewithal to sustain their gardens for some time yet. But perhaps two dozen of Victoria's ninety-odd important historic gardens are now, or soon will be, in some danger.

Owners themselves are by no means always at fault. A paucity of information about historic gardens has made it difficult for owners, and the general public, to understand not only what such things are but how to look after them. Partly as a consequence many owners, including municipal and government officials, are not aware of the heritage value of their gardens. There is little doubt that, having been made aware, many would respond positively.

Camperdown Botanic Gardens: invaders from a different age encroach on this once lovely place

It would be foolish to expect a very large number of Victoria's old gardens to have retained their original design and planting. The surviving few are probably not representative, of course, and had a wide choice been available a different group might well have been singled out for conservation. Certainly a number of very important gardens have survived – the Royal Botanic, Rippon Lea and Barcelona Terrace (Fitzroy) gardens among them. But the remaining gardens of historical significance must be protected at all costs. Although some of them were, perhaps, the most ordinary of gardens in their own day, they have become precious as the number of their contemporaries has gradually dwindled.

Those that are close to being lost should be recorded as a matter of urgency. Unlike buildings, gardens may very quickly deteriorate and the sooner such gardens are surveyed the more information they will produce. With every few years, more evidence vanishes. The box-hedged parterre at Ercildoune would almost certainly reveal a pattern now that may not be possible to determine in four or five years time. The same applies to at least a dozen other gardens. The most important requirements for the owners of those gardens that remain in reasonable condition are a rationale for conservation, sound information and advice, and financial assistance.

A SATISFACTORY philosophical approach to caring for historic gardens in this country is still some distance off. It is important, though, that owners of historic gardens think carefully about the future of these treasures. The curators of public gardens should be made to expose their policy to public scrutiny, and private owners should be encouraged to discuss and set down their views in order to clarify their aims.

Looking after historic gardens is quite different from caring for old buildings, and those responsible for buildings should recognize the difference. The latter are essentially static. This is not to say that buildings do not undergo changes. But they are inanimate objects and given the right conditions may look the same from one generation to another. Gardens will not. They are a living system – growing and decaying – and their organic nature adds to the challenge and excitement of conserving them. When the landscape designer left those vast terraces at the Villa d'Este, Tivoli, in the fifteenth century he left a garden that was an elaborate parterre. Its intricate pattern was meant to be viewed and enjoyed from the higher terraces. Today, nothing of this aerial view remains. The plants have grown to colossal size and the garden is now a series of shady avenues.

If a cornice falls off a building it may take a week to replace. If a tree is blown down it may not be possible to replant it in exactly the same place, and perhaps two hundred years will pass before it looks the way its predecessor did the previous week.

Not only are gardens organic, but they also develop empirically. Rarely is a garden laid out in one effort. Generally it changes according to taste, growth rates, plant failures and so on. This is no better demonstrated that at Stowe, in England, where whole buildings have been moved as trees grew and the scale of the garden altered.

It may be argued that trying to save any sort of garden is a contradiction in terms for, unlike some of its produce, a garden cannot be preserved – bottled up – at a particular moment. There is no anomaly in the situation, however, if we understand what gives a garden significance and, in planning ways to hold on to it, accept that certain changes are inevitable.

The question of significance is vital, because pinpointing a garden's most important features makes the task of retaining them very much easier. Is the whole layout of great interest? Or is only one major tree? Perhaps a collection of garden buildings is important; perhaps the association of a garden with a notable personality or a memorable historic event. Could it be the earliest, largest or remotest example of its type? Whatever a garden's significance, it must be identified.

There will be difficult decisions for everyone who is responsible for an historic garden. The owner of Barunah Plains, Hesse, has had to face up to a knotty problem. Should he clear out from his property all the hedges of boxthorn planted by the pioneering Russell family, eliminating thereby the danger of reinfesting the locality with an intractable noxious weed? Or should he retain some for their historical interest and because they are favoured by small native birds for nesting?

Palm trees were planted in many nineteenth-century gardens and are sometimes taken to suggest William Guilfoyle's involvement in a design (they were certainly important elements in some of his gardens). Should a modern bias against these plants – or any others – be sufficient reason for their removal? Can owners be expected to be so objective as to disregard their own preferences in such matters? How then should important historic gardens be treated?

For most historic gardens a 'pure' restoration (to their precise condition in a specific period) is neither justified nor desirable, even where it is possible. But a few special cases call for exceptional effort. Rippon Lea, for instance, was famed even in the nineteenth century as one of Melbourne's greatest gardens. It is well documented in hundreds of nineteenth-century photographs and many descriptions. Its ownership by the National Trust carries with it a responsibility to conserve it in a way that will help explain to the public the tastes, customs and lifestyle of a wealthy nineteenth-century family. But it is rarely that such a purist approach need be adopted for the conservation of historic gardens; rarely are all the circumstances right for such an approach.

A more practical and acceptable procedure for most gardens is to recognize every period in their development as making an important contribution to their appearance. By implication it is acceptable, provided that the elements giving the garden its historic importance are respected, to make certain changes to a garden. By and large this is an approach which has been adopted at Como, where modern designers including Ellis Stones and John Stevens have contributed new elements to otherwise derelict parts of the garden. One of the outstanding gardens in Australia today is that at Bolobek near Mount Macedon. Its creator, the botanical artist and garden-writer Joan Law-Smith, has used the basic structure of a large Edwardian garden and overlaid it with her own ideas. The result is a perfect fusion of two periods. This approach was very nicely summed up by H. F. Clarke, the inaugural President of the

Garden History Society in Britain when he said in 1969:

By and large, I should imagine that the restorer should avoid a too pedantic approach to period accuracy, especially in planting. What I should imagine to be the more important, is scale and an understanding of the original designer's intentions, an awareness of the continuity of time scale, and finally a feeling for what has been called those minutely organized particulars which link art and science, the past and the present.

All too often, however, historic gardens are left without any particular policy or approach. Lacking clear and precisely defined guidelines, a garden can easily lose its most valuable features or be altered beyond recognition. One need only look

The pool and rockwork designed by Ellis Stones for Como

again at the various additions made to the Fitzroy Gardens in the past fifty years to see the result of such an approach. The change in these gardens has been slow and subtle but there will only need to be a few more 'new attractions' before the peaceful quality we all admire and enjoy will be replaced by a razzmatazz fun-park atmosphere.

Although really referring to private gardens, the Duke of Devonshire, owner of Chatsworth, had this to say on the subject in 1976: 'If lions have to be introduced to make a garden attractive to the public, then far better for that garden to go; its style and integrity will not be loved, understood nor appreciated.' Gardens can very easily become convenient sites for commercial entertainment alien to horticultural, aesthetic and historical considerations alike. It is something we must seriously guard against in all our historic gardens.

HAVING DETERMINED a sensible and practical policy that respects a garden's integrity, owners and curators find that certain information becomes necessary. Such information and assistance are often quite difficult to obtain. Few professional design consultants have the expertise to work in this field. The Australian Institute of Landscape Architects should be encouraged to maintain a list of members who are knowledgeable and experienced in this area, and courses training professional designers should stimulate student interest in the special requirements of historic gardens.

The standard of garden employees steadily declined after the First World War. Many immigrants with the necessary qualifications and experience have since then been seduced into the nursery industry, which is more lucrative and gives greater status than gardening. From 1968, however, the situation has steadily improved with the commencement of the first training and apprenticeship scheme for the horticultural trades in Victoria. The initial group of certificated gardeners emerged from the course in 1971 and at present there are about a thousand apprentice gardeners throughout the state. Although the majority of those passing through the courses are ambitious for promotion and interested in senior management, there is an encouraging trend for young people to remain in practical gardening.

One of the most obvious gaps in available information concerns lists of appropriate plants for nineteenth-century gardens. Both the National Trust and the Australian Garden History Society are endeavouring to overcome this problem. Although some owners of old gardens and those wishing to re-create gardens are inclined to use appropriate planting, they have considerable difficulty not only in knowing what is correct, but also where to obtain the plants. It is almost impossible, for instance, to buy the full range of araucarias commonly used in Victorian gardens. The recent interest in palms and ferns has made the purchase of a wide range of these plants possible once again, but there are still many species unavailable.

At the Australian Garden History Society conference in Melbourne in March 1980 a list of twenty nurseries specializing in old plants was presented – though even the owners of these establishments are sometimes unable to name cultivars or even species accurately.

THE DEGREE OF financial strain involved in the preservation of historic gardens varies greatly with their size, nature and ownership. What some would regard as a burden, others do not. Public gardens can almost always do with additional funding, but essentially gardens such as the botanic gardens in Hamilton, Warrnambool and Ballarat seem to manage quite well. Those in smaller municipalities are possibly in need of assistance. Reduced funding in some instances might even keep some of the novelties at bay. It is not always easy to know, however, whether gardens are neglected through a shortage of money or because those in charge of them lack a sense of commitment.

The gardens that suffer most acutely from financial problems are undoubtedly the larger private gardens. All of these would once have employed considerable labour, where most now have little or no assistance apart from what the resident family can provide. Modern labour-saving devices such as weedicides, automatic sprinklers and ride-on mowers have helped to ease the burdens created by loss of labour. So too has the simplification of garden layouts. Massed annual displays, which are very labour-intensive, are now uncommon in private gardens and the trend has been to remove small beds from lawns and to plant the main beds thickly with trees, shrubs and ground cover to reduce maintenance. This has altered the character of many gardens but usually is an acceptable and practical device. Many would argue that the removal of the rather ostentatious floral displays from many nineteenth-century gardens is an improvement. The owners of Mooleric at Birregurra, for instance, have dispensed with all the flower beds that were once cut into the lawns. But the garden still retains its essential Guilfoylean character in layout and dominant planting – only some of the frills have been removed. Como, a garden of 2 hectares which employs three gardeners, has successfully – although some might say monotonously – used ivy as a ground cover over large areas in an endeavour to reduce maintenance and to carpet areas where grass would not grow.

Financial assistance does not only mean cash handouts. Very often these can only be a temporary prop, which will keep a place going for a few more years. Gardens rely to a much greater extent than buildings on continual maintenance, and one-off grants are useless except to help stabilize a garden building, install something specific like a water reticulation system – or as a last resort.

Of far greater benefit, and a more acceptable and equitable form of financial assistance for private owners, would be complete or partial tax deductibility against gross income for gardeners' wages and other expenses directly related to maintaining an historic garden. Municipal rate relief for gardens of approved historic importance would also benefit owners. Both tax and rate remission schemes have a number of important advantages. First, they overcome the difficulty of administrative costs associated with ongoing maintenance grants. Second, they provide an incentive to owners to engage labour and maintain their gardens, thereby committing substantial private financial resources. Third, they allow the whole community to

Still very much a Guilfoyle garden: Mooleric at Birregurra

contribute indirectly to the upkeep of part of our national estate. The amount lost in tax revenue would depend on the number of gardens eligible for concession status, but clearly this would be an infinitesimal amount compared with the costs of running large public gardens, which are entirely financed from the public purse. Such a scheme would allow private gardens to be maintained largely at the expense of the owner – who after all derives most of the benefit – but with some community contributions. Continuing private ownership should be encouraged at all costs. There is overwhelming evidence that private ownership is both cheaper and more satisfactory in the long run than public or corporate ownership. Apart from this, the special genre of a private garden can all too easily be lost when it becomes public property.

Of course, tax or rate relief implies some sort of official acknowledgement of a garden's importance. The National Trust in Victoria maintains a register of significant historic gardens. But it is not a statutory list and the Trust has no statutory powers or money to assist owners. The Historic Buildings Preservation Council in Victoria is the state's statutory body in this field as it maintains a list of important historic buildings for which it provides grants and loans for urgent works. Once on the list, owners have certain responsibilities, and permits are necessary for all alterations to the listed buildings. The Historic Buildings Preservation Council does not place gardens as such on its register, although in defining the curtilage of a house it generally includes the garden where this is obvious.

In making a grant the H.B.P.C. sometimes requires that the building involved be opened to the public on a certain number of days each year for a specified length of time. The owner is also required to enter into a covenant with the Minister for Planning not to demolish the building for the same period. Presumably similar requirements could apply to gardens if they were listed and received grants. However, apart from showing some interest in providing money for specific projects such as garden buildings or conservation studies, the H.B.P.C. has been hesitant to do more.

Gardens can already be given some legal protection under the *Town and Country Planning Act* 1961. By using the provisions of clauses 8, 8A and 8B of the Third Schedule of that Act a local planning authority can place certain constraints on an owner. Some concerned local councils have thus provided a degree of protection for historic buildings, but the Act has not been widely invoked for the protection of gardens. To its credit the Shire of Gisborne has used the Third Schedule to protect the garden and environs of the Gisborne property Fersfield. The house and garden in this instance had been separated by subdivision from the original driveway, which consisted of a beautiful elm avenue and clipped hawthorn hedges. Even though two owners are involved, the planning protection means that any development along the driveway must be compatible with the relationship of the driveway to the original garden.

The only other piece of Victorian legislation that has any real relevance to the protection of gardens is the *Government Buildings Advisory Council Act* 1972. This Act enables the Council to have some say in the future of government-owned buildings, and there is no reason why these should not include garden structures. Since most rural botanic gardens are on Crown land this could conceivably give the Council considerable control over garden buildings in these places. Perhaps buildings such as the bougainvillea rest house in the Royal Botanic Gardens may be saved in the future by the invoking of this Act.

There are many owners who would resist the establishment of a statutory register of historic gardens. There might, however, be less opposition to a list that did not place any obligation on an owner but was a basis for grants and loans. Only when a grant or loan was given would the owner have some reciprocal responsibility. Gardens are far more personal things than buildings, and a less formal type of listing procedure might therefore be more appropriate.

Opening private gardens to the public can also provide income to be reinvested in them. Some owners are reluctant to forgo the privacy of their gardens, and have indicated that they would prefer to see them decline than offer public access. This is understandable but also unfortunate, since public viewings can provide an excellent source of revenue. At an open day held on a fairly remote Western District property in 1980, an estimated seven thousand people visited the garden (the house was not open) and paid $1 per head for the privilege. The proceeds would not by any means have covered the annual costs of maintaining that garden, but we have here an indication of the potential that might be tapped by private owners especially. Although this was a 'once only' opportunity to see one of the state's most outstanding landscapes, the success of the occasion does demonstrate that with good publicity and

Opposite: Under provisions of the Town and Country Planning Act 1961, any development along the driveway at Fersfield, Gisborne, must relate satisfactorily to the original garden

occasional openings, a source of funds is open at least to the major gardens.

For a number of years now the owners of historic buildings have been made aware of the importance of such structures, and this has encouraged and promoted the concept of custodianship. At the same time the public has also become interested in the conservation of buildings – a factor adding strength and credibility to the case for conserving them, as well as being supportive to owners. It is to be hoped that the present interest in historic gardens throughout the state will encourage a greater awareness on the part of both garden-owners and the community. The process of generating concern must of necessity be a long-term one, but this has already begun. The publication of the book *The Great Gardens of Australia* (Howard Tanner and Jane Begg, 1976) and the showing of the exhibition 'Converting the Wilderness: The Art of Gardening in Colonial Australia' (1979–80) have opened many people's eyes to both the wealth of gardens in Australia and their important contribution to the national estate. It is expected that in the next ten years many more books on historic gardens in Australia will become available and accelerate this interest.

While there is a limited number of historic gardens still flourishing, there are refreshing signs of a new zeal for ensuring their future. Nurseries specializing in old plants are opening, research into a number of different aspects of garden history is in progress, gardens are being restored, and a new society has been created, one of whose aims is to assist in the conservation of important gardens. Private gardens that will eventually become historic are also in the making. Pirianda in the Dandenong Ranges and the new extension to the Royal Botanic Gardens at Cranbourne will in time be great botanical repositories. There is every reason to be confident. But there is also every reason to be vigilant – to hold on to the vestiges of an especially fascinating part of our inheritance from the men and women who shaped Victoria.

Sources/Index

BIBLIOGRAPHY

UNPUBLISHED MATERIAL

Black Papers. MS 8996, La Trobe
Collection, State Library of Victoria.
Bolwell, J. K. Parks and Gardens of the
City of Melbourne. B. Arch. thesis,
University of Melbourne, 1970.
Broadbent, James. The Landscape
Garden in N.S.W. Unpublished
paper, 1982.
Department of Crown Lands and
Survey. Records relating to Crown
Reserves.
Drysdale, Anne. Diary, 1839–54. MS
9249, La Trobe Collection, State
Library of Victoria.
Foster, John. The Carlton Gardens.
Unpublished paper, c. 1978.
—— The Fitzroy Gardens. Unpublished
paper, c. 1978.
Hattam, Kate. Historic Gardens in
South West Victoria and South
Australia. Unpublished report to
Australian Heritage Commission,
1978.
Jones, George. Our Botanic Gardens –
a Brief History. Unpublished paper,
1981.
Leahy, Philip. Central Park – brief
history. Unpublished paper, 1982.
McBriar, M. Gardens of Federation
and other Edwardian Houses in
Melbourne circa 1890–1914. Dip. L.D.
thesis, Royal Melbourne Institute of
Technology, 1980.

Memoirs of Frances Annie Moore
1864–1961. MS 9187, La Trobe Collection,
State Library of Victoria.
National Trust of Australia (Victoria).
Various files.
Pickford, J. et al. Squares of Melbourne.
B. Arch. thesis, University of Melbourne,
n.d.
Potts, David. Unpublished research
notes, history department, La Trobe
University.
Ramsay (Andrew Mitchell) Papers.
MS 11021, La Trobe Collection, State
Library of Victoria.
Sanderson, Ruth. Rippon Lea: The
Development of the Garden. M.L.A.
research paper, University of
Melbourne, 1980.
Victorian Horticultural Society. Minute
book 1859–73 (Victorian Gardeners'
Mutual Improvement Society).

NEWSPAPERS AND JOURNALS

Architects' Journal, January 1976.
Argus.
Association for Preservation Technology Bulletin,
vol. IV, 1972; vol. II, 1973; vol. VII, 1975.
Australasian.
Australian Gardener, 1907–10.
Bacchus Marsh Express.
Castlemaine Representative.
Country Life, 1968–81.
Daylesford Advocate.
Daylesford Express.
Ekistics, July/August 1978.
Garden, May 1977; October 1978.
Gardener's Chronicle, 1862–85.
Gardener's Magazine, 1826–43.
Garden Gazette.
Garden History Society Occasional Paper
no. 1, 1969.
Geelong Advertiser.
Illustrated Australian News.
Illustrated Sydney News.
Journal of the Australian Garden History Society.
Journal of the Garden History Society (U.K.).
Journal of Horticulture, 1873–84.
*Journal of the Royal Victorian Institute of
Architects*, 1903, 1904.
Landscape Architecture, April 1969; May
1976; May 1979.
Landscape Design, February 1979.
Leader.
Melbourne Punch, September, December 1880.
Portland Guardian.
Town Planning Review, 1975.
*Victorian Farmers' Journal and Gardeners'
Chronicle.*
Victorian Historical Magazine, February 1940.
Weekly Times.

BOOKS

Adams, David (ed.). *The Letters of Rachel Henning.* Sydney, 1963.
Australian Broadcasting Commission. *The Essential Past.* Sydney, 1969.
Australian Council of National Trusts. *Historic Homesteads of Australia.* 2 vols. Melbourne, 1969; Sydney, 1976.
Australian Council of National Trusts. *Historic Houses of Australia.* Melbourne, 1974.
Australian Gallery Directors Council and Howard Tanner. *Converting the Wilderness: The Art of Gardening in Colonial Australia.* Sydney, 1979.
Blainey, Geoffrey. *The Tyranny of Distance.* Melbourne, 1966.
Bligh, Beatrice. *Cherish the Earth.* Sydney, 1973.
Blomfield, Reginald. *The Formal Garden in England.* London, 1892.
Boldrewood, Mrs Rolf (Margaret Browne). *Flower Garden in Australia.* Melbourne, 1893.
Boldrewood, Rolf. *Ups and Downs: A Story of Australian Life.* London, 1878.
Boyd, Robin. *Australia's Home.* Melbourne, 1952.
Bradfield, R. A. *Castlemaine: The North-End.* Castlemaine, n.d.
Brown, P. L. (ed.). *Clyde Company Papers*, vol. V (1851–53). Melbourne, 1963.
Bunce, Daniel. *The Australian Manual of Horticulture.* 3rd edn. Melbourne, 1851.
Casey, Maie. *An Australian Story 1837–1907.* London, 1962.
Clifford, Derek. *A History of Garden Design.* London, 1962.
Cooper, J. B. *The History of Malvern.* Melbourne, 1935.
Evans, Wilson P. *Port of Many Prows.* Melbourne, 1969.
Froude, J. A. *Oceana.* London, 1886.
Garran, Andrew (ed.). *The Picturesque Atlas of Australasia.* Sydney, 1886.
Grant, James. *The Narrative of a Voyage of Discovery.* London, 1803.
Harris, John (ed.). *The Garden: A Celebration of One Thousand Years of British Gardening.* London, 1979.
Haydon, G. H. *Five Years' Experience in Australia Felix.* London, 1846.
Hebb, Isaac. *The History of Colac and District.* Melbourne, 1970.
Hibberd, Shirley. *Rustic Adornments for Homes of Taste . . .* London, 1857.
Hussey, Christopher. *The Picturesque.* London, 1927.
Kelly, William. *Life in Victoria.* Kilmore (Vic.), 1977 (first published London, 1859).

Kiddle, Margaret. *Men of Yesterday.* Melbourne, 1961.
[Kirkland, Mrs]. 'Life in the Bush, by A Lady' in *Chambers Miscellany.* London, 1844.
Lasdun, Susan. *Victorians at Home.* London, 1981.
Loudon, J. C. *Encyclopedia of Cottage, Farm and Villa Architecture.* London, 1853.
—— *Encyclopedia of Gardening.* London, 1827.
—— *The Suburban Gardener and Villa Companion.* London, 1838.
Luffmann, C. Bogue. *The Principles of Gardening in Australia.* Melbourne, 1903.
McCorkell, H. A. (ed.). *The Diaries of Sarah Midgley and Richard Skilbeck.* Melbourne, 1967.
McCrae, Hugh (ed.). *Georgiana's Journal.* 2nd edn. Sydney, 1966.
Melbourne City Council. *History – Features – Statistics of Melbourne's Gardens.* Melbourne, n.d. [c. 1975].
Mundy, G. *Our Antipodes.* London, 1852.
National Trust of Australia (Vic.). *Proceedings of the First Garden History Conference.* Melbourne, 1980.
National Trust (U.K.) *The Conservation of the Garden at Stourhead.* London, 1978.
Pescott, R. T. M. *The Royal Botanic Gardens Melbourne.* Melbourne, 1982.
—— *W. R. Guilfoyle: the Master of Landscaping.* Melbourne, 1974.
Pevsner, Nicholas. *The Picturesque Garden and its Influence Outside the British Isles.* Washington, 1974.
Polya, R. *Nineteenth Century Plant Nursery Catalogues of South-East Australia: A Bibliography.* Bundoora (Vic.), 1981.
Robinson, William. *English Flower Garden.* London, 1883.
—— *The Wild Garden.* London, 1870.
Shepherd, Thomas. *Lectures on Landscape Gardening in Australia.* Sydney, 1836.
Shillinglaw, John J. (ed.). *Historical Records of Port Phillip 1879* (ed. C. E. Sayers). Melbourne, 1972.
Sinclair, James. *The Beauties of Victoria in 1856: Notices of Two Hundred of the Principal Gardens Round Melbourne.* Melbourne, n.d.
—— *Every Man His Own Gardener.* Melbourne, n.d. [c. 1866].
Smith, James (ed.). *Cyclopedia of Victoria.* 3 vols. Melbourne, 1903–5.
Stewart, John J. *Historic Landscapes and Gardens – Procedures for Restoration.*

American Association for State and Local History, Technical leaflet no. 80, n.d.
Stuart, David C. *Georgian Gardens.* London, 1979.
Sutherland, Alexander (ed.). *Victoria and its Metropolis*, vol. 3. Melbourne, 1888.
Tanner, H. and Begg, J. *The Great Gardens of Australia.* Melbourne, 1976.
Taylor, Geoffrey. *The Victorian Flower Garden.* London, 1952.
Thacker, Christopher. *The History of Gardens.* London, 1979.
Trollope, Anthony. *Australia and New Zealand.* London, 1873.
Tuckey, J. H. *An Account of a Voyage to establish a colony at Port Philip [sic] . . . in 1802-3-4.* London, 1805.
Tunnard, Christopher. *A World With a View: An Enquiry into the Nature of Scenic Values.* New Haven, 1978.
Twopeny, R. E. N. *Town Life in Australia.* Sydney, 1973 (first published London, 1883).
Walling, Edna. *Cottage and Garden in Australia.* Melbourne, 1947.
Watts, Peter. *The Gardens of Edna Walling.* Melbourne, 1981.
Whitworth, R. P. *Massina's Popular Guide to the Melbourne International Exhibition of 1880-1.* Melbourne, 1880.
Willis, Margaret. *By Their Fruits – A Life of Ferdinand von Mueller.* Melbourne, 1949.

SOURCES OF ILLUSTRATIONS

Sequence of pictures in multiple layouts is top to bottom, column by column

2: Peter Watts. National Trust of Aust. (Vic.)
7: Hester L. Massie, 1887. By courtesy of Dr Alan Roberts
8: Burnley Horticultural College collection
9: La Trobe Collection, State Library of Victoria
11: Sargood album, 1880. National Trust of Aust. (Vic.)
14: Docker family collection
15: Ed Haigh, 1861. La Trobe Collection, S.L.V.
17: Hester L. Massie, 1889. By courtesy of Dr Alan Roberts
18: Map Collection, S.L.V.

19: Shire of Daylesford and Glenlyon
20: Unknown artist, c. 1843-44. La Trobe Collection, S.L.V.
21: Alexander Sutherland (ed.), *Victoria and its Metropolis* (vol. 2), 1888
22a: Peter Watts. National Trust of Aust. (Vic.)
22b & 23: John Patrick
24: Brian Hatfield. National Trust of Aust. (Vic.)
25: National Trust of Aust. (Vic.)
26a & b: J. C. Loudon, *The Suburban Gardener and Villa Companion*, 1838
27: Thomas Turner, c. 1868. Mitchell Library, Sydney
28: Peter Watts. National Trust of Aust. (Vic.)
29: Holtermann Collection, Mitchell Library, Sydney
30: Edward La Trobe Bateman, 1854. La Trobe Collection, S.L.V.
31: Charles Nettleton, n.d. La Trobe Collection, S.L.V.
32a: McArthur family collection
32b: National Trust of Aust. (Vic.), by courtesy of Mrs G. L. Lloyd-Smith
33a: Peter Watts. National Trust of Aust. (Vic.)
33b: By courtesy of David Potts
34a: Armytage family album. National Trust of Aust. (Vic.), by courtesy of Mrs Caroline Shepherd
34b: Map Collection, S.L.V.
35: Burnley Horticultural College collection

37a: G. W. Evans, 1808–9. Mitchell Library, Sydney
37b & d: Charles Norton, 1844 & 1847. Stewart Collection, by courtesy of Mrs D. C. Stewart
37c: W. Lyttleton, 1835. State Library of Tasmania; this copy by courtesy of the Tasmanian Club, Hobart
38a & c: Charles Norton, 1846 & 1848. Stewart Collection, by courtesy of Mrs D. C. Stewart
38b: W. Tibbits, c. 1875. Geelong Art Gallery
39: *Victoria: Parliamentary Papers* (vol. 3), 1873
40a: Hon. V. N. Hood, 1911. La Trobe Collection, S.L.V.
40b: Brian Hatfield. National Trust of Aust. (Vic.)
41a: By courtesy of Mr and Mrs J. R. Morrison
41b: Royal Historical Society of Victoria
42a: Burnley Horticultural College collection
42b: De Guchy and Leigh, 1866. La Trobe Collection, S.L.V.
43a: Palmer family collection
43b: Archives, Royal Botanic Gardens and Herbarium, Melbourne
44a: Dr J. H. Willis
44b: Peter Watts. National Trust of Aust. (Vic.)
45: Sargood album, 1903. National Trust of Aust. (Vic.)
46a: National Trust of Aust. (Vic.)
46b: Hon. V. N. Hood, 1916. La Trobe Collection, S.L.V.
47a: 'Lauderdale', *Victoria's Representative Men at Home*, n.d.
47b: Geelong Historical Records Centre
48a: Watkin family collection
48b: Geelong Historical Records Centre
49a: Family collection
49b: Sargood album, 1903. National Trust of Aust. (Vic.)
50: La Trobe Collection, S.L.V.
51a: National Trust of Aust. (Vic.)
51b: Robert O'Hara Burke Memorial Museum, Beechworth
52 & 53a: *Charlie Hammond's Sketch-book*, 1980
53b: Richard Aitken and Geelong Historical Records Centre
53c: Richard Aitken and City of Geelong
54: Burnley Horticultural College collection
55: Irvine Green. National Trust of Aust. (Vic.)
56: La Trobe Collection, S.L.V.

57: Department of Crown Lands and Survey
58: Borough of Koroit
59: *Cyclopedia of Victoria* (vol. 2), 1904
60: Archives, Royal Botanic Gardens and Herbarium, Melbourne
61: La Trobe Collection, S.L.V.
62: Meade postcard. La Trobe Collection, S.L.V.
63: Burnley Horticultural College
64: Brian Hatfield. National Trust of Aust. (Vic.)
65a: Charles Nettleton, n.d. La Trobe Collection, S.L..V.
65b: La Trobe Collection, S.L.V.
66: Richard Aitken collection
67: Brian Hatfield. National Trust of Aust. (Vic.)
68a: National Trust of Aust. (Vic.)
68b & c: La Trobe Collection, S.L.V.
69: National Trust of Aust. (Vic.)
70a: City of Ballaarat
70b: Peter Watts. National Trust of Aust. (Vic.)
70c: *Niven's Guidebook and Souvenir of Ballarat*, 1885
71: Meade postcard. La Trobe Collection, S.L.V.
72: Brian Hatfield. National Trust of Aust. (Vic.)
73: Kate Leviny, 1900. Castlemaine Art Gallery and Historical Museum
74a: Peter Watts. National Trust of Aust. (Vic.)
74b: Rose postcard. La Trobe Collection, S.L.V.
75: La Trobe Collection, S.L.V.
76a & b: Peter Watts. National Trust of Aust. (Vic.)
77a: Rose postcard. La Trobe Collection, S.L.V.
77b & 78: Brian Hatfield. National Trust of Aust. (Vic.)
79: Ernest Cameron, n.d. La Trobe Collection, S.L.V.
80: Brian Hatfield. National Trust of Aust. (Vic.)
81: National Trust of Aust. (Vic.)
82a & b: Campbell family collection
83: Brian Hatfield. National Trust of Aust. (Vic.)
84a & b: La Trobe Collection, S.L.V.
84c: Mark Strizic. National Trust of Aust. (Vic.)
84d: Peter Watts. National Trust of Aust. (Vic.)
85a: Brian Hatfield. National Trust of Aust. (Vic.)
85b: Peter Watts. National Trust of Aust. (Vic.)
86a: Brian Hatfield. National Trust of Aust. (Vic.)

86b: Peter Watts. National Trust of Aust. (Vic.)
87a: Campbell family collection
87b: Peter Watts. National Trust of Aust. (Vic.)
88: Stokes family collection
89a: Peter Watts. National Trust of Aust. (Vic.)
89b: Brian Hatfield. National Trust of Aust. (Vic.)
90: Charles Norton, n.d. Stewart Collection, by courtesy of Mrs D. C. Stewart
91: Brian Hatfield. National Trust of Aust. (Vic.)
92: Jones family collection
93a: G. Bond, 1872. Carter family collection
93b: Stewart Collection, by courtesy of Mrs D. C. Stewart
93c: Map Collection, S.L.V.
94a: Peter Watts. National Trust of Aust. (Vic.)
94b: Brian Hatfield. National Trust of Aust. (Vic.)
95a, b & c; 96a & b; 97a, b & c: Peter Watts. National Trust of Aust. (Vic.)
98a: D. Walster. National Trust of Aust. (Vic.)
98b: Peter Watts. National Trust of Aust. (Vic.)
99 & 100a: Brian Hatfield. National Trust of Aust. (Vic.)
100 b & c: Peter Watts. National Trust of Aust. (Vic.)
101: Brian Hatfield. National Trust of Aust. (Vic.)
102 & 103b: Peter Watts
103a: Mark Strizic
104: By courtesy of Miss Ella Welsh
105a: Brian Hatfield. National Trust of Aust. (Vic.)
105b: Peter Watts. National Trust of Aust. (Vic.)
106a: Burnley Horticultural College collection
106b & 107: Peter Watts. National Trust of Aust. (Vic.)
108: Brian Hatfield. National Trust of Aust. (Vic.)
109: Holtermann Collection, Mitchell Library, Sydney
110: Artist unknown, n.d. Agar family collection
111a: Jamieson family collection
111b: *Pastoral Homes of Australia*, 1910
112: Winter Cooke family collection, by courtesy of Mrs S. Winter Cooke
113a: Brian Hatfield. National Trust of Aust. (Vic.)
113b: Winter Cooke family collection, by courtesy of Mrs S. Winter Cooke

114 & 115a: Hon. V. N. Hood, c. 1910 & 1915. La Trobe Collection, S.L.V.
115b: Brian Hatfield. National Trust of Aust. (Vic.)
116: Eugène von Guérard, 1867. Dixson Library, Sydney
117a: Eugène von Guérard, 1867. By courtesy of Lady Johnston
117b: Eugène von Guérard, 1861. McArthur family collection
117c: Artist unknown, n.d. Docker family collection
118a: Peter Watts. National Trust of Aust. (Vic.)
118b & c: Brian Hatfield. National Trust of Aust. (Vic.)
119a & b: Peter Watts. National Trust of Aust. (Vic.)
119c: Brian Hatfield. National Trust of Aust. (Vic.)
120: By courtesy of Mr and Mrs Philip Russell
121a: McArthur family collection
121b: 'Lauderdale', *Victoria's Representative Men at Home*, n.d.
121c: Brian Hatfield. National Trust of Aust. (Vic.)
122a: Hood family collection
122b: Alexander Sutherland (ed.), *Victoria and its Metropolis* (vol. 2), 1888
123a: Peter Watts. National Trust of Aust. (Vic.)
123b: Ritchie family collection
124: Brian Hatfield. National Trust of Aust. (Vic.)
125a & b: Peter Watts. National Trust of Aust. (Vic.)
126a & b: Scott family collection
126c; 127a, b & c; 128a: Peter Watts. National Trust of Aust. (Vic.)
128b & 129a: By courtesy of Mr Niel Black
129b & 130a: Peter Watts. National Trust of Aust. (Vic.)
130b: Lang family collection
131a & c: Brian Hatfield. National Trust of Aust. (Vic.)
131b: Lang family collection
132a: Dennis family collection
132b; 133a & b: Peter Watts. National Trust of Aust. (Vic.)
134a: Kruger album. La Trobe Collection, S.L.V.
134b: Peter Watts. National Trust of Aust. (Vic.)
135a: Hon. V. N. Hood, 1915. La Trobe Collection, S.L.V.
135b: By courtesy of Monsignor Ken Morrison, seated, as a student, at centre front of the photograph
136a & c: Peter Watts. National Trust of Aust. (Vic.)

136b: Watkin family collection
137a: Brian Hatfield. National Trust of Aust. (Vic.)
137b: By courtesy of Mrs J. Thornton
137c; 138a & b; 139a: Peter Watts. National Trust of Aust. (Vic.)
139b: Palmer family collection
140a: Brian Hatfield. National Trust of Aust. (Vic.)
140b: Aerograph Survey Pty Ltd
141a: Ramsay family collection
141b; 142a & b: Andrew Mitchell Ramsay Papers. La Trobe Collection, S.L.V.
143a & b: Fairbairn family collection
144a: Peter Watts. National Trust of Aust. (Vic.)
144b: Russell family collection
145a: *Pastoral Homes of Australia*, 1930
145b: Russell family collection
146: Jones family collection, by courtesy of Miss Gwen Jones
147a: *Pastoral Homes of Australia*, 1910
147b & 148: Brian Hatfield. National Trust of Aust. (Vic.)
149: Ruth Sanderson and *Landscape Australia*
150: Burnley Horticultural College collection
151 & 152: Hon. V. N. Hood, n.d. & 1913. La Trobe Collection, S.L.V.
153, 155 & 156: Peter Watts. National Trust of Aust. (Vic.)
157: Brian Hatfield. National Trust of Aust. (Vic.)
158a: Mark Strizic
158b & 159: Peter Watts. National Trust of Aust. (Vic.)
160: Mark Strizic
161a: By courtesy of Mr A. Manifold
161b: Graham Cornish. National Trust of Aust. (Vic.)
162: Artist unknown, 1880. By permission of The Exhibition Trustees
163: Peter Watts. National Trust of Aust. (Vic.)
164a: Burnley Horticultural College collection
164b & 165: Brian Hatfield. National Trust of Aust. (Vic.)
166a: *Garden Gazette*, 1903
166b: Peter Jones. National Trust of Aust. (Vic.)
167a: *Garden Gazette*, 1903
167b: Map Collection, S.L.V.
168a: Burnley Horticultural College collection
168b: By courtesy of Dr John Foster
169a & b: Burnley Horticultural College collection
170: La Trobe Collection, S.L.V.
171: Map Collection, S.L.V.

172a & b: Brian Hatfield. National Trust of Aust. (Vic.)
173a: Peter Watts. National Trust of Aust. (Vic.)
173b: © Crown (State of Victoria) Copyright. Aerial photograph reproduced by permission of the Surveyor-General, Victoria
174a: Burnley Horticultural College collection
174b & c: *Report of the Principal of the School of Horticulture (C. Bogue Luffmann) 31st December, 1899*
175a: Burnley Horticultural College collection
175b: *Australasian*, 20 July 1907
176a: Brian Hatfield. National Trust of Aust. (Vic.)
176b: Peter Watts. National Trust of Aust. (Vic.)
177 & 178: City of Malvern, by courtesy of Mr Philip Leahy
179a & b: Peter Watts. National Trust of Aust. (Vic.)
179c: Irvine Green. National Trust of Aust. (Vic.)
180: Professor T. C. Chambers
181 & 182a: National Trust of Aust. (Vic.)
182b: Map Collection, S.L.V.
183: W. Tibbits, 1884. La Trobe Collection, S.L.V.
184: Sargood album, 1880. National Trust of Aust. (Vic.)
185a: 'Lauderdale', *Victoria's Representative Men at Home*, n.d.
185b: Sargood album, 1880. National Trust of Aust. (Vic.)
185c: *Garden Gazette*, 1902
186a & b: Armytage family album. National Trust of Aust. (Vic.), by courtesy of Mrs Caroline Shepherd
187: National Trust of Aust. (Vic.), by courtesy of Mrs G. L. Lloyd-Smith
188: Armytage family album. National Trust of Aust. (Vic.), by courtesy of Mrs Caroline Shepherd
189a: W. Tibbits, 1875. National Trust of Aust. (Vic.)
189b: W. Tibbits, 1878. Private collection, Melbourne
190a: Professor T. C. Chambers
190b & c; 191: Peter Watts. National Trust of Aust. (Vic.)
192a & b; 193: Sargood album, 1880; 1903. National Trust of Aust. (Vic.)
194a: Ruth Sanderson, 1980
194b: National Trust of Aust. (Vic.)
195a: Peter Watts. National Trust of Aust. (Vic.)
195b: Sargood album, 1903. National Trust of Aust. (Vic.)

INDEX

Numbers in italic refer to illustrations